Human–Computer Interaction Series

HCI is a multidisciplinary field focused on human aspects of the development of computer technology. As computer-based technology becomes increasingly pervasive—not just in developed countries, but worldwide—the need to take a human-centered approach in the design and development of this technology becomes ever more important. For roughly 30 years now, researchers and practitioners in computational and behavioral sciences have worked to identify theory and practice that influences the direction of these technologies, and this diverse work makes up the field of human-computer interaction. Broadly speaking it includes the study of what technology might be able to do for people and how people might interact with the technology. The HCI series publishes books that advance the science and technology of developing systems which are both effective and satisfying for people in a wide variety of contexts. Titles focus on theoretical perspectives (such as formal approaches drawn from a variety of behavioral sciences), practical approaches (such as the techniques for effectively integrating user needs in system development), and social issues (such as the determinants of utility, usability and acceptability).

For further volumes:
http://www.springer.com/series/6033

Alexander Osherenko

Social Interaction, Globalization and Computer-Aided Analysis

A Practical Guide to Developing Social Simulation

Alexander Osherenko
Socioware Development
Augsburg, Germany

ISSN 1571-5035   Human–Computer Interaction Series
ISBN 978-1-4471-7079-2   ISBN 978-1-4471-6260-5 (eBook)
DOI 10.1007/978-1-4471-6260-5
Springer London Heidelberg New York Dordrecht

Printed on acid-free paper

Springer is part of Springer Science+Business Media (www.springer.com)

Preface

The modern world is globalizing, and modern people enjoy the advantages of globalization. They travel from one continent to another, do sports in different world stadiums, attend international conferences, etc.

However, globalization brings not only advantages but can be also problematic. For example, human communication in times of globalization is not trivial and carries the risk of misinterpretations and misunderstandings.

This book addresses this problem and presents a comprehensive, multidisciplinary study of intercultural Social Interaction (SI) and intercultural Social Simulation (SS). Its ultimate aim is to demonstrate the development of an SS software that assists human experts to comprehend intercultural processes and thus to facilitate intercultural communication in the context of Human–Computer Interaction (HCI).

The book describes a generic, domain-independent approach to developing computer systems that realize intercultural SS. It discusses SI and SS from the perspective of different disciplines and puts special focus on intercultural aspect of discussion.

The book is a monograph where most of the findings are verified using the author's own software. It is not only computer scientists who can benefit from this book, but also researchers, research workers, practitioners, professionals in cognitive science, for example, linguistics, philosophers, or neurologists, since it covers a broad spectrum of research such as research of SI and SS in the social linguistics, the social philosophy, or neurobiology.

The idea of this book emerged from my postdoctoral application to the Japan Society for the Promotion of Science. The book explores existing approaches to SI and SS and reveals significant determinants of processing. For example, it explains reasons for consideration of the notion "identity" in simulation systems or why it is indispensable to maintain the simulation context and consider a physical space in SS. The book shows how these aspects can be implemented computationally.

To perform intercultural simulation and to develop computational prototypes of simulation systems, this book discusses the means to acquire intercultural data. It describes the own framework for statistical processing and prototyping that tackles necessary data and composes computer prototypes. This discussion is accompanied by practical recommendations on realization of the proposed algorithms and by the program code.

Although this book, as with many scientific books, is not an entertainment or an easy endeavor in the strictly conventional sense of these words, it can be nevertheless very engaging—it contains, besides specific guidelines for developers of the SS, software different cultural facts, mundane information, and colloquial explanations that are worth consideration by all scientists of the modern globalized world.

Augsburg, Germany   Alexander Osherenko
September 2013

Acknowledgments

I am very indebted to the Japan Society for the Promotion of Science and in particular to Prof. Toyoaki Nishida (Kyoto University) that initiated this research. I hope that I achieved satisfactory results.

I am very grateful to Giovanni Caire (Telecom Italia S.p.A.) who sacrificed his precious time to thoroughly answer my questions about specifics of building multi-agent systems in JADE.

I would like to thank my parents. This work would have been impossible without their support.

Contents

Acronyms

AMS   Agent Management System
AS   Asperger Syndrom
ASC   Autism Spectrum Conditions
ASD   Autism Spectrum Disorder
ARFF   Attribute-Relation File Format
BDI   Belief-Desire-Intention
BPD   Borderline Personality Disorder
CBR   Case-Based Reasoning
DF   Directory Facilitator
ECA   Embodied Conversational Agent
EEG   Electroencephalography
FOAF Friend of a Friend
GUI   Graphical User Interface
HCI   Human–Computer Interaction
HRI   Human–Robot Interaction
HMM Hidden Markov Model
LCD   Liquid Crystal Display
LIWC Linguistic Inquiry and Word Count
MAS   Multiagent System
NL   Natural-Language
PD   Prisoner's Dilemma
PMCC Product Movement Correlation Coefficient
RMA   Remote Management Agent
SAL   Sensitive Artificial Listener
SI   Social Interaction
SN   Social Network
SS   Social Simulation
SVM   Support Vector Machine
WS   WebService
UML   Unified Modeling Language

List of Figures

List of Tables

List of Tables

Part I
Multidisciplinary Part

This part describes preliminaries of Social Interaction (SI) and is addressed to every person interested in the intercultural research of SI and Social Simulation (SS). It focuses on challenges and advantages of simulation of SI, discusses various definitions that will be necessary for understanding concepts and solutions in the rest of the book, outlines multidisciplinary approaches that explain existing methods of SI, explores intercultural scenarios of SI. and emphasizes significant details of SS such as modeling dimensions. All in all, this part prepares the reader to discussion of computational solutions in the next developmental part.

Chapter 1
Introduction

Discovering new things, recovering unknown, adventures, ingenuity—these are things that engage the humankind for ages. Assuming unexpected under seemingly known subjects, the mankind spends significant amounts of intellectual energy to advance to new scientific horizons. Even tiny things such as atoms or molecules are inspected, and their observation uncovers an astonishing picture of the invisible world that was not tangible so far.

Surprisingly, a supply of unexpected things that seems to be empty is not exhausted. Every day, sciences make new discoveries, and the humankind wonders about them. New findings were actually just in close vicinity but hidden. What is the reason? How can such blindness be explained?

Well, some subjects that seem trivial are only simple at the first glance. A table is a table, a chair is a chair. These banal things are used in the everyday life, and they do not need special attention.

Similarly, a human communication is a human communication. Humans communicate everyday with other peers, and it seems to be unnecessary to investigate communication deeper. Communication is such a simple, self-explanatory thing that accompanies human life that is unnecessary to question. Why should known things be carefully inspected although they seem to be known sufficiently good?

However, it is a fallacy. Different sciences, for example, psychology or sociology examine human communication for centuries, and this research is though not finished. Now the situation becomes more complicated because of globalization! The modern world is inhabited by different persons that are situated on a considerable distance from each other. These persons travel from one continent to another, do sports in different world stadiums, and attend international conferences. They meet representatives of other cultures, debate with them, and seem to know what to do since they learned it as children in their home country. However, is this communication fully realized? Do interactants comprehend this intercultural communication completely?

Let us revise once more what is happening. The modern world is globalizing—it is indisputable. People want to benefit from globalization and enjoy advantages

A. Osherenko, *Social Interaction, Globalization and Computer-Aided Analysis*,
Human–Computer Interaction Series, DOI 10.1007/978-1-4471-6260-5_1,
© Springer-Verlag London 2014

of multicultural communication. It is also unquestionable. Everything seems to be trivial and simple.

But stop! Intercultural communication only seems to be simple. It can be merely a deflection, and the real situation is very different. Indeed, unanswered questions still exist. Is interpersonal communication explored enough and further exploration would be obsolete? What is the reason of misunderstandings in foreign cultures although the sojourners are doing everything correctly so as they would do at home? Why do the sojourners feel not accepted in the foreign culture? What is the accepted form of something that seems to be known for years and still must be reacquainted in the new culture?

The seeming simplicity of human communication is only illusive, and the truth is not evident. In fact, sciences studied only the tip of the iceberg, and there is much work to do especially now in the globalizing modern world. People participating in intercultural communication are not always persons with the same cultural background. The norms, behaviors, status values are different. Everything is different, and many things have to be questioned.

These news are depressing. Indeed, acquirement of new knowledge about lives of foreign people. What for? Surprisingly, the humankind does not give up and comprehend this challenge as a new adventure. Uncertainty does not lead to stopping investigation but just pursues an ambition to resolve it.

Of course, interacting with representatives of foreign cultures is not always straightforward: particular aspects of intercultural interaction can have only the known designation but different meanings, and those who are mastering this communication should pay attention not only to visible matters, but also to invisible issues questioning each moment of own behavior. What is seen in the foreign culture can be only a mirage, and the real interpretation is deceived by delusive, seemingly familiar things. How can different cultures circumvent difficulties of intercultural communication?

1.1 Examples

Much effort is spent on discussing communication. Maybe, because communication or, more scientifically, SI accompanies the humans all life long.

SI is learned as a child. Children call it differently, but they mean something very familiar. Children play with each other and communicate with each other. Children smile to other peers or quarrel with them; children ask for something or complain to adults. Everything (playing, communicating, quarreling, asking, complaining) is SI (Fig. 1.1).

Children grow up and go to the university. In their studies, they dispute with international students, present solutions, and communicate with their mentors. And it is also SI (dispute, presentation, communication) (Fig. 1.2).

Fig. 1.1 Children in social interaction. Based on stock image from PhotoDune, reprinted with kind permission

Fig. 1.2 Students in an international class. Based on stock image from PhotoDune, reprinted with kind permission

After the university, the graduates start to work and unconscientiously participate on the workplace in another kind of SI (Fig. 1.3). A manager gives them instructions on performing a task. Colleagues (also foreign) ask them for advice in performing a task or wish a support; different tasks require brainstorming; a Christmas party should be organized. Unexpectedly, it is also SI (interacting with the manager, advices, brainstorming, the party).

A manager of a company participates in another sort of SI. The manager is responsible for groups or organizations. On their behalf, the manager must conduct negotiations with other affiliations also abroad (Fig. 1.4) and choose a strategy that would be beneficial for manager's affiliation. SI takes place on her workplace (negotiations, strategy choice).

A friend talking to a handicapped person is also involved in SI (Fig. 1.5). She has to inform the person about the necessary treatment but abstain from patronizing. Again, choosing proper methods to inform the person about the treatment makes SI up.

Fig. 1.3 Interacting with a manager. Based on stock image from PhotoDune, reprinted with kind permission

Fig. 1.4 Negotiating. Based on stock image from PhotoDune, reprinted with kind permission

SI is also present if employees, say medical doctors, are going abroad to counsel their foreign colleagues (Fig. 1.6). The doctors have to behave not only professionally but also personally convincing, although everything is new in this situation and there are so many unknowns to think about. The doctors should convey their opinion to the foreign colleagues and speak "the host language": the language that considers appropriate communication manners and shows the respect for things that are valuable in the foreign culture. Again, hosts' comprehension, conversation form, valuable objects constitute intercultural SI.

After retirement, SI is not finished. If the retirees discuss their treatment with doctors, SI takes place between the doctors and the retirees (Fig. 1.7).

If retirees explain matters to grandchildren, SI just takes place in form of discussions and explanations (Fig. 1.8).

Wherever you look, everywhere is SI, and it has to be understood.

Fig. 1.5 Interacting with a disabled boy. Based on stock image from PhotoDune, reprinted with kind permission

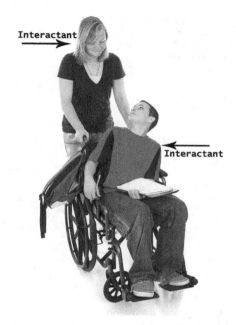

Fig. 1.6 Counseling doctors in an operating room. Based on stock image from PhotoDune, reprinted with kind permission

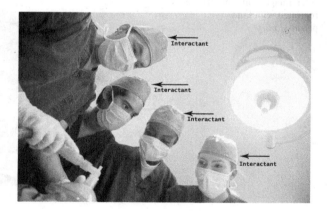

1.2 Definitions

Definition 1.1 The term *intercultural communication* is defined as a set of actions, cognitive states, etc. that involves human actors of different cultures interacting with each other.

Definition 1.2 The term *Social Interaction* (SI) is defined as the behavior of two or more humans. If the humans represent different cultures, SI is intercultural.

Fig. 1.7 Social interaction in a hospital. Based on stock image from PhotoDune, reprinted with kind permission

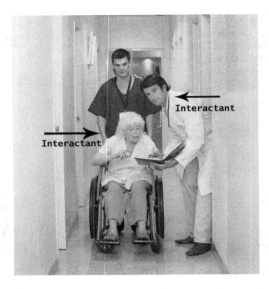

Fig. 1.8 Social interaction after retirement. Based on stock image from PhotoDune, reprinted with kind permission

Definition 1.3 The term *Social Simulation* (SS) describes computer-aided approaches that simulate SI. If SI is intercultural, SS is also defined as intercultural.

NB: This book addresses in the most cases both culturally homogeneous SI with interactants representing one culture and intercultural, culturally heterogeneous SI with interactants belonging to different cultures. The same regards SS. Thus, for better readability, this book refrains from the complete notation repeating "intercultural" but limits itself to the compact notation "SI and SS" meaning "(intercultural) SI" and "(intercultural) SS," respectively.

Definition 1.4 The term an *SS system* describes a computer system that simulates SI.

Definition 1.5 The term an *agent* is defined following Merriam-Webster[1] as "one that acts or exerts power." In this book, an agent represents a human that participates in SI.

Definition 1.6 The term an *Embodied Conversational Agent (ECA)* is defined as a software agent that interacts with its environment through an intelligent user interface, for example, by means of a Natural-Language (NL) interface. For instance, an ECA is a software piece in a computer-aided simulation representing a human that processes NL data.

Definition 1.7 The term a *meta-agent* is defined as an agent that performs secondary tasks in an SS system; for example, it maintains a dialogue or facilitates the execution in an SS system.

Definition 1.8 The term a *Social Network* (SN) is defined colloquially as a community, either physical or virtual, containing members that are connected with each other by certain cognitive relationships.

Definition 1.9 The term a *scenario of SI* or *SI scenario* defines a situation where humans communicate with each other, for instance, to perform a task.

1.3 Goal and Motivation

This book elaborates on intercultural SI and intercultural SS. These fields of study have significant importance in the field of Human–Computer Interaction (HCI) as numerous researchers claim (Yang et al. 2010; Nakano et al. 2012; Kleijnen 2010; Duran and Arnold 2013; Humphreys and Imbert 2011; Piu 2010).

Hence, this book draws on existing findings of SI and SS describing a uniform methodology for developing SS from the multidisciplinary perspective. This book considers various aspects of SI that were already examined by different sciences. It describes an approach to developing SS systems that involve interactants of various cultures. This book examines empirical basis for SS and presents data for it. It discusses peculiarities of SS to pay attention to.

Moreover, this book can be seen as an assistant for an expert in a particular discipline, for example, in psychology, that is familiar with intercultural problems but looks for a numerical evidence of particular facts to verify certain hypotheses. Although the book targets in the first place experimenters on SI and developers

---

[1]www.m-w.com.

of SS systems, it can be also engaging for a general audience since it discusses unexpected, maybe amusing facts from the life of intercultural community.

This book addresses aspects that accompany experiments on SI. It discusses colloquial interpretations of intercultural scenarios and computational implications for SS systems. Abstaining from details of particular domains, this book serves as a practical guide for building SS systems. The book shows computational interpretations of SI scenarios, discusses an architecture of prototypical SS systems, and concludes with concrete programming drafts of the final SS systems. This book provides ready programmatic fragments of software prototypes.

Therefore, following Diekmann (2007, pp. 33–40), this book can be used:

1. to perform explorative studies that investigate unknown areas, social structures, and interdependencies and to develop computer-aided intercultural SS systems that verify the tentative structure and explain potential relations of unknown fields, for example, in revealing reasons of new intercultural behaviors in the modern world;
2. to carry out descriptive studies that explore numerical relations, for example, frequencies or average values of social activities, and to implement computer-aided intercultural SS systems that show numerical relations of social activities;
3. to verify hypotheses and theories of SS, to prove possible interdependencies, for instance, between variables or properties, to develop intercultural SS systems that prove new hypotheses and theories of SS with new strategies, for example, strategies of coping with misunderstandings among intercultural interactants;
4. to conduct evaluation studies that define, for example, application-specific influence of particular actions on effectiveness criteria and to implement computer-aided intercultural SS systems that can show the influence of SI dynamically.

1.4 Methodology

Intercultural communication is admittedly complicated but not intractable.

Trial-and-error (Radnitzky et al. 1993) is a possible approach to learning and tackling with other cultures that can be considered in this book. This technique does not discuss something hypothetically, but defines concrete steps to approach to success. In trial-and-error, if a try was unsuccessful, experimental settings should be adjusted, and the try repeated until the trial-and-error succeeds.

Trial-end-error can seem to be too time-consuming or too costly. Of course, this procedure is not ideal, but it always brought success in the past. For example, recall experiments with flying objects that crashed—and now there are airplanes that fly many years without accidents. Medicine made significant progress—life span has grown dramatically. All these achievements seemed impossible, and trial-and-error was uneasy and thorny, but successful.

Trial-and-error is also not too costly. Indeed, there can be errors that detain success of experimentation. Recall experimentation in spaceflights that cost human lives and much money—and now even space tourists fly in space shuttles or experiments in the medicine with devastating consequences, for example, a medication that is considered as the best on the market has a side-effect that prevents a more positive effect of another substance. And now the quality of life of even incurable patients has grown dramatically.

Clearly, not every experiment deduces high error costs or disappointments if it is performed correctly. The main problem of experiments in new fields is, besides necessary knowledge, imperfection of experimental means and facilities. To deduce such knowledge in intercultural experiments, computer-aided simulation can be used. It allows one to simulate experiments at minimal risks and perform trial-and-error. In intercultural SS, computers simulate results of a tentative intercultural communication between different humans and perform trial-and-error.

1.5 What This Book Is Not

The computer-aided approaches in this book can merely assist an expert, for example, in the cognitive science with their expertise in a particular discipline in providing necessary empirical evidence in required simulation experiments. Hence, the approaches in this book are not intended to replace experts. Even less, the proposed approaches describe universal computer systems that answer all possible intercultural questions and replace a human expert.

1.6 Research Questions

This book addresses the following research questions:

1. What is an advantage of SS and how can this advantage be gained in SS systems?
2. How can SS be organized computationally and what computationally feasible models can be used insofar?
3. What is an approach to acquire data for intercultural SS and what heuristics can be utilized for this purpose?

1.7 Book Outline

The book is organized in two parts.

The Multidisciplinary part discusses issues of SI and SS from the perspective of different sciences: sociology, social psychology, sociolinguistics, anthropology, learning, communication studies, social philosophy, neurobiology, medicine, social robotics, and computer science.

Chapter 2 presents related work on SI and SS. It outlines shortcomings of previous approaches and summarizes findings that can be utilized in SS.

Chapter 3 shows different scenarios of SI and SS that can be realized in SS systems. It also discusses the corresponding pseudocode algorithms.

The Developmental part is more interesting for computer scientists.

Chapter 4 focuses on approaches for data acquisition that can be used to explore introduced scenarios of SI and to perform SS. It discusses heuristics to data acquisition and also the corresponding empirical data.

Chapter 5 elaborates on a framework for statistical processing and prototyping, SocioFramework, that maintains computational means to prepare informational basis of SI and to prototype SS systems.

In Chap. 6, prototypes of SS systems such as NL dialog systems are shown and their implementations are discussed. Moreover, this chapter describes the prototyping principle and a generic approach to prototyping SS systems based on interaction specifications.

Chapter 7 discusses evaluation of the introduced approach to SI and SS. It reconsiders scenarios of Chap. 3 and shows programmatic elements that constitute created prototypes of SS systems.

The book concludes in Chap. 8 with theoretical, application-related, and practical contributions, answers research questions, resolves drawbacks of existing approaches to SI and SS, and presents future work.

References

Diekmann, A. (2007). *Empirische sozialforschung. Empirical social research*. Hamburg: Rowohlt Taschenbuch Verlag. ISBN:978-3-499-55678-4. http://amazon.com/o/ASIN/3499556782/.

Duran, J. M., & Arnold, E. (Eds.) (2013). *Computer simulations and the changing face of scientific experimentation*. Cambridge: Cambridge Scholars Publishing. ISBN:978-1-443-84792-6. http://amazon.com/o/ASIN/1443847925/.

Humphreys, P., & Imbert, C. (Eds.) (2011). *Routledge studies in the philosophy of science. Models, simulations, and representations* Londong: Routledge. ISBN:978-0-415-89196-7. http://amazon.com/o/ASIN/0415891965/.

Kleijnen, J. P. C. (2010). *Design and analysis of simulation experiments (international series in operations research & management science), softcover reprint of hardcover* (1st ed.) Berlin: Springer. ISBN:978-1-441-94415-3. http://amazon.com/o/ASIN/144194415X/.

Nakano, Y., Neff, M., Paiva, A., & Walker, M. (Eds.) (2012). *Lecture notes in artificial intelligence. Intelligent virtual agents: 12th international conference, IVA 2012*, Santa Cruz, CA, USA, September, 12–14, 2012. Berlin: Springer. ISBN:978-3-642-33196-1. http://amazon.com/o/ASIN/3642331963/.

Piu, A. (2010). *Simulation and gaming for mathematical education: epistemology and teaching strategies* (1st ed.). New York: IGI Global. ISBN:978-1-605-66930-4. http://amazon.com/o/ASIN/160566930X/.

Radnitzky, G., Bartley, W. W., & Popper, K. (Eds.) (1993). *Evolutionary epistemology, rationality, and the sociology of knowledge*. Chicago: Open Court. ISBN:978-0-812-69039-2. http://amazon.com/o/ASIN/0812690397/.

Yang, H. S., Malaka, R., Hoshino, J., & Han, J. H. (Eds.) (2010). *Lecture notes in computer science. Entertainment computing: 9th international conference, ICEC 2010*, Seoul, Korea, September 8–11, 2010. Berlin: Springer. ISBN:978-3-642-15398-3. http://amazon.com/o/ASIN/3642153984/.

Chapter 2
Related Work on Social Interaction and Social Simulation

Many sciences elaborate on SI and SS and discuss their aspects. Although these can vary much depending on the discussing science, a generic approach to prototyping SS systems must reconcile all of them.

Hence, the objective of this chapter is twofold. First, it gives an overview of existing approaches in SI and SS from the perspective of different disciplines and summarizes findings that will be considered in the proposed approach in the next chapters of this book. Second, it gives an inspiration for experiments in various sciences that can be performed by researchers in the field of SI.

Since existing approaches are not always easy to categorize exactly because of the semantic overlap of several sciences, for example, "Sociology"–"Social psychology" (sociology overlaps with psychology), the final categorization is met in favor of the most weighty discipline. Alternatively, since descriptions of certain related approaches, for example, in Straub et al. (2007), spread across related work in several disciplines, certain aspects of these approaches are discussed in several sections.

2.1 Sociology

Sociology explores societal peculiarities of SI (Turner 2011; Carbaugh 2005). For instance, sociology finds a definition of SI in the network society (van Dijk 2005; Castells 2005, 2009; Bondebjerg 2001; Hopper 2007).

The network society identifies particular entities of SI. The network society consists of organic and virtual communities where organic communities are the units that are typically considered as elements of a society—an individual, a household, a group, or an organization that participates in a face-to-face communication; in contrast, virtual communities are not tied to the particular time, place, or other physical condition and are loose affiliations of special interest, target, and discussion groups, for instance, on the Internet.

A. Osherenko, *Social Interaction, Globalization and Computer-Aided Analysis*, Human–Computer Interaction Series, DOI 10.1007/978-1-4471-6260-5_2, © Springer-Verlag London 2014

Drew et al. (2006) discuss social research methods in SI and emphasize the role of language in social experiments. Language stays in the focus of this discussion, and particular chapters of this volume present different aspects of its use.

Maynard and Schaeffer (2006) address in Chap. 2 standardization in interaction and use of survey interviews for this purpose. A survey interview is a questionnaire completed by an interviewer based on respondent's answers and can be seen as a form of SI. The authors state that survey interviews span "disciplines (especially psychology, political science, and sociology), national boundaries, government and business organizations, public and private sectors, and so on." Correspondingly, a survey interview measures "demographic characteristics" and aggregates "attitudes and opinions in many societies and subsocieties around the world" by sampling a population and estimating various characteristics of it.

Research suggests that standardization of interviews is necessary to avoid errors elicited by the interviewers. For instance, a standardized survey interview shows not only turns of an interviewer (IV) and a respondent (R) but also temporal details of speech delivery such as pauses:

```
(3) AW01:364
1    IV:    Generally speak^ing do you usually think of
            yourself as a
2           re^publican (0.4)demo[crat ] independent? Or=
3    R:                           [republican          ]
4    IV:    =something else[:? re[publican? ]
5    R:                    [       [republi  ]can
```

In this survey interview, the upper arrow ^ presents intonation raise, (0.4) the duration of a pause, overlaps between utterances are indicated in brackets, contiguous utterances are linked by equal signs (=), question mark is a rising inflection, (:) stretching of a sound. Hence, standardized surveys in SI and SS consider not only factual content, but also delivery aspects such as temporal.

Anssi Peräkylä discusses in Chap. 6 (Peräkylä 2006) how video recordings can contribute to understanding SI in a dialogue. These video recordings show, on the one hand, professional AIDS counseling and, on the other hand, everyday actions (greetings). The main objective of this ethnographic study is to show the gap between theories of practitioners and conversation analysis presented in the video recordings. The scholar concludes that mundane actions depend on the social status and emotional closeness of interactants what can be used in the study of SI.

Steven E. Claymann elaborates in Chap. 9 of Clayman (2006) on NL interviews and discusses the relevance of interaction. This chapter describes possible actions in the interviews such as eliciting a particular answer, but also tasks, norms, and constraints of journalists' questions must conform. The scholar concludes that news discourse depends both on societal institutions and on their relationships.

Fu and Zhang (2011) explore virtual worlds in the context of urbanization and address corresponding social aspects. The scholars show a framework that considers social communication and personal opinions and describe a case study that distinguishes interpersonal interaction, behavior patterns, SI, and communication context. Another case study shows an approach to visualization of a virtual world that presents the infostructure of the virtual city under consideration of particular emotions and culture defined by Hofstede (2001).

Meister and colleagues (Meister et al. 2005) discuss SS in a Multi-Agent System (MAS) that maintains groups of agents and composes shift schedules of an organization under consideration of sociological preferences. The system acts according to capital sorts in the sociological theory of Pierre Bourdieu (1983, 1985) and performs negotiations between negotiation partners in a hospital. Partners' choice is strongly influenced by personal and typified experiences that can be defined, for example, by agents' personality and emotions.

Summarizing revealed findings in SI and SS, sociology distinguishes topology of SN, NL, relationships, emotions, context, MAS, personality, behaviors, virtual world.

2.2 Social Psychology

Poggi and D'Errico (2011) discuss SI in social psychology in the context of society and culture and argue that cognitive processes are influenced by social relationships and emotions felt toward another person. In scholars' opinion, SI depends not only on verbal but also nonverbal behavior and can be constituted by a computer and a human. SI can consider "social" emotions such as pride or admiration.

Berry et al. (2011), Shiraev and Levy (2006) pay careful attention to SI. They discuss behavior (including social behavior, psycholinguistical, and emotional) and present culture-related approaches to understanding it. Moreover, the scholars describe applications of these approaches to such domains as intercultural relations and communication, work and health giving serious consideration to the issues of SI.

The volume by Fiedler (2007) presents an overview of social communication and presents a framework that considers social relationship and domain knowledge. In Chap. 2, Kashima et al. (2007) point out that the today's globalizing world is affected by "clashes of civilizations" and there is a need for comprehension and mutual understanding on both sides of SI. Accordingly, SI proceeds in particular socio-cultural circumstances that correspond to certain cultural dynamics. In Chap. 4, Lucian Conway and Schaller (2007) provide evidence that communication is necessary and sufficient for culture representatives and describe cognitive issues of SI. In Chap. 13, Snyder and Stukas (2007) explore interpersonal processes in the context of settings and situations. They study how SI is influenced by contextual features and how expectations based on stereotypes and other category-based generalizations affect it. They articulate contextual variations and how these variations can change SI.

Straub et al. (2007) present a comprehensive study of intercultural communication and competence. They discuss basic aspects and definitions, disciplinary and theoretical practices, methods, domains, applications, and approaches to facilitating intercultural competence.

In Sect. 2.10, Miller and Babioch (2007) state that all significant sociopsychological phenomena rely on communicative processes particularly in the intercultural context. They explore understanding of communication and state that consists of social cognition as a part of personal behavior and also of group-relations characterized through SI. Moreover, social cognition is so fundamental for a person that babies lacking communication suffer emotional, cognitive, and social impairments. Verbal and nonverbal signals of communication are influenced through culture-specific aspects.

The scholars discuss various aspects of SI such as interpersonal and intergroup communication. They underline coincidentally that intercultural communication cannot be only defined by personal issues of interactants such as self-conception, but is determined by a social environment such as a communication in a dyad or in a small group. Moreover, communication relies on situational constraints or on sociopsychological conception of others that should be considered in SI.

Friedlmeier (2007) explores in Sect. 2.11 approaches to cross-cultural studies and distinguishes four corresponding trends:

1. Homogeneity
   Existing studies of cross-cultural differences assume a generalized structure of a culture with its norms, values, and behaviors. However, a more differentiated multilevel consideration is necessary.
2. Adaptability
   Existing cross-cultural studies would benefit from empirical studies. For example, revealed cultural differences can be validated through interactive acquisition in a psychological context.
3. Completeness
   A drawback of existing cross-cultural studies is their incompleteness according to the number of properties describing cultural groups, which complicates comprehension of considerable interdependencies. An important method of resolving this problem can be consideration of individual behavior in such studies.
4. Dynamics of cultural changes
   In times of globalization, cultures are changing under influence of intercultural exchange, migration, demographics, etc. Hence, an approach to modeling such a change is necessary that considers theoretical models of these changes and changes of individual behavior.

The scholar overviews approaches to empirical acquisition of psychological properties at the cultural and personal levels. For example, he cites the work of Hofstede (2001), providing numerical values of five cultural dimensions in Costa and McCrae (1991). To measure these dimensions, the scholar follows Matsumoto et al. (2008), which explores differences in display rules of different emotions.

Helfrich-Hölter (2007) presents in Sect. 3.6 different approaches to experimental elaboration of SI. She discusses methodological settings of cultural experiments such as differential and generalization studies.

Differential studies explore the influence of culture on behavior where culture is defined through particular factors, for example, cultural dimensions in Hofstede (2001). In such studies, a particular task completion is supposed to be influenced by cultural aspects, for instance, identification of a semantic meaning of a word of a certain print color depending on collectivistic/individualistic culture of subjects.

Generalization studies explore how psychological interdependencies revealed in one culture are applicable to other cultures. To answer this question, generalization studies systematically investigate if particular experimental variables behave in the same manner in certain situations in all cultures. For instance, if similar situations induce similar effects on intercultural norms or intercultural competence. At the same time, the scholar discusses constraints of experimentation and methodological errors. To validate the studies, she explores its representativeness and considers such properties of subjects as education, dialect, demographics, etc.

Marinetti et al. (2011) study emotions in SI. The scholars present an overview of the SI research and argue that SI depends on social factors, for instance, on the relationship between interactants. They elaborate on SI differentiating between the face-to-face and video-mediated communication and consider the interactive context. Characterizing processes in SI, the scholars describe such behavioral patterns as mimicry or synchrony that can regulate interpersonal exchange. In conclusion, the authors state that natural interaction with humans must focus on dynamic models of SI that consider emotions not statically but dynamically. These emotions are influenced by the social and cultural context of SI.

Xiaomeng and Yue (2010) discuss psychology and micro-blogging in Twitter. Claiming that SI is influenced by micro-blogging, the scholars argue that micro-blogs can be seen as a representation of SI in that they propagate ideas and social dynamics.

Farrington-Darby and Wilson (2009) discuss findings in the work psychology using an example of a system for a rail network control. In their opinion, the success of controllers that maintain the system depends not only on technical knowledge but also on social skills and interactions. To perform their studies, the scholars rely on findings of ethnography and sociology that were obtained using such methods as interviews, surveys, and observations. The scholars conclude that although non-task-related SI plays an important role in task completion, SI is indispensable for passing task-related concepts and scenarios between team members. In future work, the scholars will explore the influence of SI on controllers' performance more exactly.

Birchmeier et al. (2011) present an interactive perspective of social psychology that focuses on the role of the computer-mediated SI. They recognize a powerful role of situation and social forces on behavior, thought, and emotions and acknowledge influence of personal determinants such as power and gender. Particular contributions of this volume take into special consideration certain aspects of computer-mediated SI and address trust, deception, and identity on the Internet as a consequence of developing relationships. The scholars present an international approach to computer-mediated communication, discuss leader emergence in on-line groups, explain exclusion in electronic-based interactions, and present the virtual social world as a changing landscape of SI. To investigate SI, the scholars play the social game, Prisoner's Dilemma (PD),[1] known from the game theory (Myerson 1997).

Summarizing revealed findings in SI and SS, social psychology distinguishes topology of SN, situations, relationships, emotions, context, culture, personality, virtual world, and demographics.

2.3 Sociolinguistics

Linguists study SI.

In their volume, Fasold and Connor-Linton (2006) explore language and linguistics in the context of communication and discuss the corresponding aspects of analysis. They elaborate on linguistic SI and emphasize the role of sociology and communications. In her contribution, Schilling-Estes (2006) claims that language depends on different social factors and demographics as well as formality of speech situation. Moreover, she states that dialect plays an important role in communication since it describes cultural and personal distinctiveness. Tannen (2006) argues in her contribution the essential influence of cultural aspects on spoken communication and claims that contempt for corresponding influence can cause miscommunication or misjudgement. To convey her opinion, the scholar uses an example of communication between a German and an American and provides a detailed analysis of conversations taking into special consideration ethnic and regional aspects. Fasold (2006) studies the politics of language in the context of controversies of language uses and forms. To substantiate his findings, the scholar analyzes relationship between the language and the identity in China and Singapore under consideration of sociological theories. Moreover, he discusses issues of controlling the content of speech and explores reasons of blasphemy, cursing, or hate speech. In her contribution, Mackey (2006) discusses second language acquisition and analyzes how adults learn languages and what problems they are confronted with. The scholar argues that this acquisition relies on sociocultural background of each particular learner and demographical issues.

Pavlenko (2007) elaborates on multilingualism and brings together insights from different disciplines such as linguistics or psychology. She emphasizes the role of demographic aspects and communicative situations in analysis. Moreover, the scholar elaborates on reasons of code-switching[2] in SI.

Busch (2009) presents a survey of SI in linguistic research and claims that linguistic research lacks means to integrate the concept of culture. Thus, he explores cultural influences on SI systematically and confronts culture with psychological notions such as beliefs.

---

[1]Prisoner's Dilemma is a conventional example in the game theory that introduces different variants of cooperation involving SI.

[2]*Code-switching* applies to switching between two or more languages in the context of a single conversation.

The study by Scollon et al. (2012) aims at comprehension of sociolinguistic issues in intercultural communication. Chapter 1 discusses the statement "culture is a verb" that emphasizes the meaning of actions in a culture. Chapter 2 elaborates on the meaning of discourse and raises questions about the discourse context, for example, about its grammar and culture. Chapter 3 introduces issues of interpersonal politeness and power and discusses communicative style in SI. It focuses on the paradox of face underlining an ambivalent tendency to present autonomy and at the same time to show involvement in groups' events. Chapter 4 addresses communicational inference that explains inferential meaning, for example, in connection with verb forms or conjunctions.[3] Discussing implications of world knowledge, prosodic timing, etc., Chap. 5 draws on issues of topic and face. Consequently, it argues a special meaning of the culture and relationships stating, for example, that people in China, Japan, Thailand, or Vietnam are "quite conscious in any interaction" with others about their social, economical, and educational status.

Gumperz (1964) explores empiric aspects of SI, in particular, the verbal relationship between speakers, their cultural background, and the interactional environment. Accordingly, he distinguishes different verbal repertoires (linguistic forms) employed in SI: grammatical and social restraints on language choice. For example, interactants can consider certain style conventions and use "aren't" instead of "ain't"; social relationships and social occasions and use, for instance, "eat" instead of "dine" in the father–son relationship; co-occurrence restrictions and use, for example, "gonna" after "ain't" and not "going to."

Performing linguistic analysis of speech behavior, Gumperz discusses studies of Khalapur and Hemnesberget.

The study of Khalapur, an agricultural village near Delhi, India, begins with demographic, environmental, economic, educational, and political details. Social communities in Khalapur are called castes, and strict rules apply to interaction of particular castes with others, except close friends and family members. Describing the Khalapur verbal repertoire, Gumperz states that Hindi as a language of educated people (village leaders) symbolizes high-status relationships. In contrast, the dialect and standard Hindi are linguistic bounds of the verbal repertoire characterized through the simplification of grammatical and phonological constraints, for example, regarding grammatical function words such as pronouns.

Another study analyzes linguistic information in Hemnesberget (or Hemnes), a commercial settlement of 1,300 inhabitants, and Mo-i-Rana, both in the Rana Fjord of Northern Norway. Mo-i-Rana emerged in 1920 from a sparsely settled region in Europe with small farmers to an important iron and steel producing center in 1960. Accordingly, the region grew from 1,000 village inhabitants through immigration from South Norway to a city with 20,000 population with stores, hotels, and cinemas.

Hence, Hemnes verbal repertoire contains the village dialect and the literary, officially recognized standard. Despite the presence of the standard, Hemnes inhabitants prefer the dialect. Unlike its Khalapur equivalent, the dialect is used both

---

[3]*Conjunctions* are grammatical items that are normally placed between two clauses such as *and*.

inside and outside geographical areas, whereas the standard is restricted to particular social relationships. There are grammatical (phonological) differences between the dialect and the standard, for example, regarding function words. It is noteworthy that although there is a traveling possibility between Hemnes and Mo-i-Rana, social events in Mo-i-Rana are of marginal interest for Hemnes' inhabitants.

Concluding his study, Gumperz compares speech variation and social relationships in Khalapur and Hemnes. Consequently, the verbal repertoires in these two regions are affected by semantic, grammatical, and phonological factors. Social implications and ritual barriers play an important role in SI. For example, a Khalapur villager obeys distinct rules of linguistic etiquette and requires special linguistic vocabularies, whereas a Hemnes inhabitant considers a limited number of social relationships in SI. Moreover, linguistic interaction in Khalapur and Hemnes is transactional and personal. Transactional interaction focuses on the socially defined goal, for example, religious service, whereas personal interaction emphasizes linguistic communication style of individuals.

Labov (2006) studies social stratification[4] of English in New York City and analyzes factors influencing SI. Consequently, he discusses problems and methods of analysis of English in social context, for example, linguistic interview that focuses on demographics of its respondents (age, race, religion, etc.). Moreover, he discusses variables of analysis in the social differentiation such as phonological (r) variable as determinant of socially related pronunciation. Subjective evaluation of variables is explored: The scholar discusses assessment depending on demographic factors such as age or gender. The vowel system of New York's inhabitants is examined in detail according to its class stratification.

Salzmann et al. (2011) discuss anthropological and linguistic issues of SI. Chapter 13 scrutinizes variations of communication according to the social class. It states that although native speakers speak the same language, the way of such speaking can be very different. For example, presidential speech differs very much from the speech of a retired woman. Considering language variation, they mention phonetic differences of speaking in the study of Gumperz (1964). The study of SI in Labov (2006) is also taken into account.

The scholars present their definition of SN. The connections between the interactants is regulated by roles (relationships). A particular role supposes certain assumptions about the meaning of messages. The researchers analyze gender-specific vocabularies and conclude, for example, that women use certain emotion words such as *fascinating* more frequently than men.

The scholars claim that languages are "seen as fundamentally very much alike but the social uses... are quite different from each culture to another." Hence, it is necessary to acquire *communicative competence*, the knowledge of what is being appropriate to say in a certain culture. Particular ways of communication are characteristic for a given speech community, a social group of persons of different

---

[4]*Social stratification* defines in this case classification of English speakers into groups based on common socio-economic conditions.

demographic properties (gender, age, social status, etc.). The same persons can belong to several speech communities and adjust their pronunciation, way of speaking, etc. continuously during communication.

The scholars define the components of communication and distinguish between the sender of the communication message, its receiver, and the audience that can perceive the message. Consequently, communication is characterized by particular time, place, and physical circumstances. The scholars follow philosopher Hymes (1962), who states that communication settings can depend on psychological settings; communication takes place under identical physical setting, varying according to the mood of its participants. Communication is influenced by its purpose, channels, code, message content, and form. Moreover, communication is characterized by other components: genres, key, etc. An important aspect of communication are attitudes toward the use of speech. For example, those who talk freely are anticipated in the United States as self-confident, whereas Apache parents maintain complete silence when meeting their children returning from boarding schools. Since such communication components and peculiarities cannot be generalized, they should be studied separately in each concrete SI scenario.

Chapter 14 elaborates on linguistic anthropology in the globalized world and discusses intercultural communication and translation. Since people in the globalized world travel often and communicate with others from different ethnic societies and groups, cultural variation needs special consideration. Even if the guest and host languages are rather similar, semantic differences in linguistic comprehension should be still taken into account; otherwise, there can arise misunderstandings, for example, in relation with words that have the same vocable but different senses in various languages. For instance, the word "compromise" in American English has a positive connotation, whereas its connotation in British English is negative.

SI and the corresponding communication behavior in various ethnic groups can vary. For example, pupils can comprehend some expressions differently (Albert 1986), and teachers should be aware of this difference. Difference in communicative behavior can be formulated in relation to attitude toward communication. For instance, although Americans and Athabaskans (tribes living in Alaska and Northern Canada) speak only English, their communication behavior following (Scollon 1981) is characteristic of their ethnic background. Other issues can be also typical for ethnic communication. For example, Americans talk freely and communicate eagerly, whereas Athabaskans seem to be uninterested in such exchange and converse sparsely.

SI differentiates between different languages of politeness and law. For instance, the language of Chinese politeness distinguishes six terms of apology ranging from "simple regret" to request for "punishment." Some languages manifest only law in talks, whereas American laws are all "written down."

In conclusion, the scholars state once more that intercultural interdependencies became essential and understanding SI with representatives of other cultures is indispensable.

Summarizing revealed findings in SI and SS:,sociolinguistics distinguishes NL, context, culture, relationships, psychological settings, and demographics.

2.4 Anthropology

By definition, anthropology studies humans and their behavior in time and space. In this regard, SI in intercultural anthropology takes into special consideration temporal and geographic aspects of communication.

Koch and Mandl (2011) discuss geosimulation in urban processes and distinguish different tasks of simulation, for example, analysis of patterns of social organization or scrutiny of temporal or spatial processes. In his contribution, Koch (2011) discusses relationships of geosimulation in space, time, and social life. He elaborates on the question why spatial relationships are so important to understand geographical phenomena. König (2011) introduces a multiagent simulation that shows a city and socio-spatial organization of its population. The scholar claims that simulation allows empirical verification of properties of residential segregation or tolerance toward different kinds of residents or land or rent prices. Giffinger and Seidl (2011) state that simulation can be used to explore models of gentrification and give explanations for such phenomena as residential location or change. The contribution of Lindner and Hill (2011) discusses simulation of informal settlements or slums to study urban development in Dar es Salaam, Tanzania. In their opinion, simulation facilitates strategic and coordinated urban planning and is therefore a major challenge for urban researchers. Goetzke and Judex (2011) introduce a simulation of urban land-use change in North Rhine-Westphalia (Germany) and study aspects of urban growth. West and Deschermeier (2011) address residential satisfaction and claim that simulation identifies social clusters of urban place in social districts.

Aruka (2011) analyzes an approach by Glaeser and Scheinkman (2001) that measures SI via group selection. Accordingly, the approach distinguishes people that live in different cities, SI between them, and their culture and age. The approach assesses SI numerically by integrating it in utility functions that rely on monetary calculations.

Ioannides (2012) discusses SI in urban environments from the perspective of economics. The scholar describes in Chap. 2 theoretical models of SI and explores them in urban settings considering cultural and geographic dimensions. In Chap. 3, the researcher elaborates on decisions of individuals to choose neighborhoods or relocate considering educational and demographic issues. Chapter 5 presents location decisions in the urban space in the context of SI. Chapter 10 concludes that SI is fundamental in many aspects for the functioning of economics.

Brooks et al. (2011) analyze in Part III social and equity issues in urban economics and explore impact of SI in neighborhoods, drug wars, homelessness, poverty, racial segregation, assimilation, and gentrification. In Chap. 9, Ross (2011) studies how SI forms urban areas and discusses its educational, social, and economic aspects. He deduces implications of research on SI from these findings. In Chap. 10, Choi and Sloane (2011) raise the question if SI fosters crime deterrence. In their opinion, SI plays a significant role in "improving community dynamics and social relationships, even among people of difference backgrounds and income classes."

van Baal (2004) introduces computer simulations for crime deterrence. In scholar's opinion, computer simulations allow one to analyze individual, collective, and dynamic aspects of deterrence simultaneously. Moreover, SS enables researchers to follow a potential offender in an SN and to assess her/his evaluation of punishment and potential behavior. Hence, SS can oppose the benefits (pleasure) of crime and the expected costs (pain) resulting in the corresponding sanctions.

Rammert (2008) explores HCI and considers relationships defined by SI. He distinguishes interaction between human actors, intra-activity between technical agents, and interactivity between people and objects. In his exploration, the scholar claims a close association with anthropological concepts defined by SI.

Tangalicheva et al. (2010) discuss SI in the context of problems of acculturation in a big city. In their study, the scholars consider theoretical fundamentals of analysis, view a city as a space of intercultural interaction, and describe means of cultural coping.

Summarizing revealed findings in SI and SS, anthropology distinguishes space, relationships, demographics, time, and topology.

2.5 Learning

Learning is another field of study that considers influence of SI (Peterson et al. 2010; Schutz et al. 2010; Pane 2009).

Saleh et al. (2005) discuss SI in grouping arrangements in a plant biology course. The scholars analyze impact of groups on learning and differentiate between homogeneous and heterogeneous groups with students of high, average, and low ability. The experiments reveal that students of low and average ability benefit most from heterogeneous grouping since learning is influenced not only by abilities as such but also by SI between group members that improves learning results.

Peele-Eady (2011) discusses SI in developing identity of African American children claiming that this development often involves cultural and linguistic aspects. She elaborates on how language and interaction can contribute to socializing children and how the interplay between language and culture can be considered insofar. The scholar takes into account the communicative context (where and when communication activities take place) and pays particular attention to the intersection of what children learn and how this knowledge takes place in forming identity considering the role-relationships between interactants.

Umata et al. (2010) conduct a remote communication experiment that analyzes the influence of 3D images on SI in the music education considering emotions and social relationships. The experiment scrutinizes performance of students before and after watching a model performance by a teacher as a 3D image. Students (members of university orchestras) practice a musical piece in advance. In the experiments, students warm up and play the piece. Afterwards, a teacher (a professional violinist) perform the same piece projected on a screen without verbal comments, and the students can watch it on a display from the 30-cm distance. Afterwards, the students repeat their performance.

To assess the learning effect, students fill in a questionnaire that aims at assessing their emotional state. Moreover, the questionnaire evaluates respect for the teacher, impression of the teacher's and student's own performances and nervousness while watching the teacher's performance. The revealed results attest that distant learning improves learning effect and can be therefore considered as a face-to-face counterpart of real learning.

Eggen and Kauchak (2012) argue following Vygotky (1978, 1986) that SI facilitates children development. For example, children learn perseverance talking (interacting) with a mother. Moreover, children interacting with a more knowledgeable person can develop understanding that there are things they cannot acquire on their own. Knowledge of a culture accumulated over thousands of years should be reused through SI rather than reinvented. In scholars' opinion, students benefit from SI because it allows:

1. to acquire necessary information, for instance, while conversing (interacting) with other students;
2. to build own ideas, for example, because conversations (interactions) facilitate sharing ideas that can make a significant push into own ideas;
3. to put thoughts into words, for example, by verbalizing ideas in talks (interactions) and by substantiating own ideas.

Chen et al. (2008) studies SI in cooperative Web-based learning environments and proposes investigation of relationships in SN to find appropriate learning partners. Claiming that SI facilitates learning and consideration of social relations can significantly improve the learning effect, the scholars elaborate on the choice of beneficial learning partners that are assigned not by a human instructor but rather on the basis of SI.

The revealed results show high potential of the proposed approach. To calculate weights in the underlying weighted graph representing SN, the scholars assess the weight of the edge on the basis of information on initiating side of SI. For example, the weight of the edge $R_{in(n)}$ is calculated as

$$R_{in(n)} = \sum C_{m,n}, \qquad (2.1)$$

where $C_{m,n}$ equals 1 if the nth learner actively interacted with the mth learner.

Thoms (2011) analyzes the impact of SI in academic blogging in large classroom environments and contrasts the instructor-driven learning with the student-centric learning. In the instructor-driven learning, the active role belongs to a human instructor, whereas the student-centric software emphasizes the role of a student and gives this student an easy possibility of providing feedback to the learned course.

The scholar proves two hypotheses: (1) A social feedback system for blogs positively impacts perceived learning;[5] (2) a social feedback system for blogs positively impacts perceived interaction.

223 students take part in the experiments. On average, the students compose five blog posts, give 20 ratings, 7.5 ratings' feedbacks, and 8.5 blog comments. To verify

---

[5]Perceived learning characterizes student's perception of learning during a course, whereas actual learning can be measured using final exam scores.

the hypotheses, the Pearson's Product Movement Correlation Coefficient (PMCC) $\rho_{X,Y}$ is calculated:

$$\rho_{X,Y} = \frac{\mathrm{cov}(X, Y)}{\sigma_X \sigma_Y}, \qquad (2.2)$$

where the variable X corresponds to the frequency of system use, the variable Y corresponds to perceived level of learning; the function cov measures how much two random variables change together.

The obtained results assert that both hypotheses are true: the feedback influences learning and improves perceived interaction.

An approach of Nuankhieo et al. (2007) analyzes learning in online environments. The authors claim that online SI introduces new behaviors that are different from the one-to-one behavior between teacher and students in a typical classroom. Additionally, they argue that online SI considers context and culture in which it occurs and claim that new understanding of SI helps instructors to establish online learning. To evaluate their approach, the scholars distinguish SI in groups with 3–4 members or peer-to-peer activities. Consequently, the learning performance depends on sense of community, social relationships between peers, and demographic information such as gender or academic status.

Martinez-Reyes and Hernández-Santana (2012) describe a game, the Virtual Maze, that promotes teamwork and SI between children, motivates them, and effectively improves learning. For this purpose, the scholars develop a virtual world that represents a labyrinth in which the students have different social tasks: navigation that can need social collaboration if a student is lost; collaboration that demands cooperation with a guide that knows the way in the labyrinth; interaction where a student performs instructions of a guide to find the way. In conclusion, the researchers acknowledge usefulness of their studies and consider experiments with children from a primary school describing possible improvements of the game.

Spadavecchia and Giovannella (2010) present a project with online monitoring and evaluation of learning processes accompanied by SI. SI between interactants proceeds in exchange of NL emails or chatting. The project distinguishes eight macro-phases, the most important of which within the scope of this book are phases V and VI that collect data about the underlying SN and the social relationships between the learners. To assess the quality of an exchange, the emails or chat posts are scrutinized automatically according to their emotional content. Since revealed results are encouraging, the authors plan to develop in future work additional tools and methods for monitoring. Moreover, they consider implementing a real-time learning system that can be utilized on a daily basis.

Watson et al. (2009a, 2009b) discuss promoting prosocial behavior of groups of children in virtual learning environments populated by autonomous social agents. The scholars describe organization of human societies and present a simple SN as a model of a primary school class. The benefits of simulation are shown using the example of bullying that is used to develop copying strategies.

Watson et al. (2009b) outlines requirements for believable agents in learning environments. Hence, agents involved in SI

1. must be empathic to react to emotions of a counterpart appropriately;
2. must be endowed with the ability to communicate with other agents;
3. be alerted when a particular condition is satisfied; express emotions;
4. respond to emotions through different coping strategies.

To evoke empathy, three factors are necessary:

1. facial and body expressions;
2. situations' consideration;
3. proximity.

Summarizing revealed findings in SI and SS, learning distinguishes knowledge, space, context, relationships, emotions, demographics, culture, time, and topology.

2.6 Communication Studies

Researchers in communication studies elaborate on problems of SI (Gertsen and Søderberg 2011; Kriyantono 2012).

For instance, Sorrells (2012) examines intercultural communication within the geopolitical, economic, and cultural context of globalization. The scholar discusses issues of culture and cultural space, elaborates on nonverbal and verbal communication, analyzes relationships in interpersonal contexts, and explores intercultural conflict and social justice. She describes problems of intercultural communication and strategies that play an important role in SI. Moreover, she presents clusters of cultures that define groups of similar cultures.

Andersen and Wang (2009) explore nonverbal factors of intercultural communication. Consequently, intercultural communication can be distinguished by chromenics, proxemics, oculesics, kinesics, haptics, physical appearance, vocalics, and olfactics. Additionally, the scholars discuss six nonverbal codes of intercultural communication including context, identity, power distance, gender, uncertainty, and immediacy. The *context* defines the vagueness of messages in cultural communication; for example, cultures with low context such as Swiss, German, or North American require explicit communication and specific details, whereas cultures with high context as China, Japan, or Korea get communication context from the physical context. The nonverbal codes correspond to Hofstede's cultural dimensions discussed thoroughly in Sect. 4.1.3: identity as the individualism/collectivism dimension, power distance as the power distance dimension, gender as the masculine/feminine dimension, and uncertainty as the uncertainty dimension. The immediacy code represents the disposition of representatives of a certain culture to more closeness, intimacy, and availability for communication. For example, cultures with high immediacy are French or Brazilian; cultures with low immediacy are Japanese, Chinese, and Korean.

Prepin et al. (2012) explore SI in the form of mutual stance defined as spontaneous expression of affect such as smiles in interaction with a person or a group of persons. Claiming that dyadic communication cannot be reduced only to speech but considers many facets, the scholars consider such characteristics of comprehensible communication as gaze or prosody. The scholars introduce a model of mutual stances that differentiates two types of behavior alignment, interactive alignment and temporal alignment. Interactive alignment results in a combination of expressive elements, for example, mimics, facial expressions, etc.; temporal alignment stresses the role of temporal factors such as interaction protocols. In their study, the scholars elaborate on two types of smiles, polite or amused. To explore smiles, 192 videos of smiling virtual character and 348 videos of real persons of both genders of mean age 30 are collected.

The results of this study attest that a believable stance model should consider both types of alignment and rely on the internal state of the agent and on reactions of the communication partner. In future, the scholars plan to integrate more information about perceptive and motor spaces resulting in, for example, facial expression of anger. Moreover, they will add information about social relationships of the interactants such as friends or strangers as well as their personalities.

Bonin et al. (2012) explore temporal distribution and semantics of laughter as part of SI in conversation analysis. In their study, the scholars address questions concerning conversation patterns, topic changes, and topic termination: (1) can recurrent interaction patterns be identified in a conversation? (2) is laughter a reliable cue of topic termination? (3) does laughter mean changes in the information flow? To answer these questions, the authors use a multimodal corpus recorded at ATR in Japan containing 713 laughters in a conversation. A conversation can have several topics, and a laugh can be solo or shared with another interactant. The corpus is transcribed with start and end time of laughters' times. For the necessary lexical analysis, the Stanford POS Tagger is used (Toutanova and Manning 2000).

The results of this study reveal the following findings: (1) there is a higher probability to find a laughter at the higher distance to the topic boundaries; (2) the shared laughter is more likely to occur as the topic termination approaches; (3) shared laughter is more probable as an indicator of the topic termination although neither solo nor shared laughter alone are reliable indicators of topic termination; (4) the lexical variety[6] is significantly higher in the laugh termination segment compared with the laugh beginning segment.[7] Since this study could not provide exhaustive answers to the research questions, they should be tackled in further research.

Ojha and Holmes (2010) present a report on humor as a manifestation of SI in a small Midwestern US organization. In their study, the scholars use an approach of ethnography of communication[8] to understand patterns of communication in particular cultures. Claiming that humor has different functions such as positive (lightening tense moments) but also negative (teasing or hurting), the scholars elaborate on

---

[6]The *lexical variety* of text measures the text variation that can be calculated as a ratio of unique words in text divided through the overall number of words.

[7]The *laugh termination segment* corresponds to the time span between the last laugh in a topic and the begin of the next topic; the *laugh beginning segment* is the time span between the first laugh in a topic and the begin of a topic.

[8]The *ethnography of communication* is an interviewing method that distinguishes interpersonal and intercultural relationships as well as social context and demographics.

qualities of humor and examine what role humor plays in organizational communication.

Over three months of study, the researchers collected four tapes of interviews and two memo pads with descriptions of moods and attitudes. This data has been transcribed, and the scholars extracted three topics of humor: everyday joking, superiority as sarcasm, and inclusive teasing. Stating that this study had "an element of surprise and freshness," the scholars acknowledge its success since this study brought helpful insights into interpretation of SI on the workplace.

Summarizing revealed findings in SI and SS, communication studies distinguish NL, context, relationships, emotions, culture, and time.

2.7 Social Philosophy

Social philosophy explores philosophical questions of SI that concern, for instance, social conflicts.

Kincaid (2012) presents a comprehensive study of philosophy of social science. In the introduction, he addresses various questions of SI regarding significant advances, for example, in thinking about the social world, the conception of agents who act in the social world and agents' autonomy, desires, intentions, and interests. In Chap. 11, Gelman and Shalizi (2012) show why philosophers consider probabilistic Bayesian models in SI. Kollman (2012) discusses in Chap. 15 computational models and their importance in philosophical discourse. Risjord (2012) argues in Chap. 16 how modern philosophers model a culture. Mallon and Kelly (2012) state in Chap. 21 a significant role of race in SI and state that "racial categories are not biological groupings but are rather social roles... sustained by cultural understandings, social conventions, and common practices of classification." These social roles influence persons that "occupy them" and are psychologically constrained. Horwitz (2012) explores in Chap. 23 social constructions of mental illness and establishes a connection between a mental illness and minds, personalities, and brains. In Chap. 24, Woodward (2012) investigates empirical implications of cooperation and reciprocity from the philosophical perspective and considers social emotions such as justice, altruism in games, for instance, PD.

Honneth (1996) discusses SI in the form of social conflicts and discusses in Chap. 5 a theory of social recognition relying on emotions, rights, and solidarity. Accordingly, the scholar distinguishes recognition as an element of relations, an emotional respect in the form of needs and emotions, a cognitive respect in the form of rights, a social esteem in the form of community of value or solidarity. This theory differentiates additionally personality, relationships, relation-to-self, and forms of disrespect.

O'Neill and Smith (2012) investigate SI in the context of social conflicts and study connection between sociology and philosophy. Part III of this volume outlines the *recognition* notion that is explored in connection with politics, contemporary societies, and the state. In Chap. 8, O'Neill (2012) elicits relations between

Northern Ireland and England and substantiates the role of historical context in the ethno-national conflict. Moreover, he explains the individual freedom and the role of self-confidence, self-respect, and self-esteem that can be achieved only through relations with others. In Chap. 9, Owen (2012) studies issues of recognition in the context of dual nationality. For example, he claims that naturalizing into a new state means for an emigrant an emotional identification and simultaneously relations of value. Since migrants "typically identify with both communities" (the origin community and the residence community), the recognition acknowledges and "helps to sustain the distinctive relationship to this relationship." In Chap. 10, Cox (2012) discusses recognition and immigration relying on the theory of modern societies in Honneth (1996). She recites important aspects of this theory and considers moral emotions such as love, respect, or esteem; social relationships, for example, family or friendship; context of SI given by demographic determinants such as origin, age, or function. Afterwards, she goes into adaptation of this theory regarding immigration practices and enumerates means of recognition. In Chap. 11, Heins (2012) elaborates on global politics of recognition and argues that only persons are "the ultimate means of moral concern" and not peoples or states. This discussion involves consideration of human feelings and human sufferings that accompanies the search for recognition.

Plant (2009) discusses different aspects of community as defined by the social philosophy, for example, community work as fact and value; individualism in community work; human needs and human nature. Accordingly, he discusses the notion of *whole man*, an actor in the community that has social contacts and roles. An individual in a community is characterized geographically and by the race to be seen as a social being (p. 72). Moreover, community influences individual's mental health (p. 83).

Göller (2007) describes modern social philosophy not as eurocentric discipline but as a variety of cultures and traditions. Correspondingly, the typical philosophical questions such as questions of self or questions of thought should be debated only in a global context and consider possibly culture-independent knowledge, cognition, norms. In his opinion, only this perspective resolves many philosophical problems. Arguing his statement, the scholar presents an overview of previous philosophical approaches, including different findings not only by European philosophers, but also by Japanese, Chinese and Indian and points out social aspects of philosophical behavior. To explore particular issues in social philosophy, the scholar considers dialogue- and communication-oriented methods.

Summarizing revealed findings in SI and SS, communication studies distinguish emotions, relationships, culture, personality, and identity (self).

2.8   Neurobiology

Neurologists discuss SI to understand factors that accompany brain processes.

For example, Astolfi et al. (2011) describe a neurobiological approach that measures brain signals using Electroencephalography (EEG) during certain social tasks

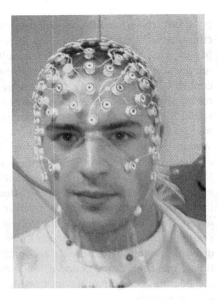

(Fig. 2.1). The motivation behind this approach is that some goals such as tasks of
SI cannot be achieved by separate individuals but only as a part of a group.

To provide a numerical evidence of SI, the scholars ask their subjects to perform
social tasks. Since a human brain never performs the same task identically even under the same conditions, brain activities of several subjects in a group are recorded
simultaneously during SI and not consequently. For this purpose, the proposed approach relies on EEG hyperscanning that defines a procedure of simultaneously
measuring EEGs of multiple subjects.

The approach shows a particular interdependence between activities of different persons' brains that were engaged in the cooperation games. In opinion of the
scholars, the obtained results open a new way of analysis of the brain functions
and facilitate comprehension of brain activities. Moreover, the authors state that a
shared feeling or a feeling of a group can be investigated comprehensively using the
revealed insights.

Naeem et al. (2012) present another useful approach to studying SI in connection
with EEG data. Hypothesizing that SI in dyads can share mutual information, the
researchers study the behavior of 12 healthy persons that perform three social tasks
in couples: (1) couples try to make own finger movements while ignoring partner's
movements; (2) couples try to synchronize their finger movements; (3) partners try
to syncopate their finger movements. Using an analytical approach to depict brain
information, the scholars show mutual EEG information in 60 brain regions. They
conclude that particular SI tasks can lead to activation of specific brain regions.

Knoch et al. (2008) explore SI in larger groups of interactants (5, 10, 20 people)
and study cognitive functions of interactants under electric stimulation of particular
brain regions. The scholars describe prior experience in this field and discuss exper-

iments on brain activity that examine the social behavior of interactants regarding social emotions such as altruism, suspect, and doubt.

To elaborate on interdependences between social behavior and brain activity, the scholars discuss results of a social Ultimatum game. The game setting is similar to PD and measures the activity of prefrontal cortices.[9] The rules of the game are the following. An interactant pair, a proposer and a responder, should split an available amount of money. The proposer makes a fair or unfair offer on how to split the money. The responder can accept or reject an offer. If the offer is accepted, the money is split as offered. If the offer is rejected, both players earn no money. Hence, the proposer chooses the amount of money that a responder can earn, and many responders are teared apart between economic interest and unfairness considerations. The scholars study the acceptance rate and draw their conclusions on how fairness/unfairness in SI influences responses in their experiments.

In other experiments, participants in the age between 21 and 26 (the mean 23 years) play the game that splits the sum of 20 Swiss Franks (CHF) in $4, 6, 8, 10$ CHF offers. 128 players are proposers, 64 players are responders, and they receive either active electric brain stimulation for the whole period of the experiment or only placebo stimulation that stimulates the brain only first 30 seconds.

The scholars examine revealed results according to the stimulation method (active or placebo). It is worth noting that in the active stimulation the acceptance rate of the most unfair offer (4 CHF) is 46.6 %, significantly higher than 25.4 % in the placebo stimulation. Concluding, the scholars claim that consideration of social factors such as fairness judgements strongly influence neurobiological SI experiments.

Anderson and Dickinson (2010) discuss a neurobiological experiment regarding decision making in social exchange in sleep deprivation. In particular, the scholars are interested in how neurobiological experiments influence the judgment ability in SI. The authors state that decision making in general is regulated by emotions and present a survey of approaches that link emotions and brain regions. To obtain experimental results, two games with financial incentives (the Ultimatum game described above and the Dictator game) and a trust game are proposed that examine fairness, trust, and trustworthiness in SI. Additionally, the games study a conflict between personal financial gain and a payoff equality focusing on decision making under conditions of sleep loss where two anonymous partners try to avoid an unfavorable inequality. The revealed results state that SI is influenced by such processes as decision making or emotions.

Summarizing revealed findings in SI and SS, neurobiology distinguishes emotions, groups, and context.

2.9 Medicine

Physicians discuss the influence of SI on human health.

---

[9]*Prefrontal cortices* are brain regions lying in front of the brain that are said to reason psychological functions of an interactant such as decision making.

Rossier and Bernardi (2009) study biological, psychological, relational, and social reasons for fertility intention[10] and analyze the gap between the fertility intention and fertility behavior. They argue that this gap can be explained by the role of individuals in SNs, i.e., is influenced by SI. To prove their hypotheses, the scholars discuss different aspects of social and demographic properties of their respondents.

Fritz et al. (2011) discuss treatment of drug-dependent individuals. The scholars claim that the most significant problem of the drug treatment is reactivation of interest in non-drug-associated activities. To cope with this problem, the researchers explore an important role of SI that would ease drug dependence.

Poutvaara and Siemers (2008) study connection of smoking and SI relying on insights from social psychology and experimental economics. The scholars analyze SI in smokers' and non-smokers' behavior and establish a model that considers utility of smoking and its loss. They perform experiments using games that give social norms special consideration. For example, an experiment studies a rule that smoking exceeds utility from SI when smoking is a social norm.[11]

Cutler and Glaeser (2007) analyze reasons of smoking and study their influence on SI on smoking behavior. The scholars identify reasons of smoking such as marriage with a smoking spouse or education and examine the dependency on demographic factors, for instance, on age or on race.

Lis and Bohus (2013) explore factors that influence SI of the patients with the Borderline Personality Disorder (BPD). Analysis of core domains of SI (social affiliation, cooperation, and hostility) reveals that patients with BPD experience typical problems of impaired social behavior: they misinterpret social situations, erroneously feel social rejection, or have difficulties in repairing cooperation. The scholars conclude that treatment of BPD should consider training of desired behavior.

Tsai and Lin (2011) describe a game-based learning approach for children with Autism Spectrum Disorder (ASD). Since ASD children have medical difficulties concerning social behavior, emotional behavior, and emotional feedback, the scholars present an approach to overcome these difficulties using an interactive game, FaceFlower, that helps autistic children to learn to convey facial expression of emotions in the context of social scenarios. The goal of the therapists that treat the ASD children is to help children to establish social relationships with other peers.

The task of the game is to complete gardening construction with peers in the limited time. The game relies on an engine that recognizes facial expressions of children that play the game. Evaluation of the approach is provided by seven experts that positively assess the game and make propositions on further improvement.

Alcorn et al. (2011) suggest an approach to treat children with ASD. The children are confronted with a virtual environment based on a touchscreen showing a virtual character that can point to an object. The ASD children practice SI when the virtual character gazes at the child and/or point to an object on the screen treating

---

[10]*Fertility intention* defines the wish to get a child.

[11]*Social norm* is a standard behavior in a human society that determines, for example, whether smoking is accepted or not.

ASD using a virtual environment. The scholars claim that virtual environments are a promising method of the ASD treatment since exercises can be practiced repeatedly. They conclude that obtained results are highly encouraging.

The approach of Ono et al. (2012) clarifies the relation between SI and mental health of members of an SN. The scholars investigate data of a consulting firm with 136 members and a care home with 50 members that were asked to fill in a questionnaire about their mental health. The questionnaire contains inquiries about the respondent's well-being including psychological, social, or physical factors.

The approach collects face-to-face data using wearable sensing devices in two Japanese organizations and analyzes the strength of relations considering SN centrality, SN topology, and duration of SI. SN centrality represents connection strength between interactants and is calculated using physical proximity between them, number of contacts, duration of SI, etc.

The approach found statistically significant negative correlations between stress measures and individual mental health, meaning that interactants, especially the elderly ones, spending more time in SI have less stress.

Moreno et al. (2012) introduce an annotation scheme for medical SI games that borrows findings from psychology. Since following (Guralnick et al. 2006) playing can show irregularities in children's behavior such as autistic behavior, the scheme contains three main categories that cover SI, physical activity, and the relation to the phase a child is in (indication of how simple the game is and if the child will play it).

The scholars perform playing experiments with 39 children where an interactive playground consists of a projector, a camera, wireless motion sensors, etc. The playing is filmed and annotated by four annotators according to the proposed scheme. The scholars conclude that the proposed annotation scheme can be used to annotate SI in future experiments.

Kandroudi and Bratitsis (2010) discuss treatment of patients with Asperger Syndrom (AS). People with AS do not have problems in their cognitive development but rather drawbacks in social skills that are usually manifested through loneliness and anxiety. Hence, patients with AS can benefit enormously from the computer-mediated treatment since as the authors state it enhances development of autonomy, encourages communication, boosts self-confidence, and reinforces optimism and respect. Moreover, only SI in computer-mediated systems offers safety to autistic people that would be otherwise considered as a threat. The scholars describe a project with computer-mediated asynchronous discussions where interactants (students) can practice their social skills. The project studies two research questions: (1) can a student with AS be involved in a meaningful interaction with other students and improve social skills? (2) if an improvement occurs, is it permanent or temporarily?

The project distinguishes three stages. In the first stage, 27 students are familiarized with journalism-related concepts such as international news. In the second stage, each student is assigned the role of a journalist. The third stage is computer-mediated where students discuss an electronic newspaper and can comment different articles in discussion forums. The time of comments and discussions is restricted:

students can only access the asynchronous discussion forum locally, twice a week, to omit influence of students' parents.

The project reveals the following answers to the research questions. (1) The obtained results attest considerable improvements of social skills—a student with AS was one of the most active students and communicated with many of his peers. (2) Although the student with AS is overwhelmed with feelings of happiness and is noticed to be more social in breaks, this improvement was completely temporary. The authors conclude thus that although project results are quite promising, more research is necessary. For example, it is necessary to study means of making improvement of social skills permanent. The other interesting aspect that can be studied in future is an adjustment of completely asynchronous discussions in synchronous collaborations in chats, which would increase psychological pressure on the patients and can have beneficial influence on the treatment.

Klein and Cook (2012) discuss emotional robot therapy in connection with the treatment of patients with cognitive impairments (dementia) in UK and Germany. The authors study how SI in care can be improved by robotic intervention. Since dementia patients often experience social and emotional isolation, the research aims to enhance care by mimicking emotional expressions and gestures using SI in emotional robots. In conclusion, the scholars state that a therapy based on SI can significantly enhance quality of life for dementia patients.

Adams and Robinson (2011) describe a project that addresses children with Autism Spectrum Conditions (ASC). Similarly to ASD children, children with ASC have difficulties with SI that can be treated using a game maintaining facially expressive android heads that follow particular strategies. In this game, a head imitates an emotion that should be mimicked by a child with ASC. Simulating emotions, the child learns to observe, control, and imitate emotions. To evaluate the approach, children with ASC are asked to label seen emotions. In conclusion, the researchers evidence encouraging results that should be considered in future.

Summarizing revealed findings in SI and SS, medicine distinguishes emotions, space, time, emotions, relationships, and topology (SN).

2.10 Social Robotics

SI is an emerging field of research in social robotics that investigates interaction between robots and humans (Murray et al. 2009).

Cangelosi et al. (2010) present a position paper that discusses trends of developmental robotics and addresses, among other things, social and communicative skills of robotic agents. The scholars state that embodied cognitive agents (e.g., robots) should be endowed with the ability to collaborative handling of objects, with the ability to learn aspects of interaction with other agents/environment, and with the ability to develop/transfer the skills by sharing them with other agents.

Williams (2012) discusses SI in the context of key cognitive capabilities of robots and claims the necessity of social intelligence to foster effective collaboration with people. Robots should display their cognitive states such as pleasure to be considered by humans as intelligent and be accepted. Moreover, an important cognitive capability that would improve human acceptance is the skill to predict and to explain human actions and behaviors.

Fink (2012) presents a literature overview and presents guidelines of design of social robots. Correspondingly, a social robot in Human–Robot Interaction (HRI) should be *anthromorphic*, meaning that it has to be humanlike to be accepted by humans. This similarity relates not only to robot appearance, but also to its behavior. Hence, enhancement of SI makes HRI more natural and therefore more effective. The behavior should be multimodal and consider gestures and emotions.

Dragone et al. (2005) present a framework that defines means to study SI between social robots, robots, and humans. The framework integrates physical robots, social robots, and humans in a shared social space participating in SI. Evaluating their approach, the scholars develop a computer system, a MAS, that relies on a Social Robot Architecture that combines the Belief-Desire-Intention (BDI) agents (Rao and Georgeff 1995). A reactive behavioral system and a social architecture allow exchange of the Foundation of Intelligent Physical Agents (FIPA)[12] messages. Social robots possess an identity that is characterized by the *character* of a robot and the *stereotype*.[13] To debug the MAS, the developers use a workbench with a BDI debug window and a BDI property window.

Gockley et al. (2005) describe an approach to designing long-time robots that consider SI in their actions. Their robotic roboceptionist, Valerie, communicates with visitors and shows an expressive computer-animated face. The roboceptionist is equipped with a Liquid Crystal Display (LCD) screen and a scanning laser that detects individuals moving around (Fig. 2.2).

Figure 2.2 shows the roboceptionist Valerie. The robot has a character and a personality and interacts with the users by maintaining a keyboard input that is processed by a rule-based NL engine. In opinion of the researchers, Valerie attracted visitors over nine months and can be improved by considering knowledge from human–human SI. Moreover, in future work the scholars recommend integration of more visitor identification and personalization as well as of more visibility of robot's emotions.

Pacchierotti et al. (2006) address design of a SI robot that guides passage behavior of visitors in an office. The scholars state that studies of different passage behaviors can foster research in SI. The tasks of the robot is detection of the visitor entry and offering the guide assistance. The robot maintains a module that functions according to a certain passing strategy considering 3D space and collision avoidance.

Sabanovic et al. (2006) introduce results of experiments on SI using robots. In their experiments, robots have two tasks: (1) augmenting SI by attending humans; (2) enhancing SI of a robotic receptionist by story-telling. An important role is

---

[12]http://www.fipa.org.

[13]The *stereotype* of robots defines the functional capabilities of a robot system.

Fig. 2.2 Roboceptionist.
©2013 IEEE. Reprinted, with
permission, from Gockley
et al. (2005)

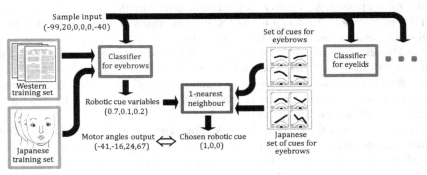

Fig. 2.3 Generator of culture-dependent facial expressions (reprinted from Trovato et al. (2012) with kind permission of Springer Science+Business Media)

played by models of "humanlike" behavior defined by appearance, emotions, personality of robots, and particular skills. In conclusion, the scholars discuss recommendations on the design of their robots that would address SI more precisely. For example, such robots will take initiative if somebody is looking at them and seeking contact.

In their approach, Trovato et al. (2012) discuss implementation of a culturally dependent social robot that communicates with humans by showing particular emotions and alters facial expressions correspondingly. The approach acknowledges differences in expressing emotions of the Japanese culture and the Western culture and claims the difficulty to substantiate the corresponding differences. Hence, to record emotional expressions for each culture, the approach collects drawings of emotions in comics relying on the Plutchick's emotional wheel (Plutchik 2002) (Fig. 2.3).

Figure 2.3 shows the model of the culture-dependent robot that uses six statistical classifiers, one for each part of face, that regulate expression of emotions and calculate a vector of motor angles. For instance, the classifier for the eyebrows calculates motor angles for lowering eyebrows typical for anger or incomprehension. 75 subjects of different genders and nationality evaluated expressions of 12 emotions and evidenced in average good system performance in 68.8 % of experiments.

Summarizing revealed findings in SI and SS, social robotics distinguishes statistical processing, emotions, personality, space, and identity.

2.11 Computer Science

Computer science is actively engaged in comprehension of SI (Nakano et al. 2012; Rahman and Sahibuddin 2010; Yu et al. 2012). Such comprehension fosters research in HCI since it means various applications in the corresponding fields. For example, Social Intelligence (Nishida 2007) and Social Informatics[14] pay special attention to the issues of SI. Ishida (2006), Daisuke et al. (2005), Indraprastha (2011) share their experience on applications of SS. Gautam et al. (2009) urge a deeper understanding of cultural phenomena in social systems and claim that SI explains different problems of economics, business organizations, and computational systems.

Sun (2005a) describes certain aspects of cognition in the context of SS. He focuses on individual cognitive modeling and discusses means of interaction implemented in a MAS. Moreover, the scholar urges better understanding of individual cognition and sociocultural processes that can be achieved by SS.

The volume is divided into a part with an overview of cognitive architectures, a part with modeling and simulating cognitive processes, and a part that discusses SS and cognitive science. Consequently, research in cognitive, and social sciences address the following questions:

1. What are essential cognitive features that should be taken into consideration in computational simulation models?
2. What are the appropriate characteristics of cognitive architectures for modeling both individual cognitive agents and multiagent interaction?
3. How important is culture in shaping individual cognition and collective behavior?

To answer these questions, in Chap. 4, Sun (2005b) describes CLARION, an architecture that extends cognitive modeling to SS. This architecture considers psychological aspects of interaction and contains subsystems for

1. motivation for actions that arise, for instance, from biological needs of agents;
2. learning that considers adjustment of simulation system, for example, on the trial-and-error basis;

---

[14]Social Informatics: http://www.social-informatics.org.

3. goal selection that includes the ability of the agents to dynamically modify their behavior according to external factors of the simulation environment.

The scholar claims that CLARION architecture allows realistic simulation of cognitive tasks due to the mentioned subsystems.

In Chap. 9, Gratch et al. (2005) address social emotions, for example, blame, and focus on their modeling to realistically represent human behavior. In SS, the scholars consider emotion models of cognitive behavior (also in nonverbal communication) and discuss face-to-face interaction in high-stress social settings. Claiming that emotions influence essential processes of cognition (decision making, planning, and beliefs), the scholars describe how coping strategies, such as denial or mental disengagement, can be influenced by emotions.

In Chap. 14, Castelfranchi (2005) addresses the crucial question of building believable SS concerning the interplay between individual and collectivistic aspects of cognitive agents such as social and cultural phenomena. Evidently, agents in a believable simulation MAS should have:

1. autonomy so that governing mechanisms of the MAS can "orchestrate" social structures;
2. "intentional stances" so that social behavior can be predicted and explained;
3. social motives such as selfishness or altruism to explain egocentric agents' behavior;
4. social sources of beliefs and goals to substantiate them in a believable SS;
5. entities of identification in a group, for instance, "we" or "they", to consider human tendency to identity;
6. social rules to organize SS according to a human society.

Thus, a believable SS relies on autonomous agents that are integrated in a social structure with its rules and norms and must therefore delegate some autonomy to organizational entities that regulate SS.

In Burns and Roszkowska (2005), the scholars discuss how social judgment can be considered in a MAS using the game theory. In their opinion, the essential entities influencing social judgments are situations with corresponding agents, their roles, relationships, and temporal issues.

The approach by Torii et al. (2004) addresses SI in the multilayer socio-environmental simulation by considering Q, a scenario description language, and CORMAS, an agent-based simulation framework that combines a physical environment and humans. The Q scenarios define sensing functions (cues) and acting functions (actions), whereas the mapping between cues/actions in Q scenarios and cues/actions in agent systems is specified by a Q adapter. A Q scenario can be attached to an existing MAS to control simulation.

Q is an extension of Scheme (Sussman and Steele Jr. 1975), a functional programming language, a Lisp dialect. CORMAS defines a framework that coordinates simulation of processes between individuals and groups and controls the resource access. For their tests, the scholars use the Fire-Fighter scenario, which defines a fireboss that starts SS and gives directions on rendezvous points of two fire fighters. Moreover, the fireboss gives directions to fire fighters on how to prevent fire and calculates their routes. If the route has to be changed because fire is encountered on the route the fire fighters report it to the fireboss and wait for the revised route according to the present environmental information.

Vollmer et al. (2010) describe an approach to SI with robot systems aiming to learn cognitive skills from a tutor based on the learner's feedback. Specifically, the research answers the following questions: what kind of the feedback should a robot (in this case, the learner) produce to adjust tutor's presentation and at which time. Claiming that infants learn from their parents, the authors try to endow robot systems with social skills by providing the feedback. In their experiments, the authors use the feedback of infants of three age groups: prelexical (8–11 months), early lexical (12–23 months), and lexical (24–30 months). A child performs a task that was demonstrated by the parents and hence mimic them. As data, the scholars use the "Motionese corpus" that consists of video-recordings of 64 pairs of parents performing manipulative tasks.

The learning task is broken into three steps. In the first step, the sequential organization and features of SI are analyzed; in the second step, a systematic annotation with timestamps of interactional events is undertaken including information about gaze, speech, pointing and reaching gestures, smiles, and actions; in the third step, the proposed hypotheses of learning are verified statistically using collected information on interactional events and their timestamps. Concluding, the researchers claim promising results and give recommendations on implementing robot systems that learn SI by mimicking.

Berger et al. (2007) discuss e-Tourism and present means to implementing SI in a virtual community. They discuss problems of online portals and state that customers feel more secure when dealing with humans rather than with automatic portals. The scholars conclude that customers need a sophisticated 3D visualization of tourism products with a virtual lounge to exchange traveling experiences.

Kisilevich and Last (2010) explore SI in the context of online communities and argue that SI depends on language and culture. The scholars analyze profiles of SN members and identify factors that influence communication such as member's education and hobbies. To record member profiles, the scholars use a questionnaire containing 100 issues that reveal the psychological type of the members.

Skraba et al. (2009) describe an approach to building an SN on the basis of implicit information rather than on explicit "friendship" declarations. By tracking interactions between users, for example, logging interactions related to a particular topic, a matrix of interpersonal communications is composed. The approach introduces a framework for analysis of SI containing three layers: a collection layer that gathers information about SI of users, an analysis layer that scrutinizes gathered information, and an API layer that presents an interface to the constructed graph of SI. The gathering layer collects information about SI by collecting SMS and email interactions. The analysis layer identifies clusters of socially related users and hence calculates social proximity between users on the basis of context and habits. The API layer makes the constructed graph available based on the FOAF/RDF format[15]

---

[15]The Friend of a Friend (FOAF) project http://www.foaf-project.org/.

to describe links in an SN. In conclusion, the scholars define their future goal in extending the set of SI types (not only SMS or email) so that their approach constructs more realistic SNs.

Danescu-Niculescu-Mizil et al. (2012) present an approach that analyzes influence of SI according to the role and power dimensions of interactants. Verifying the hypothesis that language coordination can be regulated through "a rich source of information about power difference in a group," the scholars use a Wikipedia corpus with 240,436 conversational exchanges between editors[16] that discuss changes to pages and articles and a US Supreme Court corpus with oral arguments before the United States Supreme Court[17] containing 50,389 verbal exchanges for 204 cases.

The scholars formulate power differences as follows:

1. In the Wikipedia corpus, admins vs. non-admins: *admins* have more power than *non-admins*;
2. In the US Supreme Court corpus, Justices vs. Lawyers: the majority of nine Justices decide a case after comments and questions of lawyers.

To measure language coordination, the scholars use a statistical approach based on the Support Vector Machine (SVM) classifier (Witten and Frank (2005)) and extract different features, for example, bag-of-words'[18] features.

Yassine and Hajj (2010) introduce a framework for composing online SN relying on statistical NL processing that analyzes emotions in comments of two users and reveals a social relationship between them. To compose an SN, the scholars employ a two-stage scheme.

In the first stage, the scholars use an unsupervised k-means classifier with $k = 3$ to identify comments of three categories depending on their emotionality: the first category identifies if a comment is emotional or not (either negative or positive) using keyword spotting;[19] the second category identifies to what extent comments are emotional using the means of semantic affinity;[20] the third category identifies comments of potential friends using statistical NL processing. Since Internet comments have their own language, for example, contain intentional misspelling, the authors consider text preprocessing and improvement of identification of the third category using the real-world knowledge (Liu et al. 2003). The classification result of this stage is 85.6 % averaged over classes.

The second stage processes comments of the third category statistically and identifies social classes of interactant pairs: close friends or acquaintances. As data, the

---

[16]http://en.wikipedia.org/wiki/Wikipedia:Administrators.

[17]http://scdb.wustl.edu/.

[18]The *bag-of-words* is a set of words in an analyzed text.

[19]*Keyword spotting* defines a technique that detects words from a particular set in a search text. For example, to identify if a text is emotional, keyword spotting searches for emotional words such as *happy* in the text.

[20]The *semantic affinity* shows the probability of particular sense of a word and is computed as, for example, the ratio of an emotional sense divided through the total number of word senses.

Fig. 2.4 Multiple people tracking from Chen et al. (2011) (reprinted with kind permission of Springer Science+Business Media)

scholars use a corpus with 850 comments annotated by three labelers with interannotator agreement of 86.6 %. To classify the pairs, the approach extracts emotion words and stylometric features such as the number of capitalized letters. Using 10-fold cross-validation, the approach classifies pairs as close friends or just acquaintances using the SVM classifier and obtains accuracy of 87 %.

Paredes and Martins (2010) show an approach that analyzes users in virtual communities interacting with each other under consideration of psychological and sociological factors. The researchers state that such communities need regulation of SI. For this purpose, the scholars develop a virtual environment with 40 users that can be regulated by changing roles of users, defining rules and information flow. The performed experiments show interaction improvement, for example, better focus on goals of particular users.

Sun et al. (2011) investigate mimicry behavior in SI and its benefits. In scholars' opinion, mimicry enhances SI since computer systems endowed with the corresponding ability seem to be more social (emphatic) and intelligent. Consequently, they also consider integrating mimicry in social systems.

Chen et al. (2011) present a study of SI in a work environment. Claiming that the software development shifts to a human-centered paradigm the SI is part of, the scholars describe numerous benefits of their approach such as improvement of individual's well-being and productivity. The approach is evaluated using the system that maintains visual sensors and a map of working environment where a particular area of the office layout has its dedicated semantic task (*Working*, *Meeting*, *Printing*, *Door*, and *Special*). Moreover, the system maintains three layers: the *Sensor* layer that tracks locations of the users, the *Behavior* layer that maintains behavior models of the users, and the *Service* layer that generates particular recommendations on the basis of user behavior, for example, to take a break after a considerable period of working (Fig. 2.4).

Figure 2.4 shows the working environment with interactants (on the left) and the topology of the corresponding SN (on the right).

Peters (2011) focuses on design of ECAs engaged in SI and considers occurring emotions. The ECAs are endowed with human-like appearances and behaviors to interact with humans in a more natural manner. In scholar's opinion, SI describes beneficial means of analysis beyond the study of certain system components in isolation. Moreover, ECAs can behave believably and adapt to important interaction details such as change of facial expressions or gestures in that they alter accordingly their inner state and behavior.

Payr and Wallis (2011) focus on a socially situated agent and its behavior participating in SI in the physical world and present findings inspired by psychological and brain research. In researcher's opinion, SI is made up from emotions that participate in it, a social agent is "intrinsically emotional" or "relationships between such (social) agents are regulated by emotion." The scholars argue that SI involves not only verbal but also a nonverbal behavior. Using different examples, they elaborate on modeling social identities and describe ECAs with a model of social relationships.

Herrera et al. (2011) studies SI in group behaviors of different size (dyads vs. quads) and various cultures (American, Arab, and Mexican). The scholars claim that different sizes of groups can influence group behavior and acknowledge that communication in a group is influenced by emotions, demographics, and social relationships. To model communication, the scholars consider cultural model by Hofstede et al. (2005) and empirical data from Baxter (1970).

In their experiments, the researchers explore interaction between humans and ECAs. They collect a corpus with conversations and annotate turn-taking, gaze, and proxemics as behavior implications using the ANVIL tool (Kipp 2005). The results show that American quads pause more at turns than American dyads in turn-taking. Americans and Mexicans gaze at each other more in quads than in dyads, while Arabs gaze less in quads than in dyads. In proxemics, representatives of all cultures stand closer to each other in quads than in dyads. Since the results of this study differ from other results in literature, the authors propose further experimentation.

das Gracas Bruno Marietto et al. (2012) introduce a theoretical study of approaches for panic behavior of crowds in SS. Correspondingly, understanding this behavior can be beneficial to verify social theories and to get clear and detailed insights into panic theories. Moreover, corresponding findings can help to design safer and more efficient designs of public places such as theaters or stadiums.

The scholars discuss four theoretical approaches: the contagion theory approach that claims that a person looses his/her personality in a crowd and behaves according to the collective behavior, the interactionalism and emergent norm theory approach that relates individual behavior to the current situation, the structuralist theory approach that explores the influence of social structure on individual behavior, and the constructivist theory approach that considers influence of social context on social phenomena, for example, influence of educational context.

Further, the article studies the use of computer simulations in panic behavior and distinguishes its parameters such as modeling type, reactive or cognitive agents, micro- and macro-level explicitation, and communication method. Simulation modeling type distinguishes analytical/mathematical models vs. complex systems in SS.

Fig. 2.5 A UML sequence
diagram for social interaction

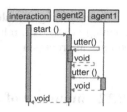

Reactive agents primarily response to stimuli from their environment whereas cognitive agents act according to cognitive aspects as the basis for their actions. The micro-level explicitation defines micro-components of simulation such as individual agents and their actions, whereas the macro-level explicitation considers general simulation components, for instance, societies. The communication method considers the way of interaction, for example, the direct message exchange that connects particular agents directly with each other or indirectly through a facilitator agent.

Approaches of Šišlák et al. (2009), Waters and Barrus (1997) use agent-based simulations as the basis for SS. Correspondingly, the comprehensible simulation allows interaction of agents in the 3D environment in the real time in a possible time-stepped mode. For this purpose, it maintains a 3D world and a wall clock defining relations to the real time.

Trajkovski and Collins (2009) address SI and SS in the context of psychology and sociology and discuss the corresponding challenges. The scholars claim that agents endowed with cognitive capabilities seem more compelling and focus on development of computer agents that experience emotions, empathy, or inference. SS can be developed as a MAS that considers cultural and temporal aspects. Moreover, SS can take into account communication and possible relationships between autonomous agents.

Zhang et al. (2009) focus on modeling cognitive agents in social systems considering urban dynamics. Accordingly, for better understanding issues of SS, researchers have to establish models that consider individual and social behaviors of interactants in simulation situations. The scholars discuss the definitions of agents and society and take the agent/society duality into special consideration: on the one side, an agent is an autonomous entity that has its own preferences and plans; on the other side, this agent is integrated in a social structure that defines groups, neighborhoods, or SNs and hence is not absolutely independent.

The approach addresses two goals. The first goal, reduction of interdependencies between agents by introducing a "meso-view" that groups agents of the same societal view. The second objective is improvement of decision making relying on psychological and sociological information.

Bersini (2012) discusses a methodology for developing SS systems that adopts Object-Oriented (OO) engineering practices using Unified Modeling Language (UML) (Fowler 2003). Correspondingly, an SS system that maintains agents participating in SI can utilize software-engineering approaches based on conventional UML diagrams, for instance, sequence diagrams (Fig. 2.5).

Figure 2.5 shows a UML diagram that defines SI between *agent1* and *agent2* that carry on a conversation by exchanging utterances.

Summarizing revealed findings in SI and SS, computer science distinguishes topology (SN), NL, relationships, emotions, context, MAS, personality, space, and statistical processing.

2.12 Summary of Findings

This chapter discussed related work in SI and SS and presented existing approaches from different sciences. Table 2.1 summarizes revealed findings and shows the corresponding keywords in parentheses.

Evidently, there are findings that can be considered as agent-specific. In contrast, there are also such findings that apply to the whole simulation and can be considered as simulation-wide.

This book discusses both agent-specific and simulation-wide findings (called hereafter modeling dimensions) in Sect. 3.5 after discussing own SI scenarios and proposes computational implementations of agent-specific dimensions in Sect. 6.4 and simulation-wide dimensions in Sect. 6.5.

2.13 Shortcomings of Previous Approaches

Table 2.1 shows findings from the perspective of different cognitive sciences and computer science. It presents a considerable amount of information that accompanies SI and SS. However, particular shortcomings of existing approaches are also evident:

1. There are no step-by-step guidelines on developing software systems that implement SS in different domains, although such software engineering guidelines are necessary for time-saving development of SS systems;
2. There is no comprehensive study of modeling dimensions that can be considered as computational dimensions necessary to build SS, although computational implementations of these dimensions are indispensable to implement computer systems (cf. trends in Friedlmeier 2007);
3. There is no generic approach to setting up experiments in the field of SS that allows prototyping simulation software for desired scenarios of (intercultural) SI;
4. There are no guidelines to prototyping SS systems of particular types, for example, dialog systems, although such guidelines (principle) are necessary to allow flexible development of SS systems.

2.14 Summary and Outlook

This chapter introduced numerous approaches to SI and SS. It presented corresponding agent-specific modeling dimensions that apply to certain agents and simulation-wide modeling dimensions that relate to the whole SS system.

Table 2.1 Findings on social interaction and simulation

Disciplines	Findings
Sociology	(1) Topology (organic/virtual communities);
	(2) NL;
	(3) Attitudes and emotions;
	(4) Explicit specifications (surveys and interviews);
	(5) Emotions (opinions, emotional patterns);
	(6) Context;
Social Psychology	(1) Social relationships, emotions;
	(2) Context (situations, stereotypes);
	(3) Topology (groups);
	(4) Culture;
	(5) Verbal, nonverbal signs;
	(6) Explicit specifications (differential and generalization studies);
	(7) Alerts (constraints and methodological errors);
Sociolinguistics	(1) Culture, values, beliefs;
	(2) NL;
	(3) Context, relationships;
Anthropology	(1) Time;
	(2) Emotions;
	(3) Culture;
	(4) Demographics;
	(5) Context (situation, demographics);
	(6) NL (genre, code);
Learning	(1) Topology (groups, relationships);
	(2) Emotions;
	(3) Context (situations, a 3D image, labyrinth);
	(4) Culture;
	(5) Knowledge (simulation-wide);
Communication Studies	(1) Context (geopolitics, demographics, chromenics, proxemics, oculesics, kinesics, haptics, physical appearance, vocalics, olfactics);
	(2) Time
	(3) Culture;
	(4) NL;
	(5) Emotions (lightening, teasing);
Social Philosophy	(1) Identity (self)
	(2) Emotions (desires, interests, individual freedom, sufferings);
	(3) Personality;
	(4) Culture;
	(5) Dynamics;
	(6) Topology (groups, relationship);

Table 2.1 (Continued)

Disciplines	Findings
Neurobiology	(1) Groups;
	(2) Context (brain signals);
	(3) Emotions (altruism, suspect, doubt, unfairness);
Medicine	(1) Context (agent-specific: demographics, race, age, physical health);
	(2) Emotions (interest reactivation, gain of nonsmoking, facial expressions, stress, loneliness and anxiety, self-confidence, optimism, respect, emotional isolation);
	(3) Repetitions (learning, training activity);
	(4) Groups (relationships, topology);
	(5) Context (simulation-wide: virtual environment, interactive playground, computer-mediated discussions);
	(6) Time (duration of SI), temporal recordings (simultaneous vs. consequential recordings);
Social Robotics	(1) NL (bag-of-words);
	(2) Emotions (acceptance, BDI);
	(3) Scenarios;
	(4) Simulation architecture (MAS);
	(5) Personality (character);
	(6) Input/output (LCD, appearance, scanning laser);
	(7) Context (agent-specific);
	(8) NL (roboceptionist, preprocessing);
	(9) Time
	(10) Statistical processing;
Computer Science	(1) Emotions (inner state);
	(2) Personality;
	(3) Culture;
	(4) Dynamic assignment of agents and behaviors;
	(5) Groups (age of children, demographics, education, hobbies, relationships);
	(6) Input/output (3D visualization, SMS, email);
	(7) Context;
	(8) NL (bag-of-words);
	(9) Topology (SN, micro- and macro-levels, communication method);
	(10) Explicit specifications (UML, social rules);
	(11) Reactive or cognitive agents;
	(11) Statistical processing;

Future work can reconsider existing approaches and present scenarios' implications giving special consideration to the intercultural setting.

References

Adams, A., & Robinson, P. (2011). An android head for social-emotional intervention for children with autism spectrum conditions. In *Proceedings of the 4th international conference on affective computing and intelligent interaction, ACII'11, part II* (pp. 183–190). Berlin: Springer. ISBN:978-3-642-24570-1. http://dl.acm.org/citation.cfm?id=2062850.2062871.

Albert, R. (1986). Communication and attributional differences between Hispanics and Anglo-Americans. In *Interethnic communication: current research* (pp. 42–59).

Alcorn, A., Pain, H., Rajendran, G., Smith, T., Lemon, O., Porayska-Pomsta, K., Foster, M. E., Avramides, K., Frauenberger, C., & Bernardini, S. (2011). Social communication between virtual characters and children with autism. In *Proceedings of the 15th international conference on artificial intelligence in education, AIED'11* (pp. 7–14). Berlin: Springer. ISBN:978-3-642-21868-2. http://dl.acm.org/citation.cfm?id=2026506.2026512.

Andersen, P. A., & Wang, H. (2009). Beyond language: nonverbal communication across cultures. In L. A. Samovar, R. E. Porter & E. R. McDaniel (Eds.), *Intercultural communication: a reader* (12th ed., pp. 264–281). Cengage Learning.

Anderson, C., & Dickinson, D. L. (2010). Bargaining and trust: the effects of 36-h total sleep deprivation on socially interactive decisions. *Journal of Sleep Research, 19*(1), 54–63. doi:10.1111/j.1365-2869.2009.00767.x. http://dx.doi.org/10.1111/j.1365-2869.2009.00767.x.

Aruka, Y. (2011). How to measure social interactions via group selection? cultural group selection, coevolutionary processes, and large-scale cooperation: a comment. In Y. Aruka (Ed.), *Complexities of production and interacting human behaviour* (pp. 141–148). Heidelberg: Physica-Verlag. doi:10.1007/978-3-7908-2618-0_6. ISBN:978-3-7908-2617-3. http://dx.doi.org/10.1007/978-3-7908-2618-0_6.

Astolfi, L., Toppi, J., De Vico Fallani, F., Vecchiato, G., Cincotti, F., Wilke, C., Yuan, H., Mattia, D., Salinari, S., He, B., & Babiloni, F. (2011). Imaging the social brain by simultaneous hyperscanning during subject interaction. *IEEE Intelligent Systems, 26*(5), 38–45. doi:10.1109/MIS.2011.61.

Baxter, J. C. (1970). Interpersonal spacing in natural settings. *Sociometry, 33*(4), 444–456. http://www.jstor.org/stable/2786318.

Berger, H., Dittenbach, M., Merkl, D., Bogdanovych, A., Simoff, S., & Sierra, C. (2007). Opening new dimensions for e-tourism. *Virtual Reality, 11*(2), 75–87. doi:10.1007/s10055-006-0057-z. http://dx.doi.org/10.1007/s10055-006-0057-z.

Berry, J. W., Poortinga, Y. H., Breugelmans, S. M., Chasiotis, A., & Sam, D. L. (2011). *Cross-cultural psychology: Research and applications* (3rd ed.). Cambridge: Cambridge University Press. ISBN:978-0-521-74520-8. http://amazon.de/o/ASIN/0521745209/.

Bersini, H. (2012). UML for ABM. *Journal of Artificial Societies and Social Simulation, 15*(1), 9. http://jasss.soc.surrey.ac.uk/15/1/9.html.

Birchmeier, Z., Dietz-Uhler, B., & Stasser, G. (2011). *Strategic uses of social technology: an interactive perspective of social psychology*. Cambridge: Cambridge University Press. http://dx.doi.org/10.1017/CBO9781139042802.

Bondebjerg, I. (2001). European media, cultural integration and globalisation. *Nordicom Review, 22*(1), 53–64. www.nordicom.gu.se/common/publ_pdf/28_bondebjerg.pdf.

Bonin, F., Campbell, N., & Vogel, C. (2012). Laughter and topic changes: temporal distribution and information flow. In *2012 IEEE 3rd international conference on cognitive infocommunications (CogInfoCom)* (pp. 53–58). doi:10.1109/CogInfoCom.2012.6422056.

Bourdieu, P. (1983). Ökonomisches Kapital, kulturelles Kapital, soziales Kapital (Economic capital, cultural capital, social capital). In R. Kreckel (Ed.), *Soziale Ungleichheiten (Social inequalities)* (pp. 183–198). Göttingen: Schwartz.

Bourdieu, P. (1985). *Sozialer Raum und "Klassen". Zwei Vorlesungen (Social space and "classes". Two lectures)*. Frankfurt a.M.: Suhrkamp.

Brooks, N., Donaghy, K., & Knaap, G. J. (Eds.) (2011). *Oxford handbooks. The Oxford handbook of urban economics and planning*. Oxford: Oxford University Press. ISBN:978-0-195-38062-0. http://amazon.com/o/ASIN/0195380622/.

Burns, T. R., & Roszkowska, E. (2005). Social judgement in multi-agent systems. In R. Sun (Ed.), *Cognition and multi-agent interaction: from cognitive modeling to social simulation* (pp. 409–416). Cambridge: Cambridge University Press.

Busch, D. (2009). The notion of culture in linguistic research. *Forum Qualitative Sozialforschung/Forum: Qualitative Social Research, 10*(1). http://www.qualitative-research.net/index.php/fqs/article/view/1242.

Cangelosi, A., Metta, G., Sagerer, G., Nolfi, S., Nehaniv, C., Fischer, K., Tani, J., Belpaeme, T., Sandini, G., Nori, F., Fadiga, L., Wrede, B., Rohlfing, K., Tuci, E., Dautenhahn, K., Saunders, J., & Zeschel, A. (2010). Integration of action and language knowledge: a roadmap for developmental robotics. *IEEE Transactions on Autonomous Mental Development, 2*(3), 167–195. doi:10.1109/TAMD.2010.2053034. http://dx.doi.org/10.1109/TAMD.2010.2053034.

Carbaugh, D. (2005). *Routledge communication series. Cultures in conversation.* London: Routledge. 9780805852349. http://amazon.com/o/ASIN/0805852344/.

Castelfranchi, C. (2005). Cognitive architecture and contents for social structures and interactions. In R. Sun (Ed.), *Cognition and multi-agent interaction: from cognitive modeling to social simulation* (pp. 219–251). Cambridge: Cambridge University Press.

Castells, M. (Ed.) (2005). *The network society: a cross-cultural perspective.* Cheltenham: Edward Elgar. ISBN:978-1-845-42435-0. http://amazon.com/o/ASIN/1845424352/.

Castells, M. (2009). *Information age series: Vol. I. The rise of the network society: the information age: economy, society, and culture* (2nd ed.). New York: Wiley-Blackwell. ISBN:978-1-405-19686-4. http://amazon.com/o/ASIN/1405196866/.

Chen, C. M., Hong, C. M., & Chang, C. C. (2008). Mining interactive social network for recommending appropriate learning partners in a web-based cooperative learning environment. In *2008 IEEE conference on cybernetics and intelligent systems* (pp. 642–647). doi:10.1109/ICCIS.2008.4670866.

Chen, C. W., Aztiria, A., Ben Allouch, S., & Aghajan, H. (2011). Understanding the influence of social interactions on individual's behavior pattern in a work environment. In *Proceedings of the second international conference on human behavior understanding, HBU'11* (pp. 146–157). Berlin: Springer. ISBN:978-3-642-25445-1. doi:10.1007/978-3-642-25446-8_16. http://dx.doi.org/10.1007/978-3-642-25446-8_16.

Choi, H., & Sloane, D. (2011). Does working together prevent crime? In N. Brooks, K. Donaghy & G. J. Knaap (Eds.), *Oxford handbooks. The Oxford handbook of urban economics and planning* (pp. 230–247). Oxford: Oxford University Press.

Clayman, S. E. (2006). Understanding news media: the relevance of interaction. In P. Drew, G. Raymond & D. Weinberg (Eds.), *Talk and interaction in social research methods* (pp. 135–154). Thousand Oaks: Sage. ISBN:978-0-761-95705-8.

Costa, P., & McCrae, R. R. (1991). The NEO personality inventory: using the five-factor model in counseling. *Journal of Counseling and Development, 69*, 367–372.

Cox, R. (2012). Recognition and Immigration. In S. O'Neill & N. H. Smith (Eds.), *Recognition theory as social research: investigating the dynamics of social conflict* (pp. 192–212). Basingstoke: Palgrave Macmillan.

Cutler, D. M., & Glaeser, E. L. (2007). *Social interactions and smoking* (Working paper No. 13477). National Bureau of Economic Research. http://www.nber.org/papers/w13477.

Daisuke, T., Toru, I., Stephane, B., & Alexis, D. (2005). Layering social interaction scenarios on environmental simulation. In D. Paul, L. Brian & T. Keiki (Eds.), *Lecture notes in computer science: Vol. 3415. Multi-agent and multi-agent-based simulation* (pp. 78–88). Berlin: Springer.

Danescu-Niculescu-Mizil, C., Lee, L., Pang, B., & Kleinberg, J. (2012). Echoes of power: language effects and power differences in social interaction. In *Proceedings of the 21st international conference on world wide web, WWW '12* (pp. 699–708). New York: ACM. ISBN:978-1-4503-1229-5. doi:10.1145/2187836.2187931. http://doi.acm.org/10.1145/2187836.2187931.

das Gracas Bruno Marietto, M., dos Santos Franca, R., Steinberger-Elias, M., Botelho, W. T., Noronha, E. A., & da Silva, V. L. (2012). In *International conference for internet technology and secured transactions* (pp. 628–633).

Dragone, M., Duffy, B. R., & O'Hare, G. M. P. (2005). Social interaction between robots, avatars humans. In *IEEE international workshop on robot and human interactive communication, ROMAN 2005* (pp. 24–29). doi:10.1109/ROMAN.2005.1513751.

Drew, P., Raymond, G., & Weinberg, D. (2006). *Talk and interaction in social research methods.* Thousand Oaks: Sage. ISBN:978-0-761-95705-8. http://amazon.com/o/ASIN/0761957057/.

Eggen, P. D., & Kauchak, D. P. (2012). *Educational psychology: windows on classrooms plus myeducationlab with pearson etext—access card package* (9th ed.). Upper Saddle River: Pearson. ISBN:978-0-132-89357-2. http://amazon.com/o/ASIN/0132893576/.

Farrington-Darby, T., & Wilson, J. R. (2009). Understanding social interactions in complex work: a video ethnography. *Cognition Technology & Work, 11*(1), 1–15. doi:10.1007/s10111-008-0118-z. http://dx.doi.org/10.1007/s10111-008-0118-z.

Fasold, R. (2006). The politics of language. In R. W. Fasold & J. Connor-Linton (Eds.), *An introduction to language and linguistics* (pp. 373–400). Cambridge: Cambridge University Press.

Fasold, R. W., & Connor-Linton, J. (Eds.) (2006). *An introduction to language and linguistics* (1st ed.). Cambridge: Cambridge University Press. ISBN:978-0-521-61235-7. http://amazon.com/o/ASIN/0521612357/.

Fiedler, K. (Ed.) (2007). *Social communication. Frontiers of social psychology* (1st ed.). London: Psychology Press. ISBN:978-1-841-69428-3. http://amazon.com/o/ASIN/1841694282/.

Fink, J. (2012). Anthropomorphism and human likeness in the design of robots and human-robot interaction. In S. S. Ge, O. Khatib, J. J. Cabibihan, R. Simmons & M. A. Williams (Eds.), *Lecture notes in computer science: Vol. 7621. Social robotics* (pp. 199–208). Berlin: Springer. ISBN:978-3-642-34102-1. doi:10.1007/978-3-642-34103-8_20. http://dx.doi.org/10.1007/978-3-642-34103-8_20.

Fowler, M. (2003). *UML distilled: a brief guide to the standard object modeling language* (3rd ed.). Reading: Addison-Wesley. ISBN:978-0-321-19368-1. http://amazon.com/o/ASIN/0321193687/.

Friedlmeier, W. (2007). Kulturvergleichende Psychologie (Cross-cultural psychology). In *Handbuch interkulturelle Kommunikation und Kompetenz (Handbook of intercultural communication and competence)* (pp. 225–236). Berlin: Metzler.

Fritz, M., Rawas, R. E., Klement, S., Kummer, K., Mayr, M. J., Eggart, V., Salti, A., Bardo, M. T., Saria, A., & Zernig, G. (2011). Differential effects of accumbens core vs. shell lesions in a rat concurrent conditioned place preference paradigm for cocaine vs. social interaction. *PLoS ONE, 6*(10), 26761. http://www.biomedsearch.com/nih/Differential-Effects-Accumbens-Core-vs/22046347.html.

Fu, Z., & Zhang, X. (2011). Designing for social urban media: creating an integrated framework of social innovation and service design in china. In *Proceedings of the 4th international conference on internationalization, design and global development, IDGD'11* (pp. 494–503). Berlin: Springer. ISBN:978-3-642-21659-6. http://dl.acm.org/citation.cfm?id=2028768.2028829.

Gautam, D., Singh, R. R., & Singh, V. K. (2009). Multi-agent based models of social contagion and emergent collective behavior. In *International conference on intelligent agent multi-agent systems, IAMA 2009* (pp. 1–5). doi:10.1109/IAMA.2009.5228082.

Gelman, A., & Shalizi, C. R. (2012). Philosophy and practice of Bayesian statistics in the social sciences. In H. Kincaid (Ed.), *Oxford handbooks. The Oxford handbook of philosophy of social science* (pp. 259–273). Oxford: Oxford University Press.

Gertsen, M. C., & Søderberg, A. M. (2011). Intercultural collaboration stories. on narrative inquiry and analysis as tools for research in international business. *Journal of International Business Studies, 42*(6), 765–786. doi:10.1057/jibs.2011.15.

Giffinger, R., & Seidl, R. (2011). Micro-modeling of gentrification: a useful tool for planning? In A. Koch & P. Mandl (Eds.), *Modeling and simulating urban processes (geosimulation)* (pp. 59–76). Berlin: LIT Verlag.

Glaeser, E. L., & Scheinkman, J. A. (2001). Measuring social interactions. In H. P. Y. S. N. Durlauf (Ed.), *Social dynamics* (pp. 83–131). Washington: Brooking Institute.

Gockley, R., Bruce, A., Forlizzi, J., Michalowski, M., Mundell, A., Rosenthal, S., Sellner, B., Simmons, R., Snipes, K., Schultz, A. C., & Wang, J. (2005). Designing robots for long-term social interaction. In *IEEE/RSJ international conference on intelligent robots and systems, IROS 2005* (pp. 1338–1343). doi:10.1109/IROS.2005.1545303.

Goetzke, R., & Judex, M. (2011). Simulation of urban land-use change in North Rhine-Westphalia (Germany) with the Java-based modelling platform Xulu. In A. Koch & P. Mandl (Eds.), *Modeling and simulating urban processes (geosimulation)* (pp. 99–118). Berlin: LIT Verlag.

Göller, T. (2007). Interkulturelle Philosophie (Intercultural philosophy). In *Handbuch interkulturelle Kommunikation und Kompetenz (Handbook of intercultural communication and competence)* (pp. 272–282). Berlin: Metzler.

Gratch, J., Mao, W., & Marcella, S. (2005). Modeling social emotions and social attributions. In R. Sun (Ed.), *Cognition and multi-agent interaction: from cognitive modeling to social simulation* (pp. 219–251). Cambridge: Cambridge University Press.

Gumperz, J. J. (1964). Linguistic and social interaction in two communities. *American Anthropologist, 66*(6_PART2), 137–153. doi:10.1525/aa.1964.66.suppl_3.02a00100. http://dx.doi.org/10.1525/aa.1964.66.suppl_3.02a00100.

Guralnick, M. J., Hammond, M. A., Connor, R. T., & Neville, B. (2006). Stability, change, and correlates of the peer relationships of young children with mild developmental delays. *Child Development, 77*(2), 312–324. doi:10.1111/j.1467-8624.2006.00872.x. http://dx.doi.org/10.1111/j.1467-8624.2006.00872.x.

Heins, V. (2012). The Global Politics of Recognition. In S. O'Neill & N. H. Smith (Eds.), *Recognition theory as social research: investigating the dynamics of social conflict* (pp. 213–230). Basingstoke: Palgrave Macmillan.

Helfrich-Hölter, H. (2007). Experimente (Experiments). In *Handbuch interkulturelle Kommunikation und Kompetenz (Handbook of intercultural communication and competence)* (pp. 352–357). Berlin: Metzler.

Herrera, D., Novick, D., Jan, D., & Traum, D. (2011). Dialog behaviors across culture and group size. In *Proceedings of the 6th international conference on universal access in human–computer interaction: users diversity, UAHCI'11, part II* (pp. 450–459). Berlin: Springer. ISBN:978-3-642-21662-6. http://dl.acm.org/citation.cfm?id=2027376.2027428.

Hofstede, G. (2001). *Culture's consequences: comparing values, behaviors, institutions and organizations across nations* (2nd ed.). Thousand Oaks: Sage. ISBN:978-0-803-97324-4. http://amazon.com/o/ASIN/0803973241/.

Hofstede, G., Hofstede, G. H., & Hofstede, G. J. (2005). *Successful strategist series. Cultures and organizations: software of the mind.* New York: McGraw-Hill. ISBN:978-0-071-43959-6. http://books.google.de/books?id=tLbt4eCcltcC.

Honneth, A. (1996). *Studies in contemporary German social thought. The struggle for recognition: the moral grammar of social conflicts* (1st ed.). Cambridge: MIT Press. ISBN:978-0-262-58147-9. http://amazon.com/o/ASIN/0262581477/.

Hopper, P. (2007). *Understanding cultural globalization.* London: Polity. ISBN:978-0-745-63558-3. http://amazon.com/o/ASIN/074563558X/.

Horwitz, A. (2012). Social Constructions of Mental Illness. In H. Kincaid (Ed.), *Oxford handbooks. The Oxford handbook of philosophy of social science* (pp. 559–580). Oxford: Oxford University Press.

Hymes, D. (1962). The ehnography of speaking. In T. Gladwin & W. C. Sturtevant (Eds.), *Anthropology and human behavior* (pp. 13–53). Washington: Anthropological Society of Washington.

Indraprastha, A. (2011). Computational model of social interaction in multiagent simulation based on personality traits. In *2011 international conference on advanced computer science and information system (ICACSIS)* (pp. 183–188).

Ioannides, Y. M. (2012). *From neighborhoods to nations: the economics of social interactions.* Princeton: Princeton University Press. ISBN:978-0-691-12685-2. http://amazon.com/o/ASIN/0691126852/.

Ishida, T. (2006). Multiagent simulation meets the real world. In *Proceedings of the fifth international joint conference on Autonomous agents and multiagent systems, AAMAS '06* (pp. 123–125). New York: ACM. ISBN:1-59593-303-4. http://doi.acm.org/10.1145/1160633.1160652.

Kandroudi, M., & Bratitsis, T. (2010). Children with Asperger syndrome and computer supported collaborative learning activities: a case study in a 3rd grade mixed class. In *2010 2nd international conference on intelligent networking and collaborative systems (INCOS)* (pp. 274–281). doi:10.1109/INCOS.2010.58.

Kashima, Y., Klein, O., & Clark, A. E. (2007). Grounding: sharing information in social interaction. In K. Fiedler (Ed.), *Social communication. Frontiers of social psychology* (1st ed., pp. 27–78). London: Psychology Press.

Kincaid, H. (Ed.) (2012). *Oxford handbooks. The Oxford handbook of philosophy of social science* Oxford: Oxford University Press. ISBN:978-0-195-39275-3. http://amazon.com/o/ASIN/0195392752/.

Kipp, M. (2005). *Gesture generation by imitation: from human behavior to computer character animation.* Dissertation.com.

Kisilevich, S., & Last, M. (2010). Exploring gender differences in member profiles of an online dating site across 35 countries. In *MSM/MUSE* (pp. 57–78).

Klein, B., & Cook, G. (2012). Emotional robotics in Elder care—a comparison of findings in the UK and Germany. In S. S. Ge, O. Khatib, J J. Cabibihan, R. Simmons & M. A. Williams (Eds.), *Lecture notes in computer science: Vol. 7621. Social robotics* (pp. 108–117). Berlin: Springer. ISBN:978-3-642-34102-1. doi:10.1007/978-3-642-34103-8_11. http://dx.doi.org/10.1007/978-3-642-34103-8_11.

Knoch, D., Nitsche, M. A., Fischbacher, U., Eisenegger, C., Pascual-Leone, A., & Fehr, E. (2008). Studying the neurobiology of social interaction with transcranial direct current stimulation—the example of punishing unfairness. *Cerebral Cortex, 18*(9), 1987–1990. doi:10.1093/cercor/bhm237. http://cercor.oxfordjournals.org/content/18/9/1987.abstract.

Koch, A. (2011). Geosimulation: Expeditions to the invisible relationships of space, time, and social life. In A. Koch & P. Mandl (Eds.), *Modeling and simulating urban processes (geosimulation)* (pp. 11–38). Berlin: LIT Verlag.

Koch, A., & Mandl, P. (Eds.) (2011). *Modeling and simulating urban processes. Geosimulation.* Berlin: LIT Verlag. ISBN:978-3-643-50036-6. http://amazon.com/o/ASIN/364350036X/.

Kollman, K. (2012). The Potential Value of Computational Models in Social Science Research. In H. Kincaid (Ed.), *Oxford handbooks. The Oxford handbook of philosophy of social science* (pp. 259–273). Oxford: Oxford University Press.

König, R. (2011). An agent-based simulation to show the effects of the size of a city on the socio-spatial organisation of its population. In A. Koch & P. Mandl (Eds.), *Modeling and simulating urban processes (geosimulation)* (pp. 39–58). Berlin: LIT Verlag.

Kriyantono, R. (2012). Measuring a company reputation in a crisis situation: an ethnography approach on the situational crisis communication theory. *International Journal of Business and Social Science, 3*(9).

Labov, W. (2006). *The social stratification of English in New York city* (2nd ed.). Cambridge: Cambridge University Press. http://amazon.com/o/ASIN/B008SLHGAK/.

Lindner, C., & Hill, A. (2011). Simulating informal urban development in Dar es Salaam, Tanzania—a CA-based simulation model for strategic and coordinated urban planning. In A. Koch & P. Mandl (Eds.), *Geosimulation. Modeling and simulating urban processes* (pp. 77–98). Berlin: LIT Verlag.

Lis, S., & Bohus, M. (2013). Social interaction in borderline personality disorder. *Current Psychiatry Reports, 15*, 1–7. doi:10.1007/s11920-012-0338-z. http://dx.doi.org/10.1007/s11920-012-0338-z.

Liu, H., Lieberman, H., & Selker, T. (2003). A model of textual affect sensing using real-world knowledge. In *IUI '03: proceedings of the 8th international conference on intelligent user interfaces* (pp. 125–132). New York: ACM Press. ISBN:1-58113-586-6. http://doi.acm.org/10.1145/604045.604067.

Lucian Conway, I., & Schaller, M. (2007). How Communication shapes culture. In K. Fiedler (Ed.), *Frontiers of social psychology. Social communication* (1st ed., pp. 107–128). London: Psychology Press.

Mackey, A. (2006). Second language acquisition. In R. W. Fasold & J. Connor-Linton (Eds.), *An introduction to language and linguistics* (pp. 433–464). Cambridge: Cambridge University Press.

Mallon, R., & Kelly, D. (2012). Making race out of nothing: psychologically constrained social roles. In H. Kincaid (Ed.), *Oxford handbooks. The Oxford handbook of philosophy of social science* (pp. 507–532). Oxford: Oxford University Press.

Marinetti, C., Moore, P., Lucas, P., & Parkinson, B. (2011). Emotions in social interactions: unfolding emotional experience. In R. Cowie, C. Pelachaud & P. Petta (Eds.), *Cognitive technologies. Emotion-oriented Systems* (pp. 31–46). Berlin: Springer. doi:10.1007/978-3-642-15184-2_3. 978-3-642-15183-5. http://dx.doi.org/10.1007/978-3-642-15184-2_3.

Martinez-Reyes, F., & Hernández-Santana, I. (2012). The virtual maze: a game to promote social interaction between children. In *Proceedings of the 2012 eighth international conference on intelligent environments, IE '12* (pp. 331–334). Washington: IEEE Computer Society. doi:10.1109/IE.2012.42. 978-0-7695-4741-1. http://dx.doi.org/10.1109/IE.2012.42.

Matsumoto, D., Yoo, S. H., & Fontaine, J. (2008). Mapping expressive differences around the world: the relationship between emotional display rules and individualism versus collectivism. *Journal of Cross-Cultural Psychology, 39*(1), 55–74. doi:10.1177/0022022107311854. http://jcc.sagepub.com/content/39/1/55.abstract.

Maynard, D. W., & Schaeffer, N. C. (2006). Standardization-in-interaction: the survey interview. In P. Drew, G. Raymond & D. Weinberg (Eds.), *Talk and interaction in social research methods* (pp. 9–27). Thousand Oaks: Sage. ISBN:978-0-761-95705-8.

Meister, M., Urbig, D., Kay, S., & Gerstl, R. (2005). Agents enacting social roles. Balancing formal structure and practical rationality in mas design. In *LNAI: Vol. 3413. Socionics. Scalability of complex social systems* (pp. 104–131). Berlin: Springer.

Miller, R., & Babioch, A. (2007). Sozialpsychologische Ansätze (Sociopsychological approaches). In *Handbuch interkulturelle Kommunikation und Kompetenz (Handbook of intercultural communication and competence)* (pp. 215–224). Berlin: Metzler.

Moreno, A., van Delden, R., Reidsma, D., Poppe, R., & Heylen, D. (2012). An annotation scheme for social interaction in digital playgrounds. In *Proceedings of the 11th international conference on entertainment computing, ICEC'12* (pp. 85–99). Berlin: Springer. ISBN:978-3-642-33541-9. doi:10.1007/978-3-642-33542-6_8. http://dx.doi.org/10.1007/978-3-642-33542-6_8.

Murray, J. C., Canamero, L., & Hiolle, A. (2009). Towards a model of emotion expression in an interactive robot head. In *The 18th IEEE international symposium on robot and human interactive communication, RO-MAN 2009* (pp. 627–632). doi:10.1109/ROMAN.2009.5326131.

Myerson, R. B. (1997). *Game theory: analysis of conflict.* Harvard: Harvard University Press. ISBN:978-0-674-34116-6. http://amazon.com/o/ASIN/0674341163/.

Naeem, M., McGinnity, T. M., Watson, D., Wong-Lin, K., Prasad, G., & Kelso, J. A. S. (2012). Inter-brain mutual information in social interaction tasks. In *2012 international workshop on pattern recognition in neuroimaging (PRNI)* (pp. 25–28). doi:10.1109/PRNI.2012.32.

Nakano, Y., Neff, M., Paiva, A., & Walker, M. (Eds.) (2012). *Lecture notes in artificial intelligence. Intelligent virtual agents: 12th international conference, IVA 2012,* Santa Cruz, CA, USA, September, 12–14, 2012. Berlin: Springer. ISBN:978-3-642-33196-1. http://amazon.com/o/ASIN/3642331963/.

Nishida, T. (2007). Social intelligence design and human computing. In *Artificial intelligence for human computing* (pp. 190–214).

Nuankhieo, P., Tsai, I. C., Goggins, S., & Laffey, J. (2007). Comparing the social interaction pattern of online one-on-one peer and small group collaboration activities. In *Ninth IEEE international symposium on multimedia workshops, ISMW '07* (pp. 441–446). doi:10.1109/ISM.Workshops.2007.80.

Ojha, A. K., & Holmes, T. L. (2010). Don't tease me, I'm working: examining humor in a midwestern organization using ethnography of communication. *The Weekly Qualitative Report, 3*(12), 54–63. http://www.nova.edu/ssss/QR/QR15-2/ojha.pdf.

O'Neill, S. (2012). The politics of conflict transformation: a recognition-theoretical reading of the peace process in Northern Ireland. In S. O'Neill & N. H. Smith (Eds.), *Recognition theory as social research: investigating the dynamics of social conflict* (pp. 149–172). Basingstoke: Palgrave Macmillan.

O'Neill, S., & Smith, N. H. (Eds.) (2012). *Recognition theory as social research: investigating the dynamics of social conflict.* Basingstoke: Palgrave Macmillan. ISBN:978-0-230-29655-8. http://amazon.com/o/ASIN/0230296556/.

Ono, E., Nozawa, T., Ogata, T., Motohashi, M., Higo, N., Kobayashi, T., Ishikawa, K., Ara, K., Yano, K., & Miyake, Y. (2012). Fundamental deliberation on exploring mental health through social interaction pattern. In *2012 ICME international conference on complex medical engineering (CME)* (pp. 321–326). doi:10.1109/ICCME.2012.6275728.

Owen, D. (2012). Recognition as statecraft? Contexts of recognition and of state membership regimes. In S. O'Neill & N. H. Smith (Eds.), *Recognition theory as social research: investigating the dynamics of social conflict* (pp. 173–191). Basingstoke: Palgrave Macmillan.

Pacchierotti, E., Christensen, H. I., & Jensfelt, P. (2006). Design of an office-guide robot for social interaction studies. In *IROS* (pp. 4965–4970).

Pane, D. M. (2009). The relationship between classroom interactions and exclusionary discipline as a social practice: a critical microethnography. In *FIU electronic theses and dissertations* (p. 109).

Paredes, H., & Martins, F. M. (2010). Social interaction regulation in virtual web environments using the social theaters model. In *2010 14th international conference on computer supported cooperative work in design (CSCWD)* (pp. 772–777). doi:10.1109/CSCWD.2010.5471871.

Pavlenko, A. (2007). *Studies in emotion and social interaction. Emotions and multilingualism* (1st ed.). Cambridge: Cambridge University Press. ISBN:978-0-521-04577-3. http://amazon.com/o/ASIN/0521045770/.

Payr, S., & Wallis, P. (2011). Socially situated affective systems. In R. Cowie, C. Pelachaud & P. Petta (Eds.), *Cognitive technologies. Emotion-oriented Systems* (pp. 501–520). Berlin: Springer. ISBN:978-3-642-15183-5. doi:10.1007/978-3-642-15184-2_26. http://dx.doi.org/10.1007/978-3-642-15184-2_26.

Peele-Eady, T. B. (2011). Constructing membership identity through language and social interaction: the case of African American children at faith missionary baptist church. *Anthropology & Education Quarterly, 42*(1), 54–75. doi:10.1111/j.1548-1492.2010.01110.x. http://dx.doi.org/10.1111/j.1548-1492.2010.01110.x.

Peräkylä, A. (2006). Observation, video and ethnography. In P. Drew, G. Raymond & D. Weinberg (Eds.), *Talk and interaction in social research methods* (pp. 81–96). Thousand Oaks: Sage. 9780761957058.

Peters, C. (2011). Editorial: "emotion in interaction". In R. Cowie, C. Pelachaud & P. Petta (Eds.), *Cognitive technologies. Emotion-oriented systems* (pp. 287–291). Berlin: Springer. ISBN:978-3-642-15183-5. doi:10.1007/978-3-642-15184-2_15. http://dx.doi.org/10.1007/978-3-642-15184-2_15.

Peterson, P., Baker, E., & McGaw, B. (Eds.) (2010). *International encyclopedia of education, 8-volume set* (3rd ed.). Amsterdam: Elsevier Science. ISBN:978-0-080-44893-0. http://amazon.com/o/ASIN/0080448933/.

Plant, R. (2009). *Community and ideology (Routledge revivals): an essay in applied social philosophy, volume 4.* London: Routledge. http://amazon.com/o/ASIN/B002OEZJ88/.

Plutchik, R. (2002). *Emotions and life: perspectives from psychology, biology, and evolution* (1st ed.). Washington: American Psychological Association. ISBN:978-1-557-98949-9. http://amazon.com/o/ASIN/1557989494/.

Poggi, I., & D'Errico, F. (2011). Social signals: A psychological perspective. In A. A. Salah & T. Gevers (Eds.), *Computer Analysis of Human Behavior* (pp. 185–225). London: Springer. ISBN:978-0-85729-993-2. doi:10.1007/978-0-85729-994-9_8.

Poutvaara, P., & Siemers, L. H. R. (2008). Smoking and social interaction. *Journal of Health Economics, 27*(6), 1503–1515. http://www.biomedsearch.com/nih/Smoking-social-interaction/18657872.html.

Prepin, K., Ochs, M., & Pelachaud, C. (2012). Mutual stance building in dyad of virtual agents: smile alignment and synchronisation. In *2012 international conference on privacy, security, risk and trust (PASSAT), and 2012 international conference on social computing (SocialCom)* (pp. 938–943). doi:10.1109/SocialCom-PASSAT.2012.134.

Rahman, N. A., & Sahibuddin, S. (2010). Social interaction in e-learning: an overview. In *2010 international symposium in information Technology (ITSim)* (Vol. 1, pp. 1–4). doi:10.1109/ITSIM.2010.5561324.

Rammert, W. (2008). Where the action is: distributed agency between humans, machines, and programs. In *Paradoxes of interactivity. Perspectives for media theory, human–computer-interaction, and artistic investigations* (pp. 62–91). Bielefeld: Transcript

Rao, A. S., & Georgeff, M. P. (1995). BDI agents: from theory to practice. In *proceedings of the first international conference on multi-agent systems (ICMAS-95)* (pp. 312–319).

Risjord, M. (2012). Models of culture. In H. Kincaid (Ed.), *Oxford handbooks The Oxford handbook of philosophy of social science* (pp. 387–408). Oxford: Oxford University Press.

Ross, S. L. (2011). Social interactions within cities: neighborhood environments and peer relationships. In N. Brooks, K. Donaghy & G. J. Knaap (Eds.), *Oxford handbooks. The Oxford handbook of urban economics and planning* (pp. 203–229). Oxford: Oxford University Press.

Rossier, C., & Bernardi, L. (2009). Social interaction effects on fertility: intentions and behaviors. *European Journal of Population / Revue européenne de Démographie, 25*(4), 467–485. http://nbn-resolving.de/urn:nbn:de:0168-ssoar-204074.

Sabanovic, S., Michalowski, M. P., & Simmons, R. (2006). Robots in the wild: observing human–robot social interaction outside the lab. In *9th IEEE international workshop on advanced motion control* (pp. 596–601).

Saleh, M., Lazonder, A., & De Jong, T. (2005). Effects of within-class ability grouping on social interaction, achievement, and motivation. *Instructional Science, 33*, 105–119. doi:10.1007/s11251-004-6405-z. http://dx.doi.org/10.1007/s11251-004-6405-z.

Salzmann, Z., Stanlaw, J., & Adachi, N. (2011). *Language, culture, and society: an introduction to linguistic anthropology* (5th ed.). Boulder: Westview. ISBN:978-0-813-34540-6. http://amazon.com/o/ASIN/0813345405/.

Schilling-Estes, N. (2006). Dialect variation. In R. W. Fasold & J. Connor-Linton (Eds.), *An introduction to language and linguistics* (pp. 311–342). Cambridge: Cambridge University Press.

Schutz, P. A., Quijada, P. D., de Vries, S., & Lynde, M. (2010). Emotion in educational contexts. In P. Peterson, E. Baker & B. McGaw (Eds.), *International encyclopedia of education* (3rd ed.). Amsterdam: Elsevier.

Scollon, S. (1981). *Advances in discourse processes. Narrative, literacy and face in interethnic communication* New York: Praeger. ISBN:978-0-893-91086-0. http://amazon.com/o/ASIN/0893910864/.

Scollon, R., Scollon, S. W., & Jones, R. H. (2012). *Wiley desktop editions. Intercultural communication: a discourse approach* (3rd ed.). New York: Wiley-Blackwell. ISBN:978-0-470-65640-2. http://amazon.com/o/ASIN/0470656409/.

Shiraev, E., & Levy, D. (2006). *Cross-cultural psychology: critical thinking and contemporary applications* (3rd ed.). Needham Heights: Allyn & Bacon. ISBN:978-0-205-47432-5. http://amazon.de/o/ASIN/0205474322/.

Skraba, R., Beauvais, M., Stan, J., Maaradji, A., & Daigremont, J. (2009). Developing compelling social-enabled applications with context-based social interaction analysis. In *International conference on advances in social network analysis and mining, ASONAM '09* (pp. 206–211). doi:10.1109/ASONAM.2009.7.

Snyder, M., & Arthur Stukas, J. (2007). Interpersonal processes in context: understanding the influence of settings and situations on social interaction. In K. Fiedler (Ed.), *Frontiers of social psychology. Social communication* (1st ed., pp. 363–388). London: Psychology Press.

Sorrells, K. (2012). *Intercultural communication: globalization and social justice*. Thousand Oaks: Sage. ISBN:978-1-412-92744-4. http://amazon.de/o/ASIN/1412927447/.

Spadavecchia, C., & Giovannella, C. (2010). Monitoring learning experiences and styles: the socioemotional level. In *2010 IEEE 10th international conference on advanced learning technologies (ICALT)* (pp. 445–449). doi:10.1109/ICALT.2010.129.

Straub, J., Weidemann, A., & Weidemann, D. (2007). *Handbuch interkulturelle Kommunikation und Kompetenz (Handbook of intercultural communication and competence)*. Berlin: Metzler. ISBN:978-3-476-02189-2. http://amazon.com/o/ASIN/3476021890/.

Sun, R. (Ed.) (2005a). *Cognition and multi-agent interaction: from cognitive modeling to social simulation*. Cambridge: Cambridge University Press. ISBN:978-0-521-83964-8. http://amazon.com/o/ASIN/0521839645/.

Sun, R. (2005b). The CLARION cognitive architecture: extending cognitive modeling to social simulation. In R. Sun (Ed.), *Cognition and multi-agent interaction: from cognitive modeling to social simulation* (pp. 79–99). Cambridge: Cambridge University Press.

Sun, X., Nijholt, A., Truong, K. P., & Pantic, M. (2011). Automatic understanding of affective and social signals by multimodal mimicry recognition. In *ACII (2)* (pp. 289–296).

Sussman, G. J., & Steele, G. L. Jr. (1975). Scheme: an interpreter for extended lambda calculus. In *MEMO 349, MIT AI LAB*.

Tangalicheva, R., Golovin, N., & Kuropjatnik, M. (Eds.) (2010). *Megkulturnaja kommunikazia i problemi akkulturisazii v krupnom gorode (Intercultural communication and problems of acculturation in a big city)*. St.-Petersburg: Isdatel'stvo Sankt-Peterburgskogo universiteta/St.-Petersburg University Press.

Tannen, D. (2006). Language and culture. In R. W. Fasold & J. Connor-Linton (Eds.), *An introduction to language and linguistics* (pp. 343–372). Cambridge: Cambridge University Press.

Thoms, B. (2011). A dynamic social feedback system to support learning and social interaction in higher education. *IEEE Transactions on Learning Technologies*, 4(4), 340–352. doi:10.1109/TLT.2011.9.

Torii, D., Ishida, T., Bonneaud, S., & Drogoul, A. (2004). Layering social interaction scenarios on environmental simulation. In *MABS* (pp. 78–88).

Toutanova, K., & Manning, C. D. (2000). Enriching the knowledge sources used in a maximum entropy part-of-speech tagger. In *Proceedings of the 2000 joint SIGDAT conference on empirical methods in natural language processing and very large corpora: held in conjunction with the 38th annual meeting of the association for computational linguistics, EMNLP '00* (Vol. 13, pp. 63–70). Stroudsburg: Association for Computational Linguistics. doi:10.3115/1117794.1117802. http://dx.doi.org/10.3115/1117794.1117802.

Trajkovski, G., & Collins, S. G. (2009). *Handbook of research on agent-based societies: social and cultural interactions*. Aarhus: Information Science Reference. ISBN:978-1-605-66236-7. http://amazon.com/o/ASIN/1605662364/.

Trovato, G., Kishi, T., Endo, N., Hashimoto, K., & Takanishi, A. (2012). A cross-cultural study on generation of culture dependent facial expressions of humanoid social robot. In S. Ge, O. Khatib, J. J. Cabibihan, R. Simmons & M. A. Williams (Eds.), *Lecture notes in computer science: Vol. 7621. Social robotics* (pp. 35–44). Berlin: Springer. ISBN:978-3-642-34102-1. doi:10.1007/978-3-642-34103-8_4. http://dx.doi.org/10.1007/978-3-642-34103-8_4.

Tsai, T. W., & Lin, M. Y. (2011). An application of interactive game for facial expression of the autisms. In *Proceedings of the 6th international conference on E-learning and games, edutainment technologies, Edutainment'11* (pp. 204–211). Berlin: Springer. ISBN:978-3-642-23455-2. http://dl.acm.org/citation.cfm?id=2040452.2040497.

Turner, T. C. (2011). *Understanding community: the implications of information flow and social interactions in online discussion groups*. New York: BiblioBazaar. ISBN:978-1-243-54756-9. http://books.google.de/books?id=6-MCywAACAAJ.

Umata, I., Oshima, C., Ito, S., Iwasawa, S., Nakamura, H., Endo, A., Nakayama, Y., & Ando, H. (2010). Do 3d images help social interaction? A study in remote music education. In *2010 4th international universal communication symposium (IUCS)* (pp. 197–200). doi:10.1109/IUCS.2010.5666223.

van Baal, P. (2004). *Onderzoekschool maatschappelijke veiligheid rotterdam. Computer simulations of criminal deterrence: from public policy to local interaction to individual behavior*. Boom Juridische uitgevers. http://books.google.de/books?id=CPGeKlNzn7EC.

van Dijk, P. J. A. G. M. (2005). *The network society: social aspects of new media* (2nd ed.). Thousand Oaks: Sage. ISBN:978-1-412-90868-9. http://amazon.com/o/ASIN/141290868X/.

Vollmer, A. L., Pitsch, K., Lohan, K. S., Fritsch, J., Rohlfing, K. J., & Wrede, B. (2010). Developing feedback: how children of different age contribute to a tutoring interaction with adults. In *2010 IEEE 9th international conference on development and learning (ICDL)* (pp. 76–81). doi:10.1109/DEVLRN.2010.5578863.

Vygotsky, L. S. (1978). *Mind in society: the development of higher psychological processes* (14th ed.). Harvard: Harvard University Press. ISBN:978-0-674-57629-2. http://amazon.com/o/ASIN/0674576292/.

Vygotsky, L. S. (1986). *Thought and language* (revised ed.). Cambridge: MIT Press. http://amazon.com/o/ASIN/B00AZ83YYQ/.

Waters, R. C., & Barrus, J. W. (1997). The rise of shared virtual environments. *IEEE Spectrum, 34*(3), 20–25. doi:10.1109/6.576004.

Watson, S., Dautenhahn, K., Ho, W. C. S., & Dawidowicz, R. (2009a). Developing relationships between autonomous agents: promoting pro-social behaviour through virtual learning environments, part I. In G. Trajkovski & S. G. Collins (Eds.), *Handbook of research on agent-based societies: social and cultural interactions* (pp. 125–138). Aarhus: Information Science Reference.

Watson, S., Dautenhahn, K., Ho, W. C. S., & Dawidowicz, R. (2009b). Developing relationships between autonomous agents: promoting pro-social behaviour through virtual learning environments, part II. In G. Trajkovski & S. G. Collins (Eds.), *Handbook of research on agent-based societies: social and cultural interactions* (pp. 229–242). Aarhus: Information Science Reference.

West, C., & Deschermeier, P. (2011). Value orientation, locational choice and residential satisfaction—a spatial econometric analysis. In A. Koch & P. Mandl (Eds.), *Modeling and simulating urban processes (geosimulation)* (pp. 119–130). Berlin: LIT Verlag.

Williams, M. A. (2012). Robot social intelligence. In S. S. Ge, O. Khatib, J. J. Cabibihan, R. Simmons & M. A. Williams (Eds.), *Lecture notes in computer science: Vol. 7621. Social robotics* (pp. 45–55). Berlin: Springer. ISBN:978-3-642-34102-1. doi:10.1007/978-3-642-34103-8_5. http://dx.doi.org/10.1007/978-3-642-34103-8_5.

Witten, I., & Frank, E. (2005). *Data mining: practical machine learning tools and techniques* (2nd ed.). San Francisco: Morgan Kaufmann.

Woodward, J. (2012). Cooperation and reciprocity: empirical evidence and normative implications. In H. Kincaid (Ed.), *Oxford handbooks. The Oxford handbook of philosophy of social science* (pp. 581–606). Oxford: Oxford University Press.

Xiaomeng, H., & Yue, C. (2010). Psychology and micro-blogging: self-presentation, social interaction and social culture. In *2010 IEEE 2nd symposium on web society (SWS)* (pp. 643–647). doi:10.1109/SWS.2010.5607369.

Yassine, M., & Hajj, H. (2010). A framework for emotion mining from text in online social networks. In *2010 IEEE international conference on data mining workshops (ICDMW)* (pp. 1136–1142). doi:10.1109/ICDMW.2010.75.

Yu, Y. C., You, S. C. D., & Tsai, D. R. (2012). Social interaction feedback system for the smart classroom. In *2012 IEEE international conference on consumer electronics (ICCE)* (pp. 500–501). doi:10.1109/ICCE.2012.6161993.

Zhang, Y., Lewis, M., Drennon, C., Pellon, M., Coleman, P., & Leezer, J. (2009). Modeling cognitive agents for social systems and a simulation in urban dynamics. In G. Trajkovski & S. G. Collins (Eds.), *Handbook of research on agent-based societies: social and cultural interactions* (pp. 104–124). Aarhus: Information Science Reference.

Šišlák, D., Volf, P., Jakob, M., & Pechoucek, M. (2009). Distributed platform for large-scale agent-based simulations. In F. Dignum, J. Bradshaw, B. Silverman & W. Doesburg (Eds.), *Lecture notes in computer science: Vol. 5920. Agents for games and simulations* (pp. 16–32). Berlin: Springer. ISBN:978-3-642-11197-6. doi:10.1007/978-3-642-11198-3_2. http://dx.doi.org/10.1007/978-3-642-11198-3_2.

Chapter 3
Scenarios of Social Interaction

Previous chapters studied related work on SI and SS. They discussed SI in the conventional humanities that exist for centuries, such as psychology or sociology, but also mentioned derived sciences that emerged only later, such as sociolinguistics or communication studies. Existing approaches to SI and SS were examined, what problems they resolve, what tasks they present, and what significant issues they address.

The previous chapters showed that SI, typically for the human behavior, can be unreasonable and difficult to comprehend or to "grasp." They took note of inexplicable matters in SI that constitute the nature of human beings. And here we are: we have a huge amount of specific information, a smorgasbord of interesting facts, thousands of peculiarities to pay attention to and many things to consider. How can we integrate them in an SS system?

Remember, this book is not only about SI as it is defined by various sciences. This book's intention is to gap a bridge between the abstract and vague, computationally unfeasible language of the humanities and the language of facts, arid language of computer science and mathematics. The main subject of this book is a multidisciplinary exploration of SI that culminates in a computational approach to SS. The main objective of this book is compilation of findings of different disciplines that discuss SI and describes a computationally feasible SS to assist a human expert to gain corresponding advantages (cf. Sect. 1.3).

Hence, a basis to study SI is necessary. This chapter discusses such a basis in the form of own scenarios of SI. In this chapter, scenarios of SI and SS from related approaches in Chap. 2 are augmented with own scenarios of SS with a focus on scenarios' interculturality. The result of this discussion, following conventional practice in the computer science, is modeling dimensions that present significant issues to be differentiated in each particular scenario. This discussion is rounded off with a pseudocode that presents scenarios' processing before this book goes into scenarios' realization.

A. Osherenko, *Social Interaction, Globalization and Computer-Aided Analysis*, 57
Human–Computer Interaction Series, DOI 10.1007/978-1-4471-6260-5_3,
© Springer-Verlag London 2014

3.1 Typical Culturally Homogeneous Scenarios of Social Interaction

This section discusses SI scenarios in which interactants are representatives of one culture, person *A* and person *B*.

1. Scenarios from Rehm (2009a, 2009b) draw on the collectivistic/individualistic dimension of a culture that describes colloquially the tendency of individuals to perform actions in group or alone (cf. the exact definition in Sect. 4.1.2):

   1.1. **Meeting someone for the first time** *A* meets *B* for the first time

   This scenario illustrates one of the most fundamental interactions that takes place in everyday communication. Consequently, first meetings in a collectivistic culture such as Japanese take longer than in individualistic cultures as German. Gesture usage is more frequent in individualistic cultures. Moreover, more body contact can be expected in individualistic cultures. Algorithm 3.1 defines the corresponding behavior depending on the culture of person *person*.

Algorithm 3.1 meeting someone for the first time

```
 1: for all person in {A, B} do
 2:     culture ← get_culture(person)
 3:     if culture is collectivistic then
 4:         set(person, long_meeting)
 5:         set(person, seldom_gesture_usage)
 6:         set(person, less_body_contact)
 7:     end if
 8:     if culture is individualistic then
 9:         set(person, shorter_meeting)
10:         set(person, often_gesture_usage)
11:         set(person, more_body_contact)
12:     end if
13: end for
```

   1.2. **negotiating** *A* negotiates with *B*

   This scenario shows different negotiation strategies and the accompanying verbal and nonverbal behavior. According to Rehm et al. (2009a), the negotiation strategy (avoidance, integrative, distributive) is influenced by a culture. In the avoidance negotiation strategy, a negotiation partner tries to avoid an undesirable negotiation; in the integrative negotiation strategy, a negotiation partner tries to find a satisfactory solution for all participants; in the distributive negotiation strategy, a negotiation partner tries to carry out his point and "win" negotiation. Algorithm 3.2 extracts persons of a negotiation (*A* and *B*) and reads their culture and negotiation strategy.

Algorithm 3.2 Negotiating

```
1: for all person in {A, B} do
2:    culture ← get_culture(person)
3:    strategy ← get_negotiation_strategy(person, culture)
4: end for
```

1.3. **Interacting with higher-status individual** Superior *A* interacts with the employee *B*

This scenario shows interaction of persons of unequal social relationship and illustrates the corresponding behaviors. Consequently, this scenario considers specific emotional and personal properties of superior *A* and employee *B* that influence such categories of behavior as proxemics (high-status individuals take more space and are less invaded by others), vocalic (high-status individuals take more, louder, interrupt more frequently), symbolically intrusive (high-status individuals may point at others or shut them up with a gesture). Algorithm 3.3 reads behavior *behavior* of person *person* depending on person's culture and behavior category.

Algorithm 3.3 interacting with a higher-status individual

```
1: for all person in {A, B} do
2:    culture ← get_culture(person)
3:    for all category in {proxemics, vocalic, symbolically_intrusive} do
4:       behavior ← get_behavior(person, culture, category)
5:    end for
6: end for
```

2. **Culture and group size**

Algorithm 3.4 shows a scenario from Herrera et al. (2011) that discusses influence of the group size by modulating behavior *behavior* according to different cultures, group sizes, and behavior categories.

Algorithm 3.4 Culture and group size

```
1: for all culture in {American, Arab, Mexican} do
2:    for all category in {turn-taking, gaze, proxemics} do
3:       for all size in {dyads, quads} do
4:          behavior ← modulate_by_size(culture, category, size)
5:       end for
6:    end for
7: end for
```

3. Scenarios of **Apology**

   Supposing a special role of social relationships between interactants in apology scenarios, the following algorithms distinguish processing depending on these relationships. Note that the term *social relationship* is used for simplicity colloquially and not from the point of view of group dynamics (Sorrentino and Higgins 1996) or the theory of relationships (VanLear et al. 2006).

   3.1. **Social relationship: friends** A accidentally hits B. A apologizes to B for that.

   Since A and B are friends, A apologizes due to cultural norms.

   3.2. **Social relationship: slight acquaintance** A accidentally hits B. A apologizes to B for that.

   A does not experience any strong negative emotions when hitting B. Moreover, according to the SI context, A and B are not antagonists. Since B shows a high negative emotion, A experiences a negative emotion (negative emotions are evidenced through corresponding observations), and hitting is interpreted by B as "accidental." A apologizes for hitting.

   3.3. **Social relationship: antagonists** A intentionally hits B. A utters apologies for that.

   A and B are antagonists, and two variants of further interaction are possible:

   (a) The probability of a negative emotion is too low, and A does not apologize to B although he should.

   (b) A apologizes to B because A is feeling a negative emotion, for example, *sorrow*. This negative emotion can be boosted by particular properties of A's personality, for example, if A is neurotic.

   3.4. **Social relationship: enemies** A intentionally hits B. A will not apologize.

   Since A and B are enemies, A does not apologize.

   Algorithm 3.5 shows a pseudocode that simulates the apology scenarios. After reading persons' cultures *culture1* and *culture2* and personalities *personality1* and *personality2*, the algorithm evaluates persons' emotions *emotion1* and *emotion2*. Then the algorithm reads the social relationship between *person1* and *person2* (variable *social_relationship*). Finally, the pseudocode calculates the resulting apology behavior using the values of read arguments.

4. Scenarios of **Harmony/sympathy** A feels harmony/sympathy for B.

   Harmony can be assessed through the number of coincident positive emotions in the course of interaction between A and B. This coincidence can be measured and mapped onto harmony/sympathy. For example, harmony can correspond to a high coincidence of positive emotions, whereas sympathy has a lower coincidence value (Algorithm 3.6).

   Algorithm 3.7 traverses through the dialogue and analyzes emotions of persons *person1* and *person2*. It modifies the coincidence value until all dialogue turns are processed.

5. Scenarios of **Trust** A trusts B.

Algorithm 3.5 apology

1: *person1* ← A
2: *culture1* ← get_culture(*person1*)
3: *personality1* ← get_personality(*person1*)
4: *emotion1* ← get_emotion(*person1*)
5: *person2* ← B
6: *culture2* ← get_culture(*person2*)
7: *personality2* ← get_personality(*person2*)
8: *emotion2* ← get_emotion(*person2*)
9: *social_relationship* ← get_social_ relationship(*person1*, *person2*)
10: *arguments* ← {*social_relationship*, *culture1*, *culture2*, *personality1*, *personality2*, *emotion1*, *emotion2*}
11: *apology_behavior* ← get_behavior(*arguments*)

Algorithm 3.6 coincidence analysis

1: *person1* ← A
2: *person2* ← B
3: **repeat**
4:    *emotion1* ← get_emotion(*person1*)
5:    *emotion2* ← get_emotion(*person2*)
6:    modify_coincidence(*emotion1*, *emotion2*)
7: **until** no turns in the course
8: *coincidence* ← get_coincidence()

In this book, *trust* is interpreted according to philosophical findings as a combination of experienced positive emotions and social relationship of persons (Kim and Park 2006) (Algorithm 3.7).

Algorithm 3.7 trust

1: *person1* ← A
2: *person2* ← B
3: *social_relationship* ← get_social_ relationship(*person1*, *person2*)
4: **repeat**
5:    *turn1* ← get_next_turn(*person1*)
6:    *emotion1* ← get_emotion(*turn*, *person1*)
7:    *turn2* ← get_next_turn(*person2*)
8:    *emotion2* ← get_emotion(*turn*, *person2*)
9:    *arguments* ← {*social_relationship*, *emotion1*, *emotion2*}
10:    modify_trust(*arguments*)
11: **until** no turns in the dialogue
12: *trust* ← get_trust()

Algorithm 3.7 traverses through the dialogue and analyzes emotions of persons *person1* and *person2*. It modifies the trust value until all dialogue turns are processed.

6. Scenarios of **Analyzing SI patterns**.

SI can mean adaptation to particular interaction style or following a certain coping strategy, for instance, in a dialogue. Burgoon et al. (2007) describe typical patterns of adaptation such as synchrony, mirroring, matching that can be interpreted according to emotional, cultural, personal determinants (Algorithm 3.8).

Algorithm 3.8 adaptation patterns

1: person1 ← A
2: culture1 ← get_culture(*person*1)
3: personality1 ← get_personality(*person*1)
4: *person2* ← B
5: *culture2* ← get_culture(*person*2)
6: *personality2* ← get_personality(*person*2)
7: **repeat**
8:    *turn*1 ← get_next_turn(*person1*)
9:    *emotion*1 ← get_emotion(*turn*, *person*1)
10:    *turn*2 ← get_next_turn(*person2*)
11:    *emotion*2 ← get_emotion(*turn*, *person*2)
12:    *arguments* ← {*culture*1, *culture*2, *personality*1, *personality*2, *emotion*1, *emotion*2}
13:    add_situation(*situations*, *arguments*)
14: **until** no turns in the dialogue
15: *pattern* ← analyze_interaction_ pattern(*situations*)

Algorithm 3.8 extracts culture and personality of *person1* and *person2*. Afterwards, it traverses a dialogue by extracting participating turns of *person1* and *person2* and analyzing their emotions. It updates the history of situations *situations* given by the calculated values. Finally, it scrutinizes the interaction pattern *pattern* by considering all previous situations.

3.2 Culturally Heterogeneous Scenarios of a Digital Globe

This section concentrates on scenarios of globalization. A perfect metaphor for such scenarios is a metaphor of a digital city. According to Ishida and colleagues (Ishida 2005; Ishida et al. 2005), a digital city is a social information infrastructure that models everyday life. This book extends the notion *digital city* to the notion *digital globe* in order to consider interaction between digital cities of various cultures. Figure 3.1 illustrates the vision of the digital globe adopting figures from interconnections of digital cities (Devriendt et al. 2008).

Fig. 3.1 Digital Globe

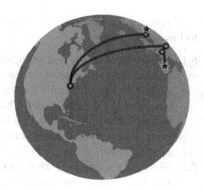

Figure 3.1 shows the digital globe with digital cities represented through circles and stars. Interactions between individual digital cities are shown as lines.

Figure 3.2 shows digital cities categorized along socio-technical and virtual–physical dimensions according to Yasuoka et al. (2010).

Figure 3.2 shows classification of world cities according to the socio-technical and virtual–physical dimensions. The socio-technical dimension shows the tendency to integrate new technologies vs. focus on community life whereas the virtual–physical dimension shows to what degree a city is a virtual world or has close ties with real cities. For example, virtual Helsinki is a city with a high technical development that does not exist in reality.

Activities in a digital city include shopping, business, transportation, education, and social welfare. In this book, the activities of the digital city are used to define scenarios of the digital globe: (1) a particular activity is examined and used to extract scenarios that are important in a multicultural setting of the digital globe; (2) dimensions are determined that should be considered in SI. Algorithm 3.9 on p. 67 shows a pseudocode for processing scenarios in the digital globe.

Fig. 3.2 Some digital cities

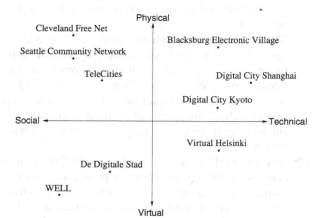

Hence, in the *shopping* activity, Messerschmidt et al. (2009) distinguishes the following scenarios:

6.1. **Navigation** This scenario allows a purchaser in a virtual online shop to obtain an optimal route of online navigation. The virtual route can be optimized according to purchaser's emotional, cultural, anf personal disposition. For example, if the purchaser has a bad mood, she/he should be navigated not to all items on the virtual shopping list, but only to the first. Thus, significant modeling dimensions of SS are emotions of the customer, culture, personality, and space consideration.

6.2. **Shopping assistance** This scenario implies suggestion of new items that are missing on the virtual shopping list. For instance, representatives of short-term cultures have a high respect for traditions (Mascarenhas et al. 2009; Hofstede et al. 2002). Thus, if an American customer as a representative of a short-term culture forgets to buy a turkey before Thanksgiving, she should be reminded of it. Alternatively, a shop on the Mexican border wishing to sell a product to an American customer should consider American traditions. Thus, significant modeling dimensions of SS can be the history of articles on the virtual shopping list that were purchased in the past but are not present on the current shopping list and the emotional state of the customer that would not allow guidance if in a bad mood.

6.3. **Special offers** This scenario considers navigating the purchaser to special offers in the online shop. Thus, significant modeling dimensions of SS are the history of purchased items to identify special offers of similar items, the emotions of the purchaser to avoid confrontation, and culture to identify culturally necessary items.

In the *business* activity, for example, interaction in the context of intercultural negotiations using e-commerce, the following scenarios can be simulated:

6.1. **Study of cultural variation of display rules** Kopelman and Rosette (2008) describe two studies that correspond to cultural variation in display rules of emotions during negotiations. Thus, significant modeling dimensions of SS are the emotions and culture of the purchaser that can help to give relevant hints to an expert.

6.2. **Mobile market research** According to Maxl et al. (2009), acceptance and usage of mobile methods are strongly dependent on psychological and cultural factors. That is why intercultural differences and similarities regarding mobile communication in Asia, North America, and Europe as well as other less outstanding regions should be considered in a compelling SS. Thus, significant modeling dimensions of SS used to improve mobile market research and enhance acceptance of trading are emotions, culture, and personalities of the customers.

6.3. **Intercultural business** According to Hil (2007), intercultural business considers cultural differences and develops an appreciation for them. Thus, significant modeling dimensions of SS are emotions of the customers during negotiations under consideration of personal/cultural/contextual issues.

In the *social welfare* activity, the Multicultural Social Work Practice (MCSW) defines according to Sue (2005) the following scenarios:

6.1. **Helping role and process** *MCSW involves acknowledging and broadening the roles that social workers play and expands the repertoire of problem-solving skills.* Thus, significant modeling dimensions of SS can be emotional and cultural issues that define strategies of problem-solving for improving interaction between a social worker and a client.

6.2. **Consistent with life experiences and cultural values** *Effective MCSW practice means using modalities and defining goals for culturally diverse clients that are consistent with their racial, cultural, ethnic, gender, and sexual orientation backgrounds.* Thus, significant modeling dimensions of SS can be emotional, cultural issues, contextual issues defining racial, ethnic, sexual, etc. orientation.

6.3. **Individual, group, and universal dimensions of existence** *MCSW acknowledges that our existence and identity are composed of individual (uniqueness), group, and universal dimensions. Any form of helping that fails to recognize the totality of these dimensions negates important aspects of a person's identity.* Thus, significant modeling dimensions of SS are emotional, personal, cultural, and contextual issues. The uniqueness dimension can be evaluated using statistical processing distinguishing that a particular emotion and personality model is not typical for a given culture.

6.4. **Universal and culture-specific strategies of helping** *MCSW believes that different racial/ethnic minorities and other sociodemographic groups might respond best to culture-specific strategies of helping.* Thus, significant modeling dimensions of SS can be emotional, personal, culture-specific, contextual (racial, ethnic) issues, and topology (groups).

6.5. **Individualism and collectivism** *MCSW broadens the perspective of the helping relationship by balancing the individualistic approach with a collectivistic reality that acknowledges our embeddedness in families, significant others, communities, and cultures.* Thus, significant modeling dimensions of SS can be social relationships between interactants, culture, groups, and topology.

6.6. **Client and client systems** *MCSW assumes a dual focus in helping clients.*[1] *In many cases, it is important to focus on individual clients and encourage them to achieve insights and learn new functional and adaptive behaviors. ... The focus for change must shift to altering client systems rather than to individual clients alone.* Thus, significant modeling dimensions of SS can be emotions, culture, groups, topology, and an alert that recommends altering helping if it detects that the chosen approach failed.

---

[1]In this case, Sue (2005) refers to the sociological term *client* and not to *clients* in the sense of computer science. Sociological *client* is defined in the Code of Ethics of the National Association of Social Workers "... 'Clients' is used inclusively to refer to individuals, families, groups, organizations, and communities."

The *social welfare* activity considers scenarios of well-being. According to Dolan and White (2007), well-being is influenced by subjective (mental-state) as well as by objective-list and desire-fulfillment measures. The subjective approach can identify current or recent moods and emotions and assess well-being on this basis; the objective-list approach can comprise the list of basic human needs and rights that have to be satisfied to guarantee well-being; the desire-fulfillment approach can be based on the decision utility that focuses on the ability to satisfy more preferences. Hence, significant modeling dimensions of SS can be emotional or cultural issues and an alert that recommends altering helping if it detects that the chosen approach failed.

Additionally, social welfare applications are confronted with the problems of counseling. Gerstein et al. (2009) describe problems of cross-cultural counseling and focus on different world regions: East/Southeast/South/Central Asia, Europe, Americas/Caribbean, South/West Africa, Middle East, Oceania. Thus, significant modeling dimensions of SS can be emotions, personality, culture, groups, and relationships of persons to help an expert to develop a beneficial counseling strategy:

6.1. **Internationalization of counseling** This aspect points to integration of research and practice derived from many cultures;
6.2. **Counseling** This aspect puts a focus on using a broad array of psychological strategies and activities aimed at the process of helping others to reach individual, group, and organizational goals;
6.3. **Techniques of counseling psychology** This aspect emphasizes the role of theory, research, and practice of counseling psychology paying special attention to cultural and diversity issues, for instance, group diversity (individual, family, group, etc.).

In the *education* activity, the following scenarios can be considered (Littleton 2010):

6.1. **Elicit knowledge from students,** *so teachers can see what the students already know and understand and so that the knowledge is seen to be "owned" by students and teachers.* For example, an e-learning scenario showing interaction between a German student in Berlin who wants to learn sinology directly from a Chinese teacher in Pekin or an Italian class that communicates with a teacher in an American digital city in order to inquire about a correct use of articles in American English.
6.2. **Respond to things that students say**, *not only so that students get feedback on their attempts but also that the teacher can incorporate what students say into the flow of discourse and gather students' contributions together to construct more generalized meanings.*
6.3. **Describe the classroom experiences** *that they share with the students in such a way that the education significance of those joint experiences is revealed and emphasized.*

The following significant modeling dimensions of SS can be distinguished in the *education* activity: emotions, personality, culture, groups, knowledge, relationships of persons to help an expert to develop a beneficial educational strategy.

In the *transportation* activity, SS can consider SI in the emergency evacuation scenarios, for example, that should coordinate rescue of people of different cultures in the channel tunnel between England and France or supervision of preparation for earthquakes in Japanese drills (Nakanishi et al. 2008). SS can be used to analyze the guidance system in that the SS system assesses emotions of the persons to rescue and gives a hint to an expert on dealing with this situation. The estimated emotions can be utilized to change guidance messages or their mode to avoid panic. For instance, the text message "Please do not hurry!" should be adapted to the person emotional state and changed into "Please do not hurry because you will pass the crowd soon!" supposed to quiet people.

The following significant modeling dimensions of SS can be distinguished in the *transportation* activity: emotions, personality, culture, groups of persons, NL to help an expert to develop a beneficial rescue strategy.

Algorithm 3.9 shows a common pseudocode for scenarios of the digital globe.

Algorithm 3.9 processing in the digital globe

1: *person* ← A
2: *emotion* ← get_emotion(*person*)
3: *culture* ← get_culture(*person*)
4: *personality* ← get_personality(*person*)
5: *context* ← get_context(*person*)
6: process_scenario(*emotion, culture, personality, context*)

3.3 Culturally Heterogeneous Controversial Scenarios

This section describes controversial scenarios of SS in which interactants are representatives of different cultures.

Cushner and Brislin (1995) discuss different intercultural interactions and present 110 problematic situations, as they call "incidents," in the following categories: the host customs, interacting with hosts, settling in and making adjustments, tourist experiences, the workplace, family, education and schooling, returning home. An incident addresses an intercultural problem and presents several problem explanations containing the best answer chosen by the majority of 60 respondents. In this book, the incidents present scenarios of intercultural SS with several explanations of behavior: the best (most probable) answer and other alternatives (probable, improbable). A common pseudocode for processing the incidents is shown in Algorithm 3.10 on p. 76.

The scholars group incidents across 18 themes and categorize them according to emotions, socialization knowledge, differences of the home and host cultures:

1. **Anxiety and related emotional states** In the changing situation of a new culture, people become anxious about their behavior.

    Example: Incident "The Trip to the Doctor" (incident 40, p. 119) tells about a son of a well-to-do family in Hong Kong that lives in America. His life is formally successful: the student was accepted for graduate studies at a prestigious American university, he found housing, etc. After a time, he began though to be disappointed in his work, was unhappy with life in America, and is personally unhappy. Finally, he experiences physical discomforts and goes to a doctor who prescribes him a strong drug. What is the reason of the personal problems?

    Best answer: The real reason of physical symptoms is personal problems of the student that often occur in adjusting to another culture.

    Alternatives:

    1.1. (improbable) The Hong Kong student gets a placebo prescription;
    1.2. (improbable) The Hong Kong student as a member of a well-to-do family considered special reception in US;
    1.3. (improbable) People who accompanied the Hong Kong student did not pay enough attention to student's problems;
    1.4. (improbable) The student should have prepared better for the intercultural journey, for example, should have attended a course of English as a second language.

    Modeling dimensions: Emotions of the student such as disappointment; context of SI that includes knowledge of the doctor indicating high risk of taking strong drugs; statistical engines to calculate outcomes' probabilities; time consideration.

2. **Emotional experiences and disconfirmed expectations** People can be disappointed if their expectations in the foreign culture differ from the real circumstances.

    Example: Incident "Do I really Want to Study This" (incident 25, p. 84) tells about an American student who studies the sign-language to translate communication between deaf people with their communication. One day, the student witnesses a communication of two deaf people who intensively complain about their interpreter. Since the student knew the interpreter as a conscientious person, he wonders about the reasons of this complain. What is the explanation?

    Best answer: Deaf people have love–hate relationship with their interpreters.

    Alternatives:

    2.1. (improbable) Student's proficiency in the sign-language is not high enough to understand the deaf students;
    2.2. (probable) The deaf students had bad experience with their interpreter;
    2.3. (improbable) The student provoked the deaf students to complain about interpreters.

    Modeling dimensions: Mixed emotions; context with knowledge about the conscientious interpreter; statistical engines to calculate outcomes' probabilities; situation snapshot with emotions of all participants.

3. **Belonging** People need a feeling that they belong to something that can be different in a foreign culture if they are considered as outsiders.

Example: Incident "Pizza for Dinner" (incident 29, p. 87) tells a story of an American student, 12 years old, who served a prepackaged pizza dinner during his visit to a Belizean family. Due to technical problems, there was a small explosion. Because nobody was affected, the host family encouraged the student to keep on. The student though was affected mentally. Soon the student's teacher arrived for a short visit. After seeing the teacher, the student burst into tears confusing the host family. What is the explanation of the tears?

Best answer: The explosion caused strong emotions of the student (uncertainty and danger) that he controlled in the presence of the host family. Controlling emotions was however the reason why the student showed them after seeing a familiar face.

Alternatives:

3.1. (improbable) The student misses his home and the family so much;
3.2. (improbable) The student is upset because he ruined the important event;
3.3. (improbable) The student is very anxious while meeting his teacher.

Modeling dimensions: Emotions of the American and the host family; statistical engines to calculate outcomes' probabilities.

4. **Ambiguity** People learn to make decisions as responses to different stimuli. In other cultures, though, stimuli and reactions can be different. To cope with it, people have to tolerate such ambiguity.

Example: Incident "Social Ease" (incident 31, p. 89) discusses a story of an American student who recently came from United States to Indonesia. She is invited to a birthday party and is excited to be meeting new friends. However, when she arrives to the party, she feels very uncomfortable. Everything is different: besides the food and drinks, it is the birthday greeting that the student is not accustomed to. There are also other things why she is feeling uneasy and awkward. Finally, she tries to cope with this situation by deciding that maybe some food would help to relax and approaches a food table. When she takes her food and drink, her drink spills on the floor. Everybody in the room begins to laugh out loud, and the American is very ashamed. What is the explanation of the laughing?

Best answer: In Indonesia, laughter is often meant to disperse tension.

Alternatives:

4.1. (improbable) Student's behavior was inappropriate;
4.2. (improbable) The hosts expected that the student brings a gift;
4.3. (improbable) The student reacts to her culture shock.

Modeling dimensions: Emotions of participants; Indonesian culture including traditions; statistical engines to calculate outcomes' probabilities; party situation.

5. **Prejudice and ethnocentrism** People in other cultures may represent other beliefs than that kept in prejudices.

Example: Incident "Island Paradise: Two Experiences" (incident 42, p. 121) tells a story of a Hawaiian that has prejudice against Samoans. He thinks that Samoans are aggressive, in sports they often use dirty tactics when losing, etc. Later, in need of work, he started a job in the Western Samoa and found out that Samoans are completely different from the negative image the Hawaiian had: they are cooperative and positive. The Hawaiian is vaguely upset and reserved and experiences physical problems. Why?

Best answer: The Hawaiian must acknowledge that his past feelings and opinions just do not seem applicable in Western Samoa, which caused him to feel anxiety and even led to psychosomatic problems.

Alternatives:

5.1. (improbable) The Samoans only seem to be calm but are actually aggressive;
5.2. (improbable) The Hawaiian is getting used to his life in Western Samoa;
5.3. (improbable) The Hawaiian experiences culture shock;
5.4. (improbable) The Hawaiian is anxious because of the problems in his homeland.

Modeling dimensions: Emotions of the Hawaiian and his Samoan neighbors; statistical engines to calculate outcomes' probabilities.

6. **Work** Cultural differences in decision making at the workplace can play a significant role in particular situations.

Example: Incident "A Development Project" (incident 60, p. 154) describes a story about a Canadian engineer who spent three years in Nigeria installing a new technical system. The system functioned very good, and the hosts were happy. However, five years after the Canadian left Nigerian, the hosts are disappointed because the system is not functioning as it should do, parts are rusted, etc. What is the reason of this disappointment?

Best answer: The Canadian did not train the Nigerians to maintain the system.

Alternatives:

6.1. (improbable) The materials used by the Canadian wore out;
6.2. (improbable) The assistance on maintaining the system was rejected;
6.3. (improbable) The system is too complicated.

Modeling dimensions: Emotions of the hosts; emotional course (history of previous emotions); statistical engines to calculate outcomes' probabilities; time consideration.

7. **Time and space** Different cultures define various perception of time and space and what is appropriate and polite in different situations.

Example: Incident "The Final Advance" (incident 9, p. 69) tells a story of a female American who was asked to represent her company at the conference at the Latin America. The American is positively excited, and everything is good: travel to the hotel, checking into the hotel, etc., until a welcome cocktail party. The American was approached by a female representative of a local firm from Latin America, who always kept the American at the close distance. The American was annoyed.

Best answer: A comfortable distance for conversations is different in every country, for example, 18 inches in United States and 10–12 inches in Latin America.

Alternatives:

7.1. (improbable) The American avoids intimacy;
7.2. (probable) The Latin American tries to make the American sojourn as uncomfortable as possible;
7.3. (improbable) The American cared much about personal hygiene of her contacts.

Modeling dimensions: Emotions of the American and her Latin counterpart; space and time consideration; context (situation); statistical engines to calculate outcomes' probabilities.

8. **Language and communication** Differences in verbal and nonverbal behavior are the most obvious difficulties of intercultural communication.

    Example: Incident "The Helpful Classmate" (incident 13, p. 69) addresses a person who is paralyzed in both her legs and partly her arms. Now she studies at a university where almost all buildings are wheelchair accessible and she can get access to them with exception of one that necessitates her asking for assistance. In this accident, the handicapped person is in the building without the handicapped facilities and wants to leave a classroom, but a wastebasket blocked the path to the door. What is the correct behavior of her classmates?

    Best answer: Disabled people can do many things and value the ability if they are not assisted.

    Alternatives:

    8.1. (improbable) The correct behavior is to leave the classroom as if the paralyzed person is not present;
    8.2. (probable) The correct behavior is to move the wastebasket out of the way;
    8.3. (improbable) The correct behavior to wait until somebody moves the wastebasket out of the way.

    Modeling dimensions: Emotions of the handicapped person before and after seeing the blocking wastebasket; space consideration; history of emotions; statistical engines to calculate outcomes' probabilities; behavior norms.

9. **Roles** Depending on the roles of interaction participants (boss, family member, etc.), there can be significant differences in behavior. Cf. *interacting with higher status individual* (item 1 on p. 58).

    Example: Incident "Healing wounds" (incident 8, p. 68) discusses a situation where an elderly patient from Saudi Arabia needs to guide him in rehabilitation exercises and the supervisor of the respected Australian clinic assigns a fairly new female therapist to the task without a prior formal introduction to the patient. However, this attempt fails, and the patient complains about the therapist's incompetence; the therapist is defeated. What is the explanation of the patient's behavior?

Best answer: Such behavior is explained as a consequence of not following the norms (traditions) of other culture: it is unacceptable for an Arab man to be assisted in personal, private tasks by a young woman not in his family.

Alternatives:

9.1. (improbable) The female therapist was not formally introduced to the patient;

9.2. (improbable) The female therapist did not explained the therapy to the patient;

9.3. (probable) The Arab patient prefers a male therapist for his therapy;

9.4. (improbable) The female therapist is not competent.

Modeling dimensions: Emotions and cultural background of the interactants; statistical engines to calculate outcomes' probabilities; traditions and norms.

10. **Importance of the group and importance of the individual** Behavior of a person depends either on personal or group interests that are determined by the particular culture. Cf. *Culture and Group Size* (item 2 on p. 59)

    Example: Incident "Trip to the mountains" (incident 11, p. 71) describes a situation where an American performs a trip with a Chinese. Because the Chinese invited his friends to this trip, the American is not pleased. Why?

    Best answer: Such behavior is explained by pointing out cultural differences between two cultures, the American (individualistic) culture and the Chinese (collectivistic) culture.

    Alternatives:

    10.1. (improbable) The chosen terrain is not suitable for hiking;

    10.2. (improbable) The American is selfish and needs more attention;

    10.3. (probable) The American is too shy.

    Modeling dimensions: Emotions of the Chinese and the American; culture (collectivistic/individualistic); statistical engines to calculate outcomes' probabilities.

11. **Ritual and superstition** Every culture defines its rituals and superstitions that influence persons' behavior.

    Example: Incident "Betting on the Bull" (incident 3, p. 59) tells a story of an American working for a multinational company in Spain who attended a bullfight. He wanted to put his money on the bull, which offended the hosts. Why?

    Best answer: The hosts consider bullfighting as a ritual, not as a sport. Thus, the hosts are offended.

    Alternatives:

    11.1. (improbable) The American assumed the hosts bet on the outcome;

    11.2. (improbable) The American was too ignorant;

    11.3. (improbable) The American announced publicly that the bull will win.

    Modeling dimensions: Emotions of the participants; cultural values; statistical engines to calculate outcomes' probabilities.

12. **Hierarchies among people; class and status** Particular cultures are particularly concerned about social class and social status that can significantly influence behavior of interactants or comprehension of their actions.

    Example: Incident "His First Job" (incident 12, p. 72) discusses a story of a 25-year-old American who took a job in the Philippines. The American became very successful: he was invited to parties and was included in the guest lists of the most important Filipino policy makers. His behavior changed, for example, he arrives at work several hours later than expected. His coworkers in the project became unhappy with his contributions to the project. What is the reason of the behavior changes?

    Best answer: The behavior changes of the American are typical for the people who experience quick raise in status.

    Alternatives:

    12.1. (improbable) The work of the American is poorly conceived;
    12.2. (improbable) The American is considered for a higher position;
    12.3. (improbable) The American keeps up close contacts to high-level managers.

    Modeling dimensions: Emotions of the American and the Filipino; the context reflecting the change of the social relationship between them; statistical engines to calculate outcomes' probabilities.

13. **Values: the integrating force** Various things have different values in particular cultures. For example, a cow is sacred in India, whereas it is a common animal in Germany. Cf. *Ritual and Superstition* (item 11 on p. 72).

    Example: Incident "Foreign Policy Discussions" (incident 10, p. 70) tells about an American who went to Germany for an oversees study. During several informal gatherings, she was asked about different issues of American foreign policy but had little to say because she was unprepared for such questions. Finally, she was not so frequently included in the gatherings. Why?

    Best answer: German students assumed that the American can comment on the American foreign policy. However, the American was not informed about it.

    Alternatives:

    13.1. (improbable) German students were baiting the American;
    13.2. (improbable) German students have authoritarianism as a national characteristic;
    13.3. (improbable) German students are very anti-American.

    Modeling dimensions: Emotions, high value of the facts from the American foreign policy; statistical engines to calculate outcomes' probabilities.

14. **Learning styles** To achieve improvements in a new culture, sojourns have to learn and adjust their behavior and way of thinking to comprehend the hosts appropriately.

    Example: Incident "The Assessment of His Efforts" (incident 83, p. 197) tells the story of a Gambian that has recently begun a postgraduate course at a British university and is quite confident of his ability to do well. However, he was very puzzled by the first assessments that acknowledged a poor quality of his contributions from the point of view of British people, for example, the Gambian did not keep to the topic, etc. The Gambian is puzzled at this since his work seemed logical and relevant to him. He asks his British friend to show him his good works and the Gambian cannot understand why they are assessed good. What is the reason of such comprehension discrepancy?

Best answer: The Gambian and the British way of thinking and communicating are very different. In some cultures, thinking and communicating can be analytical and highly indirect, whereas Western way is distinguished through step-by-step and deductive approach.

Alternatives:

14.1. (improbable) The Gambian is intellectually not capable;
14.2. (improbable) The British educational system is too rigorous for the Gambian;
14.3. (improbable) The Gambian is confused by the settling-in period.

Modeling dimensions: History of emotions of the Gambian before and while inspecting his work; means to adjust cognitive models dynamically; statistical engines to calculate outcomes' probabilities.

15. **Categorization** People are used to categorize information they get. However, people of different cultures anticipate different categories for similar information, which can cause confusion.

    Example: Incident "Special Educational Needs" (incident 98, p. 212) discusses a story of a Chinese that completed her doctoral studies in the US and obtained a teaching position in an American University. She married and born a daughter. The daughter's aides taught the daughter to pronounce "ahh-so" what infuriated the Chinese. Why is the Chinese angry?

    Best answer: Many Americans do not differentiate between Chinese and Japanese and put persons with similar characteristics into the same categories. That is why they confused the Chinese daughter with a Japanese and learnt her to say "ahh-so" what is for many Americans a stereotype of a Japanese. However, due to historical animosities between two countries, the Chinese do not want to be considered as Japanese. The reason of the anger of the Chinese mother was that the Chinese daughter was erroneously considered as a Japanese.

    Alternatives:

    15.1. (improbable) The Chinese desired more parent–teacher collaboration;
    15.2. (improbable) The Chinese thinks that the American mocks her daughter;
    15.3. (improbable) The Chinese cannot accept the fast-paced American lifestyle.

    Modeling dimensions: Emotions of the Chinese; historical context that prohibit the linkage between China and Japan; statistical engines to calculate outcomes' probabilities.

16. **Differentiation** Various cultures categorize information in their own manner. Consequently, sojourners that differentiate information using categories they know from the home country have to get accustomed to the new category differentiation in order to be not treated as naïve or ignorant.

    Example: Incident "The proposal process" (incident 58, p. 152) discusses a meeting with two friends, a person from New Zealand and a person from Philippines, each presenting their proposal on a project. The first proposal was known to the others in the meeting and has gone without big modifications; the second proposal was changed significantly, and the Filipino was requested by the principal to review the proposal. The Filipino is upset, why?

    Best answer: Filipino culture considers only one social relationship: either a friend or a critic, so the same person cannot be both a friend and a critic. However, these expectations were violated in the meeting.

    Alternatives:

    16.1. (improbable) The Filipino has no time because he goes to the library;
    16.2. (improbable) The Filipino is jealous because his proposal did not pass on without major modifications;
    16.3. (improbable) The Filipino was asked by the principal to prepare his proposals better.

    Modeling dimensions: Emotions; culture of interactants with a ban of multiple social relationships; statistical engines to calculate outcomes' probabilities.

17. **In-group/out-group distinction** Human cultures have tendency to build in-group/out-groups. In-group members are humans with whom interaction is sought. In contrast, the out-group members are often held at a distance and are often targets of rejection.

    Example: Incident "Next-Door Neighbors" (incident 27, p. 86) Two English teachers work in Barcelona, Spain. They want to learn their neighbors better and invite them to different occasions. However, they are not invited to the functions of the neighbors and feel uneasy because they think they are not accepted. What is the explanation of the missing invitations?

    Best answer: In Mediterranean cultures, there is a strong identification with the family, and friends are generally not allowed to attend family parties. Hence, the English teachers are not rejected, but an invitation to family parties is not appreciated.

    Alternatives:

    17.1. (improbable) The neighbors wary an intimate contact to the foreigners;
    17.2. (improbable) The neighbors do not know how to entertain the foreigners;
    17.3. (improbable) The neighbors are offended by the foreigners.

    Modeling dimensions: Emotion, culture of the teachers and the neighbors; traditions of the host culture; statistical engines to calculate outcomes' probabilities.

18. **Attribution** People observe behavior of others and reflect upon their own behavior. Each culture presents its own judgment, called attribution, of what is appropriate and inappropriate.

Example: Incident "Trip to the Public Market" (incident 53, p. 140) tells a story of an Australian who arrived to a Central America country on a job assignment. She went to a public market and stopped at a stall looking at the dresses and talking in Spanish with the owner. Upon leaving the stall without buying something, the Australian is addressed by the owner in the unpleasant tone and begins to develop negative feelings about her job and the country. What is the reason for the negative feelings?

Best answer: There is a tendency to overestimate vivid events such as a conversation with the owner and misinterpret anger of the stall owner as prejudice or jealousy. Sojourners can ask themselves if they overinterpret an event they were directly involved in.

Alternatives:

18.1. (improbable) The Australian has a poor command of the local language and is overstressed;

18.2. (probable) The Australian was a target of the jealousy by the stall owner;

18.3. (improbable) The Australian damaged a dress;

18.4. (probable) The Australian targeted anger of the stall owner.

Modeling dimensions: Emotions of the Australian and the stall owner, situation given by the public market indicating a vivid situation; time and space consideration; statistical engines to calculate outcomes' probabilities.

Algorithm 3.10 shows a pseudocode that summarizes SS of the above incidents.

Algorithm 3.10 processing of the incidents

1: *person* ← A
2: *emotion* ← get_emotion(*person*)
3: *culture* ← get_culture(*person*)
4: *personality* ← get_personality(*person*)
5: *context* ← get_context(*person*)
6: *history* ← get_history(*person*)
7: *situation* ← get_situation(*person*)
8: calculate_outcome(*emotion, culture, personality, context, history, situation*)

Gannon (2007) presents other situations of intercultural interaction and discusses its 93 paradoxes. This comprehensive study has three parts organized in an introduction chapter and nine chapters that address different aspects of multicultural interaction. Each chapter is divided in turn into subsections and concludes with subsection "Discussion questions" and subsection "Exercises" that present questions and exercises to be discussed in a class; these questions and exercises are considered in this book as descriptions of hypothetical scenarios of simulation that can serve as inspirations for further studies (cf. Sect. 3.6).

This book describes not all paradoxes but only those that would benefit more from SS. Thus, sometimes identification of modeling dimensions is omitted since they become obvious after a thorough discussion. Algorithm 3.9, a pseudocode for processing scenarios in the digital globe, can be used as a basis for an SS system implementing the paradoxes (see p. 67).

The following paradoxes can be used to identify significant modeling dimensions:

- **Chapter 2: Conceptualizing and perceiving culture** This chapter discusses the basics of cultures. Besides multiple definitions, this chapter addresses how individuals perceive a culture.

   Conceptualizing culture – Paradox 2.1: Why are there so many definitions of culture? Every person defines a culture in its own manner depending on personal preferences. However, since this book focuses on a computer-aided SS, an appropriate approach to defining a culture should consider computationally feasible culture definitions, for example, according to Hofstede (2001).

   Perceiving culture – Paradox 2.9: Do proper introductions and greetings simultaneously require kissing, bowing, and shaking hands? Every person has his own idea of appropriateness of such additional actions as kissing during introductions and greetings. To assess this appropriateness, it is necessary to identify psychological determinants that accompany introductions and greetings. For instance, if SS identifies specific emotions during introduction of a certain person using bowing, it can point out that such bowing is appropriate/inappropriate.

   Modeling dimensions: Emotions; culture model with particular traditions; statistical engines evaluating appropriateness/inappropriateness.

- **Chapter 3: Leadership, motivation, and group behavior across cultures** This chapter describes behavioral issues across cultures.

   Leadership – Paradox 3.2: Who is more effective, the instrumental–visionary–transformational leader or the headman? A successful leader is defined differently in particular cultures. An SS system has to track social relationships between members of a group and the emotions of group members. To assess productivity of a group conducted by the leader, each scenario should define a productivity measure, e.g., the number of positive emotions of the group members divided by the commercial productivity of the group.

   Motivation – Paradox 3.5: Is the relationship between motivation and ability additive or multiplicative in the prediction of individual success and performance? To answer this question, three things are necessary. First, definition of numeric measures of motivation and ability. Second, separation of personal determinants from other issues that can influence this calculation. Third, a definition of a numeric comparison criterion to determine "additivity" and "multiplicativity."

   First, the motivation measure can be defined as the probability of positive emotions that are experienced by a particular individual when performing a certain task. The ability measure can be evaluated as a time period taken by a particular individual to complete the task normalized through the average time period needed to complete this task.

Second, separation of personal determinants requires broad experimentation. Hence, it can be necessary to compare personality traits of individuals before and after experimentation to differentiate a constant determinant given by a specific culture from other determinants such as gender, age, etc.

If motivation and ability can be mapped onto numerical values, it is straight-forward to provide a comparison criterion; whether it is additive or multiplicative can be assessed arithmetically using available numerical motivation and ability measures.

Group behavior – Paradox 3.9: In general and in small groups, do the personalities of individuals primarily reflect the influence of culture? To answer the question, it is necessary to separate cultural determinants from other behavior issues, for example, using techniques in Rehm et al. (2009a). Moreover, it can be necessary to compare personality traits of individuals before and after interaction to differentiate determinants given by a specific culture. For the same purpose, statistics can be recorded that track behavior of demographically varying individuals (gender, age, etc.).

Modeling dimensions: The context defining formal/real social relationship between group members and the appropriate productivity measure; demographics; ability/productivity measures.

- **Chapter 4: Communicating across cultures** Interaction across cultures takes place in its most evident form as a verbal communication. However, there are also other more subtle means of communication including issues of time, space, eye movements, body motions, haptics, physical appearance, speaking, smelling, etc.

    Language – Paradox 4.1: How can knowing the language of another culture be a disadvantage? This question addresses the basics of successful communication: what is more beneficial, linguistic knowledge or knowing the norms, values, and behaviors of a particular culture. The ability to communicate with members of the foreign culture in their language is a big advantage in communication and indicates a great familiarity with foundations of the foreign culture. However, even a comprehensive linguistic knowledge can turn into disadvantage if the moral basis of the foreign culture is disrespected. Knowledge about such norms can prevent from many problematic situations even more than the language proficiency.

    Context and beyond – Paradox 4.5: Can a culture be simultaneously monochronic and polychronic? Monochronicity vs. polychronicity can be generally defined as doing one thing at a time vs. multitasking. Gannon lists examples of monochronicity and polychronicity in an organization. Accordingly, employees in a monochronic culture do one thing at a time or adhere to plans, whereas employees in a polychronic culture do many things simultaneously or change plans often.

    Symbolism – Paradox 4.7: How can the same phenomenon represent different symbolic meanings? Some phenomena possess different symbolic meanings in different cultures. For example, bullfight in Spain is a ritual that can end up with killing of the bull and should remind on "full and vitally engaging life." In

contrast, in the bullfight in Portugal the killing of the bull is outlawed and is symbolically "a community manifestation of bravery that serves to unite the audience
and the team." Hence, the same verbal term (bullfight) can have different meanings in each concrete culture; this term means high moral feelings and sacrifice in
Spain and bravery in Portugal. To distinguish between rituals and manifestation
of bravery, SS should show emotions of the interactants.

Modeling dimensions: Knowledge, time, space, NL, norms, values, moral
emotions.

- **Chapter 5: Crossing cultures** This chapter describes issues inherent in going
abroad, for example, culture shock.

   **Culture-based Ethics: Relativism and Universalism – Paradox 5.1. Are
ethical norms and standards universal or relative to the situation?** Gannon
claims that individualistic cultures tend to accept universal standards that hold in
every situation, whereas collectivistic cultures emphasize relative standards that
apply only to particular situations. Hence, we answer the question by collecting
statistics of norms and situations using SS and resolve the question depending on
these statistics.

   **Generic Cultures and Ethics – Paradox 5.2: Are there universal entities
across generic cultures, or do ethics vary by generic cultures?** This question
can be answered by simulating scenarios that focus on ethical issues of particular
cultures. For example, if certain emotions are equal in different cultures when
communicating particular issues, these issues can be considered as universal.

   **Expatriate Paradoxes – Paradox 5.3: Is the general stereotype of the host
culture valid?** Gannon claims that the host community can be considered gen-
erally as homogeneous, although with some exceptions such as the cannibalism.
This book answers the paradox question by claiming that the culture can provide
a general disposition toward particular determinants of behavior, where behavior
of representatives of certain culture can be adjusted according to the particular
personality.

   Understanding Cross-Cultural Interactions via Cultural Sensemaking
There are no paradoxes in this section. Gannon reports that interactants use their
experience to choose an interaction scheme that corresponds to an optimal practice in each particular situation. However, this choice can be not simple in a mono-
cultural situation, and it is much more difficult in the situation where several cultural understandings interact with each other.

   To deal with this case, instead of trying to find a solution using conventional
solutions, it can be beneficial to consider a revolutionary method that contains
action pieces for the most standard situations. Actions in the pieces can include
different information such as social or emotional. To find optimal solution in each
situation and explain cultural differences, SS can compare such pieces with each
other.

   Reentry into the Home Culture There are no paradoxes in this section. Gannon reports that visitors and expats that returned to their home culture uniformly
tell about the enriched experience, for example, improved work skills. A reentry scenario can answer the question if enriched experience is objective or it is a
subjective comprehension.

Modeling dimensions: Productivity measure (extended knowledge), emotions, norms, culture (collectivistic), personality.

- **Chapter 7: Multiethnicity, religion, geography, and immigration** This chapter describes paradoxes of globalization focusing on properties of interactants of different cultures, for example, multiethnicity.

  Multiethnicity – Paradox 7.1: Do multiethnic groups impede rather facilitate the formation of national cultures? There is a controversy about this question. On the one side, ethnic groups often struggle with each other, and conflicts occur periodically, for example, involving white Americans or Hispanic Americans. On the other side, prosperous societies such as American benefit much from ethnic groups, for example, American universities benefited much from German Jewish professors fleeing from Europe prior to World War II. Accordingly, this question can be studied in an SS that requires information about the ethnic context and also a measure that would evaluate the gain.

  Religion – Paradox 7.5: Must religion be anthropomorphic?[2] (see also p. 35) This difficult question can be reformulated as follows. How would a character in SS argue to another character that something is a godlike thing?

  For example, what properties of a human must be represented by a godlike thing? what human emotions, e.g., admiration or astonishment, would arouse in an observer when a godlike thing performs things that can be considered as miracles by the most people?

  For example, Christianity. Is Christianity an anthropomorphic religion? Yes, it is Evans (1996). Jesus Christ can experience human emotions since Christianity describes Jesus Christ as a human-like person. However, Jesus Christ can also perform miracles. An SS scenario that answers the question if Jesus Christ represents a anthropomorphic religion can study emotions of interactants.

  Geography – Paradox 7.7: Do geographic maps reflect cultural beliefs? Gannon emphasizes the role of geography in cultures. For example, many Americans would tend to draw US in the center of a world map with completely unrealistic size, whereas America is not a center of the world, and it is not very large.

  In SS, this scenario can be simulated as follows: SS would collect imaginary maps of the world. To assess the perception of the world, SS would, for example, lay the real map of the world on the imaginary map and calculate numerical similarity between the real and imaginary maps.

  Immigration – Paradox 7.9: Will the issue of immigration derail globalization? Gannon claims that immigration has both positive and negative features and it is problematic to give an intelligent answer to this question. To simulate this scenario, the problem can be expressed more concretely by asking a question that concerns some aspect of immigration. For example, "How do immigrants contribute to the introduction of new practices from the host country?"

---

[2]*Anthropomorphic*—described or thought of as having a human form or human attributes (Merriam-Webster); for example, most religions of the world are anthropomorphic because they attribute human-like features to God.

To assess the contribution, the skills of the immigrants of a particular host country can be recorded during a long period of time, and the gain of immigration as integral increase or decrease of the number of these skills can be evaluated.

Modeling dimensions: Context including information on ethnic groups and the skills of particular immigrants; a measure that corresponds to the gain of an ethnic group; space (maps), emotions.

3.4 One-Person Scenarios

This section describes one-person scenarios of SS. Although SI assumes communication with more than one person, discussion of one-person scenarios is necessary to identify significant issues of SI that should be reflected in a believable SS.

The following one-person scenarios of SI can be considered:

1. **Feeling pain, schadenfreude, envy, discomfort, disgust** The most scenarios of SI consider emotions to facilitate a believable SS. The better emotions are analyzed, the more plausible is the SS. For instance, some SS systems can detect, besides six basic emotions (Ekman 2007), also emotions in E/A space (cf. findings in Takahashi et al. 2009).
2. **Linking emotions and goal priority** To link emotions and a goal priority in SI, a history of occurred emotions can be collected. The stored history can be mapped onto a value representing a goal priority. For instance, the goal "Eat ice" is associated normally with a pleasant emotional course and is mapped therefore onto a high goal priority. In contrast, the goal "Eat meat" is associated by a vegetarian with unpleasant emotions and gets therefore a low goal priority.
3. **Experiencing mixed emotions** Literature in different sciences claims that there exist emotions of different kinds experienced simultaneously (mixed emotions). For example, Weigert (1991) acknowledges this statement and claims that mixed emotions are defined by ambivalence and influenced by social aspects and culture. Moreover, TenHouten (2007) argues the *existence of two opposing emotions at once* relying on social and cultural aspects. Becker-Asano (2008) claims that *although it is not agreed that secondary emotions can be described in terms of a mixture of primary ones, it is nevertheless agreed that two or more emotions, primary or secondary, may coexist at any given time moment.*

   An example of a mixed emotion is love–hate (cf. an incident with deaf students, item 2 on p. 68).
4. **Experiencing blended emotions** A blended emotion, e.g., anger or fear, is an emotion with concealed real intensity (Buisine et al. 2006). To tackle such scenarios, SS can scrutinize the intensity of emotions analyzed on the basis of external signals such as NL utterances and emotions on the basis of internal signals, for instance, brain or bodily responses.
5. Power and Dalgleish (2008) describe the following scenarios:

   5.1. *Anna gets very anxious about things in her life. Her feelings of fear and anxiety always make her feel sad and depressed as she dwells on what she has missed out on as a result of her problems. Such feelings of sadness in turn make her anxious that things will never change, and she becomes caught in a self-perpetuating cycle of emotions of anxiety, fear, and sadness. The first example, then, illustrates the cyclical coupling of two basic emotion states that reciprocally activate each other. Such coupling can also occur when an emotion module activates itself, as in fear of fear or depression about depression.*

Anna experiences negative feelings such as anxiety, fear, and sadness over a long period of time. Analysis of specific patterns of emotions can give an expert a hint on interpretation of such a situation under consideration of Anna's labile personality.

5.2. *Looking back over events from when he was a young student, Ed becomes nostalgic. He feels happy, as he remembers the good times he had but, at the same time, sad as he dwells on the fact that those times are in the past. The second example illustrates how two emotions can be generated by the same event often giving rise to a complex emotion such as, in this case, nostalgia.*

Ed feels happiness when he remembers good times that can give rise to nostalgia. Ed's emotions can be influenced by his personality.

6. **Meeting with a friend** The emotion is typically considered as positive. The scenario tracks the past experience represented through a similar emotional course and connected with a meeting with a friend; the major entries in the emotional course indicate that the past meetings were accompanied in most cases by positive emotions.

7. **Death of a colleague** The emotion is typically considered as negative. The scenario can rely on the past experience represented through a similar emotional course and connected with a death of a colleague. Emotional analysis can confirm negative emotions.

8. **Beating heart, redden**:
    These emotions can be considered either as positive or as negative. For example, *redden* can be positive, for example, caused by arrival of an important person or can be negative, for instance, caused by fear of this person.

9. **Getting goose pimples while listening to music** Spitzer (2002, Chap. 15, p. 397): Getting goose pimples while listening to music can be explained in the same manner as in the scenario *beating heart* or *redden*: goose pimples can be manifestation of emotions analyzed using physiological or neurobiological information.

10. **Having a bad/good mood** Following Ekkekakis (2012), emotion is considered as a short affective experience, whereas a mood is typically a longer process. Accordingly, an emotion is an entry in the emotional course, and a mood is its abstract.

11. **Phineas P. Gage before/after the "horrible accident" processing.** Neurobiologist Damasio (1994, p. 3) discusses the "horrible accident" with Phineas P. Gage in which "an iron rod" terribly injured his head.

Phineas P. Gage was a healthy person without any mental damage before the accident. After the accident, Phineas P. Gage was seriously injured, and particular regions of his brain are impaired. Thus, before the accident, Phineas P. Gage can store his past experience in the emotional course, and his reminiscences can be saved for future processing. However, after the accident, the emotional course with reminiscences is missing, and the learned model that analyzes emotional data is damaged. Consequently, Phineas P. Gage (p. 7) "devises many plans of future operation, which are no sooner arranged than they are abandoned." Phineas P. Gage is difficult to recognize—new behavior comes in strong conflict with the behavior before the accident since he always fulfilled his plans.

12. **Experiencing other feelings such as *spiritual*, *aesthetic*, *ethical*, or *moral* feelings.** Statistical engines can be trained to identify every emotion on the basis of available data, for example, neurobiological, lexical, etc. For instance, detecting the emotion *depression* can correlate with the moral emotion *shame*. See also Sabini (1998).

13. **Experiencing jet lag** Jet lag is "a condition that is characterized by various psychological and physiological effects (as fatigue and irritability), occurs following long flight through several time zones, and probably results from disruption of circadian rhythms in the human body" (Merriam-Webster). Jet lag influences psychological balance and can have negative consequences, for example, it can reduce the sport performance of international sportsmen (Landrigan et al. 2004; Harrison and Horne 2000).

    Jet lag can disappear—according to the rule of thumb, it takes one day to recover for each time zone crossed. This scenario shows the necessity of an inner-clock or the body clock representing biological processes (Kolla and Auger 2011; Kantermann 2008).

In summary, modeling dimensions in all one-person scenarios are the following:

1. Emotions;
2. Statistical or semantic engines to process data, for example, to deduce emotions;
3. Time;
4. Personality;
5. History (emotional course).

A pseudocode for SS in one-person scenarios is shown in Algorithm 3.11 using an example of emotional processing.

Algorithm 3.11 Processing in one-person scenarios

1: Initialize processing (statistical processing, time)
2: Train statistical engines
3: Read necessary models (culture, personality)
4: Emotion ← Deduce emotion (pain, mixed, spiritual, etc.)
5: Add situation to history (emotional course)

Algorithm 3.11 shows processing in one-person scenarios. It preprocesses data, for example, extracts statistical features and trains statistical or semantic emotional engines to classify emotions. It sets time. The algorithm reads necessary models, for example, cultural or personal, to deduce emotions and adds the detected situation to the history, for instance, an emotional course.

3.5 Summary of Significant Modeling Dimensions

This chapter presented a comprehensive study of scenarios of SI and SS the objective of which was identification of modeling dimensions, significant determinants of processing. It introduced agent-specific modeling dimensions that consider certain aspects of particular agents and also simulation-wide modeling dimensions that reflect important issues of SS systems (cf. findings in Sect. 2.12).

Summarizing revealed findings, the following agent-specific dimensions could be identified (cf. implementation of agent-specific dimensions in Sect. 6.4):

- Identity
  Many scenarios, especially philosophical, emphasize a significant role of identity in SI.
- Emotions
  Emotions should participate in SS as many scenarios show. For example, emotions of an interactant show the priority of certain actions identified on the basis of time, space, eye movements, body motions, haptics, physical appearance, speaking, smelling.
- Personality
  To anticipate a general disposition of a character in SS, a personality dimension is necessary. For instance, if A has a neurotic personality, A should be simulated as a neurotic person.
- Culture
  Since particular aspects of SI are defined by character's culture, the culture model is indispensable in analysis of SI. For example, if superior A is a representative of a culture with high power distance, the supervisor should be addressed by his title.
- Input/Output
  In some cases, SS requires feedback from the interactants or shows simulation results or interactants's appearance, and so SS should maintain means to input or output data. Input from the interactants can be supplied, for example, in the form of neurological/physiological data or bodily data used for statistical processing. Output can be performed, for example, as an image showing particular data in a dialog window.
- Statistical engines
  Statistical processing is indispensable in SS systems. Since requirements on according processing can be multifold, an SS system should realize multiple statistical engines that can be used to analyze SI information. In descriptions of the

incidents in Sect. 3.3, scenario outcomes, for example, explanations, can have different probabilities (best answer, probable, improbable). To calculate these outcomes, an SS system should maintain the corresponding statistical engines. Statistical processing can be utilized not only in particular agents, but also in the whole SS system (see item *Statistical processing* in the simulation-wide dimensions).

- Natural-language processing
  Although SI can be performed using different sources of information, the most natural manner of SI between humans is communication using NL turns. To react believably to interactants' inputs, information processing should take into consideration NL processing.
- Social relationships
  Comprehensible SI and SS should consider social relationships. For example, some actions are appropriate only between close friends, whereas the same actions can be inappropriate among colleagues.
- Context (agent-specific)
  The agent-specific context of SI and SS can define the race, age, education, marital status, social class, religion, etc. that should be considered in SS. Moreover, interactants can have different races in a multiethnic scenario of SS.
- Knowledge (agent-specific)
  The agent-specific knowledge refers to the facts held by a particular agent. For example, this knowledge can define particular abilities of an agent.
- Time (agent-specific)
  Some scenarios, for example, the jet lag scenario considers the temporal component. For instance, an SI interactant is more likely to be unbalanced if she experiences jet lag that disappears in the course of time.

While the previous dimensions of SI tend to describe simulation determinants regarding one individual, the following dimensions (history, knowledge, time, etc.) refer to the whole simulation and different interactants. Correspondingly, SS should consider the following simulation-wide dimensions of modeling (cf. implementations of simulation-wide dimensions in Sect. 6.5):

- Explicit specifications
  An SS system simulating a specific scenario of interaction defines system behavior that should be reflected explicitly and persistently to facilitate transparency in system development. For example, the incident "The Helpful Classmate" addresses a scenario with a paralyzed person, where the SS prototype should maintain different interactants and their behavior. To aid the development, the SS system can be composed on the basis of a humanly comprehensible interaction specification.
- History
  Some scenarios process a history of SI or the course of previous states. For example, the emotional course contains previous emotions of an interactant. Some scenarios consider a history of states of an interactant before and after a particular event. Moreover, some scenarios define even more general necessity, snapshots of interaction that should be consolidated in a whole course of several events.

- Space

  Some scenarios of SS consider the physical space as a significant aspect of SI. For example, the proximity measure in Ono et al. (2012) to assess SN using wearable devices. The incident "Last Advance" provided an obvious influence of space consideration in SI and SS.

- Context (simulation-wide)

  The simulation-wide context defines circumstances in which SI takes place. For example, in an incident the market place represents the SI context that should be considered in the SS system.

- Knowledge (simulation-wide)

  Knowledge plays a significant role in SS and can refer to common knowledge, for instance, the real-world knowledge (Liu et al. 2003). Knowledge can define intentions of an interactant, for example, knowledge about the behavior or the attended action strategy.

- Time (simulation-wide)

  Some scenarios, for example, the jet lag scenario considers the temporal component. For instance, an SI interactant is more likely to be unbalanced if she experiences jet lag that disappears in the course of time. Consequently, some scenarios of SI rely on time in SS.

- Social network, topological issues

  SS systems maintain different agents connected according to specific topology. Different aspects of simulation, for example, micro- or macro-level explicitation can be taken into consideration by developing a SS prototype with particular topology. For instance, the micro-level explicitation defines an SS system with interactants as individual agents, whereas a macro-level explicitation defines whole cultural societies as interactants.

- Statistical processing

  SS systems often require means to statistical processing information, for example, in approach by Trovato et al. (2012) to control face expressions.

Development of every software, for example, an SS system is a potentially error-pruning issue. Adopting a good practice of software development that defines asserts (particular conditions) that should be tracked in SS systems, this book distinguishes intercultural alerts. Consequently, the simulation-wide modeling dimensions are augmented with:

- Alerts

  In some cases, SS should assert agent-specific or simulation-wide alerts that represent certain conditions that should be tracked in SS. For instance, an alert should be issued if some cultural tradition in SS is violated.

- Statistical processing

  In many situations of SS, a computational apparatus is necessary that requires statistical processing of information either agent-specific or simulation-wide. For instance, eyebrows of a robotic head should be moved according to statistical data.

Note that the indicated modeling dimensions are only recommendations that can be endorsed in design of an SS system. Correspondingly, certain dimensions with their models and properties can be omitted, or other dimensions can be added. For example, the scenario "interacting with higher-status individual" in Sect. 3.1 does not typically need a temporal consideration and therefore the dimension *Time*. Moreover, some modeling dimensions are not common enough for consideration in every SS system such as motivation and ability measures in paradox 3.5 on p. 77 and can be therefore neglected.

Chapter 6 explains how SS systems implement a flexible architecture and how particular dimensions necessary for simulating a certain SS scenario can be realized by SS systems.

3.6 Inspirations for Further Scenarios

This section finishes this chapter and concludes with inspirations that can be used for developing new intercultural SS scenarios (Table 3.1).

In Table 3.1, column *Country* lists the discussed country or geographical area; column *Cushner and Brislin (1995)* (*incident*) refers to incidents of intercultural communication in Cushner and Brislin (1995); column *Gannon (2007)* (*paradox*) references paradoxes of intercultural communication in Gannon (2007); column *Gannon and Pillai (2012)* (*chapter*) refers to a chapter in Gannon and Pillai (2012) that discusses a particular country. Note that Table 3.1 contains rows with empty information such as the row for Costa Rica. Such "unuseful" rows are provided however for reference purposes—an approach to supplying useful data on the basis of cultural clusters will be discussed in Sect. 4.4.

3.7 Summary and Outlook

This chapter discussed scenarios of SI and SS focusing on their interculturality. It considered, among others, both culturally homogeneous scenarios and culturally heterogeneous scenarios that distinguish interactants of one or more cultures. Since it did not reveal further findings on dimensions of modeling besides those in Sect. 2.12, further concentration on modeling dimensions is dispensable.

Future work will reconsider SS scenarios in Table 3.1 for identification of significant determinants that are not considered yet in Sect. 3.5. These scenarios can consider discussion questions and exercises from Gannon (2007) as descriptions of hypothetical scenarios of simulation that can serve as inspiration for further studies. More scenarios of interaction across cultures can be found in Smith et al. (2006), Gannon (2000), Gannon and Pillai (2012).

Table 3.1 Inspirations for further scenarios

No.	Country	Cushner and Brislin (1995) (incident)	Gannon (2007) (paradox)	Gannon and Pillai (2012) (chapter)
1.	Albania	–	3.4, 7.3	5
2.	Argentina	–	8.3	33
3.	Australia	8, 32, 53	2.5, 7.11, 9.9	34
4.	Austria	–	4.3	–
5.	Bangladesh	–	–	–
6.	Belgium	–	–	22
7.	Brazil	15, 16, 77	10.1, 10.4, p. 76	32
8.	Bulgaria	–	–	–
9.	Cambodia	94	–	–
10.	Canada	35, 56, 60, 62	3.1, 4.12	14
11.	Chile	–	–	–
12.	China	2, 11, 24, 55, 69, 72, 89, 98	4.4, 5.1	25, 26
13.	Colombia	39	5.1, 5.5	–
14.	Costa Rica	–	–	–
15.	Czechia	–	–	–
16.	Denmark	–	–	11
17.	Ecuador	–	–	–
18.	Egypt	4, 20, 35	–	–
19.	Estonia	–	–	–
20.	Finland	–	2.5, 4.3	10
21.	France	64	p. 137, 7.3, p. 172, 9.6	15
22.	Gambia	83	–	–
23.	Georgia	–	–	–
24.	Germany	10, 101	2.4, 2.8, 2.12	12
25.	Great Britain	7, 17, 36, 48, 83	p. 161	17
26.	Greece	49, p. 332, p. 337	–	5
27.	Guatemala	17	–	–
28.	Hawaii	42, 54, 90, 100	–	–
29.	Hong Kong	14, 40	–	26
30.	Hungary	–	–	–
31.	Indonesia	4, 31, 67, 74	p. 60	–
32.	India	84	2.12, pp. 42–43	28, 29
33.	Iran	79	p. 76	–
34.	Ireland	14	p. 152	13
35.	Israel	49	p. 123	20
36.	Italy	103, pp. 265–267	–	21

Table 3.1 (Continued)

No.	Country	Cushner and Brislin (1995) (incident)	Gannon (2007) (paradox)	Gannon and Pillai (2012) (chapter)
37.	Jamaica	–	–	–
38.	Japan	1, 26, 37, 54, 63–64, 68, 70–71, 76, 80, 86–87, 105–107, 110	2.4, 2.9, pp. 56–59, 4.2, 4.5, 8.5, 9.7, 10.10	3
39.	Kazakhstan	–	–	–
40.	Korea (South)	6, 65, 78	3.7, 4.1, 10.1	8
41.	Kuwait	–	–	–
42.	Libya	107	–	–
43.	Luxembourg	–	–	–
44.	Malaysia	44, 67, 86, pp. 320–321	p. 161	18
45.	Malta	–	–	
46.	Mexico	20, 23, 56, 96, 102	–	
47.	Morocco	–	–	
48.	Namibia	–	–	–
49.	Netherlands	–	4	
50.	New Zealand	38, 49, 51, 58	5.1	–
51.	Nigeria	60, 96	–	19
52.	Norway	–	–	–
53.	Pakistan	–	7.11	–
54.	Panama	–	–	–
55.	Peru	–	–	–
56.	Philippines	12, 19, 23, 34, 48, 50, 58, 82, 100, 109	–	–
57.	Poland	–	10.9	7
58.	Portugal	32, 88	4.7	31
59.	Qatar	–	–	
60.	Romania	–	–	
61.	Russia	–	8.5	24
62.	Salvador	–	–	–
63.	Samoa	18, 41–42	–	–
64.	Saudi Arabia	8, 66	–	4
65.	Singapore	47, 54, 67	7.1	27
66.	Slovenia	–	9.1	–
67.	Slovakia	–	–	–
68.	South Africa	–	–	–
69.	Spain	3, 27, 52, 57	4.7	30
70.	Surinam	–	–	–

Table 3.1   (Continued)

No.	Country	Cushner and Brislin (1995) (incident)	Gannon (2007) (paradox)	Gannon and Pillai (2012) (chapter)
71.	Sweden	52, 57	–	9
72.	Switzerland	43, 81	–	–
73.	Taiwan	11	–	–
74.	Thailand	28	4.3, 4.5	2
75.	Trinidad	–	–	–
76.	Turkey	49	8.3	5
77.	Uruguay	–	–	–
78.	United States	1–3, 5–6, 10, 12–14, 16, 20, 23–26, 28–31, 36–37, 39–40, 43–45, 47, 50, 55, 61, 63, 65–70, 73–75, 78–80, 82, 84, 86–89, 91–93, 95–96, 98, 101–106, 109–110	2.5, 2, 7, 3.1, 3.2, 3.7, 4.1, 4.5, 4.8, 5.5, 5.9, 6.3–6.4	16
79.	Venezuela	93	–	–
80.	Vietnam	38, 94	–	6
81.	Yugoslavia	–	–	–
82.	Zambia	–	–	–
83.	Zimbabwe	–	8.1	–
Regions:				
84.	Arab countries	83, 105	p. 76, 4.11	–
85.	Central America	22, 30, 52, 62, 94	–	–
86.	East Africa	108	–	35
87.	Latin America	9, 61	–	4
88.	Middle East	7, 46, 64	–	4
89.	West Africa	–	–	35
90.	Australian continent	s. Australia	s. Australia	34
91.	African continent	–	–	35

References

Becker-Asano, C. (2008). *WASABI: affect simulation for agents with believable interactivity*. Dissertationen zur künstlichen Intelligenz. AKA. ISBN:978-3-898-38319-6. http://books. google.de/books?id=8ABvlwHBCQIC.

Buisine, S., Abrilian, S., Niewiadomski, R., Martin, J. C., Devillers, L., & Pelachaud, C. (2006). Perception of blended emotions: from video corpus to expressive agent. In *Intelligent virtual agents* (pp. 93–106). Berlin: Springer.

Burgoon, J. K., Stern, L. A., & Dillman, L. (2007). *Interpersonal adaptation: dyadic interaction patterns*. Cambridge: Cambridge University Press. ISBN:978-0-521-03314-5. http://amazon.com/o/ASIN/0521033144/.

Cushner, K., & Brislin, R. W. (1995). *Intercultural interactions: a practical guide (cross cultural research and methodology)* (2nd ed.). Thousand Oaks: Sage. ISBN:978-0-803-95991-0. http://amazon.com/o/ASIN/0803959915/.

Damasio, A. (1994). *Descartes' error*. London: Vintage Books.

Devriendt, L., Derudder, B., & Witlox, F. (2008). Cyberplace and cyberspace: two approaches to analyzing digital intercity linkages. *Journal of Urban Technology, 15*(2), 5–32.

Dolan, P., & White, M. P. (2007). How can measures of subjective well-being be used to inform public policy? In *Perspectives on psychological science* (Vol. 2, pp. 71–85). Oxford: Blackwell. http://pps.sagepub.com/content/2/1/71.full.

Ekkekakis, P. (2012). The measurement of affect, mood, and emotion in exercise psychology. In *Measurement in sport and exercise psychology* (pp. 321–332). Champaign: Human Kinetics.

Ekman, P. (2007). *Emotions revealed, second edition: recognizing faces and feelings to improve communication and emotional life* (2nd ed.). New York: Holt Paperbacks. ISBN:978-0-805-08339-2. http://amazon.com/o/ASIN/0805083391/.

Evans, C. A. (1996). *New Testament tools and studies: Vol. 24. Life of Jesus research: an annotated bibliography*. Leiden: Brill Academic. ISBN:978-9-004-10282-8. http://amazon.com/o/ASIN/9004102825/.

Gannon, M. J. (Ed.) (2000). *Cultural metaphors: readings, research translations, and commentary* (1st ed.). Thousand Oaks: Sage. ISBN:978-0-761-91337-5. http://amazon.com/o/ASIN/0761913378/.

Gannon, M. J. (2007). *Paradoxes of culture and globalization*. Thousand Oaks: Sage. ISBN:978-1-412-94045-0. http://amazon.com/o/ASIN/1412940451/.

Gannon, M. J., & Pillai, R. R. K. (2012). *Understanding global cultures: metaphorical journeys through 31 nations, clusters of nations, continents, and diversity* (5th ed.). Thousand Oaks: Sage. ISBN:978-1-412-99593-1. http://amazon.com/o/ASIN/1412995930/.

Gerstein, L. H., Leung, S. M. A., Ægisdóttir, S., Norsworthy, K. L., & Heppner, P. P. (2009). *International handbook of cross-cultural counseling: cultural assumptions and practices worldwide*. Thousand Oaks: Sage. ISBN:978-1-412-95956-8. http://books.google.de/books?id=erw9SJ3v3NUC.

Harrison, Y., & Horne, J. A. (2000). The impact of sleep deprivation on decision making: a review. *Journal of Experimental Psychology. Applied, 6*(3), 236–249. doi:10.1037/1076-898x.6.3.236. http://mres.gmu.edu/pmwiki/uploads/Main/C1T1.pdf.

Herrera, D., Novick, D., Jan, D., & Traum, D. (2011). Dialog behaviors across culture and group size. In *Proceedings of the 6th international conference on universal access in human–computer interaction: users diversity, UAHCI'11, part II* (pp. 450–459). Berlin: Springer. ISBN:978-3-642-21662-6. http://dl.acm.org/citation.cfm?id=2027376.2027428.

Hil, C. W. (2007). *International business: Competing in the global marketplace* (6th ed.). Boston: McGraw-Hill Colege. http://amazon.com/o/ASIN/B001ESR5VY/.

Hofstede, G. (2001). *Culture's consequences: comparing values, behaviors, institutions and organizations across nations* (2nd ed.). Thousand Oaks: Sage. ISBN:978-0-803-97324-4. http://amazon.com/o/ASIN/0803973241/.

Hofstede, G. J., Smith, D. M., & Hofstede, G. (2002). *Exploring culture: exercises, stories and synthetic cultures*. Boston: Nicholas Brealey.

Ishida, T. (2005). Digital cities III, information technologies for social capital: a cross-cultural perspective. In P. van den Besselaar & S. Koizumi (Eds.), *LNCS* (Vol. 3081, pp. 166–187). Berlin: Springer. http://ice.kuis.kyoto-u.ac.jp/~ishida/pdf/lncs06i.pdf.

Ishida, T., Aurigi, R., & Yasuoka, M. (2005). World digital cities: beyond heterogeneity. http://citeseerx.ist.psu.edu/viewdoc/summary?doi=?doi=10.1.1.10.2772.

Kantermann, T. (2008). *Challenging the human circadian clock by daylight saving time and shiftwork*. http://nbn-resolving.de/urn:nbn:de:bvb:19-94289.

Kim, U., & Park, Y. S. (2006). The scientific foundation of indigenous and cultural psychology. In U. Kim, K. S. Yang & K. K. Hwang (Eds.), *International and cultural psychology. Indigenous and cultural psychology* (pp. 27–48). New York: Springer. doi:10.1007/0-387-28662-4_2. ISBN:978-0-387-28661-7. http://dx.doi.org/10.1007/0-387-28662-4_2.

Kolla, B. P., & Auger, R. R. (2011). Jet lag and shift work sleep disorders: how to help reset the internal clock. *Cleveland Clinic Journal of Medicine, 78*(10), 675–684. doi:10.3949/ccjm.78a.10083. http://www.ccjm.org/content/78/10/675.abstract.

Kopelman, S., & Rosette, A. (2008). Cultural variation in response to strategic emotions in negotiations. *Group Decision and Negotiation, 17*, 65–77. doi:10.1007/s10726-007-9087-5.

Landrigan, C. P., Rothschild, J. M., Cronin, J. W., Kaushal, R., Burdick, E., Katz, J. T., Lilly, C. M., Stone, P. H., Lockley, S. W., Bates, D. W., & Czeisler, C. A. (2004). Effect of reducing interns' work hours on serious medical errors in intensive care units. *The New England Journal of Medicine, 351*(18), 1838–1848. doi:10.1056/NEJMoa041406. http://www.nejm.org/doi/full/10.1056/NEJMoa041406.

Littleton, K. (2010). Social interaction and learning. In P. Peterson, E. Baker & B. McGaw (Eds.), *International encyclopedia of education* (3rd ed., pp. 255–276). Amsterdam: Elsevier.

Liu, H., Lieberman, H., & Selker, T. (2003). A model of textual affect sensing using real-world knowledge. In *IUI '03: proceedings of the 8th international conference on intelligent user interfaces* (pp. 125–132). New York: ACM Press. ISBN:1-58113-586-6. http://doi.acm.org/10.1145/604045.604067.

Mascarenhas, S., Dias, J., Afonso, N., Enz, S., & Paiva, A. (2009). Using rituals to express cultural differences in synthetic characters. In *AAMAS '09: proceedings of the 8th international conference on autonomous agents and multiagent systems*, Richland: International Foundation for Autonomous Agents and Multiagent Systems (pp. 305–312). ISBN:978-0-9817381-6-1.

Maxl, E., Döring, N., & Wallisch, A. (Eds.) (2009). *Mobile market research* (1st ed.). New York: Halem. ISBN:978-3-938-25870-5. http://amazon.de/o/ASIN/3938258705/.

Messerschmidt, F., Lattner, A. D., & Timm, I. J. (2009). Customer assistance services for simulated shopping scenarios. In *Proceedings of the third KES international symposium on agent and multi-agent systems: technologies and applications, KES-AMSTA '09* (pp. 173–182). Berlin: Springer. ISBN:978-3-642-01664-6.

Nakanishi, H., Ishida, T., & Koizumi, S. (2008). Virtual cities for simulating smart urban spaces. In M. Foth (Ed.), *Handbook of research in urban informatics* (pp. 256–268). Aarhus: Information Science Reference. ISBN:978-1-605-66152-0. http://amazon.com/o/ASIN/160566152X/.

Ono, E., Nozawa, T., Ogata, T., Motohashi, M., Higo, N., Kobayashi, T., Ishikawa, K., Ara, K., Yano, K., & Miyake, Y. (2012). Fundamental deliberation on exploring mental health through social interaction pattern. In *2012 ICME international conference on complex medical engineering (CME)* (pp. 321–326). doi:10.1109/ICCME.2012.6275728.

Power, M. J., & Dalgleish, T. (2008). *Cognition and emotion: from order to disorder*.

Rehm, M., André, E., Bee, N., Endrass, B., Wissner, M., Nakano, Y., Lipi, A. A., Nishida, T., & Huang, H. H. (2009a). Creating standardized video recordings of multimodal interactions across cultures. In M. Kipp, J. C. Martin, P. Paggio & D. Heylen (Eds.), *Multimodal corpora* (pp. 138–159). Berlin: Springer. ISBN:978-3-642-04792-3.

Rehm, M., Nakano, Y., André, E., Nishida, T., Bee, N., Endrass, B., Wissner, M., Lipi, A. A., & Huang, H. H. (2009b). *From observation to simulation: generating culture-specific behavior for interactive systems*. New York: AI & Soc.

Sabini, J., & Silver, M. (1998). *Emotion, character, and responsibility*. Oxford: Oxford University Press.

Smith, P. B., Bond, M. H., & Kagitcibasi, C. (2006). *Sage social psychology program. Understanding social psychology across cultures: living and working in a changing world*. Thousand Oaks: Sage. ISBN:978-1-412-90366-0. http://amazon.com/o/ASIN/1412903661/.

Sorrentino, R. M., & Higgins, E. T. (Eds.) (1996). *Handbook of motivation and cognition, volume 3: the interpersonal context* (1st ed.). New York: Guilford. ISBN:978-1-572-30052-1. http://amazon.com/o/ASIN/1572300523/.

Spitzer, M. (2002). *Musik im Kopf: hören, musizieren, verstehen und erleben im neuronalen Netzwerk (Music in the head: hearing, music-making, understanding and comprehension in the neural network)*. Stuttgart: Schattauer. ISBN:978-3-794-52174-6. http://amazon.com/o/ASIN/3794521749/.

Sue, D. W. (2005). *Multicultural social work practice* (1st ed.). New York: Wiley. ISBN:978-0-471-66252-5. http://amazon.com/o/ASIN/0471662526/.

Takahashi, H., Kato, M., Matsuura, M., Mobbs, D., Suhara, T., & Okubo, Y. (2009). When your gain is my pain and your pain is my gain: neural correlates of envy and schadenfreude. *Science, 323*(5916), 937–939. http://www.sciencemag.org/cgi/content/full/323/5916/937.

TenHouten, W. D. (2007). *Routledge advances in sociology. A general theory of emotions and social life*. London: Routledge. ISBN978-0-415-36310-5. http://books.google.de/books?id=I9hRPE453lkC.

Trovato, G., Kishi, T., Endo, N., Hashimoto, K., & Takanishi, A. (2012). A cross-cultural study on generation of culture dependent facial expressions of humanoid social robot. In S. Ge, O. Khatib, J. J. Cabibihan, R. Simmons & M. A. Williams (Eds.), *Lecture notes in computer science: Vol. 7621. Social robotics* (pp. 35–44). Berlin: Springer. ISBN:978-3-642-34102-1. doi:10.1007/978-3-642-34103-8_4. http://dx.doi.org/10.1007/978-3-642-34103-8_4.

VanLear, C. A., Koerner, A., & Allen, D. M. (2006). In A. L. Vangelisti & D. Perlman (Eds.), *The Cambridge handbook of personal relationships* (pp. 91–110). Cambridge: Cambridge University Press.

Weigert, A. J. (1991). *Suny series in the sociology of emotions. Mixed emotions: certain steps toward understanding ambivalence*. New York: State University of New York Press. ISBN:978-0-791-40600-7. http://books.google.de/books?id=uH0srBp2W4YC.

Yasuoka, M., Ishida, T., & Aurigi, A. (2010). The advancement of world digital cities. In H. Nakashima, H. Aghajan & J. C. Augusto (Eds.), *Handbook of ambient intelligence and smart environments* (pp. 939–958). New York: Springer. ISBN:978-0-387-93808-0.

Part II
Developmental Part

This part is addressed to computer scientists. It discusses the development of the SS systems and describes acquisition of intercultural data. This part discusses a framework that performs statistical processing of the data and examines SS systems and programmatic drafts that realize scenarios of SI. It introduces a principle to prototype SS systems and formalisms to describe SI scenarios. Moreover, this part examines an approach to evaluate composed SS systems concluding with contributions of this book.

Chapter 4
Acquisition of Intercultural Data

This chapter describes approaches to acquiring intercultural data for scenarios of SI and SS in Chap. 3. Intercultural data in the proposed approach can be deduced numerically using emotional-, personality-, and culture-related information. Other information must be supplemented colloquially relying on verbal information about a particular culture, for example, information about its traditions, rites, and rituals.

This chapter proposes two methods to acquire intercultural data for SI and SS numerically, a bootstrapping psychological approach and a case-based approach. The first method takes data of one dimension, for example, emotional, as a basis and spreads it toward the personality-related dimension. For example, emotional data in the SAL corpus is used as a basis (Sect. 4.1) and used to deduce the missing data, for example, personality-related using different heuristics.

The second method (the case-based method) relies on the idea that the necessary data can be deduced from descriptions of cases, for example, descriptions of intercultural incidents. The case-based solution will be discussed thoroughly in Sect. 4.3.

4.1 Acquisition on the Basis of Emotion-Related Data

This section describes a heuristic to acquiring personality-related data from an emotional corpus. Emotion-related data is represented in this book as the audio-visual Sensitive Artificial Listener (SAL) corpus (Douglas-Cowie et al. 2007). SAL is a set of affective NL dialogues where a wizard representing four psychologically different characters (optimistic and outgoing Poppy, confrontational and argumentative Spike, pragmatic and practical Prudence, depressing and gloomy Obadiah) tries to draw users into their own emotional state. The corpus consists of 27 dialogues (Fig. 4.1).

Figure 4.1 shows a frame from the SAL corpus, the audio channel, and the corresponding textual transcription.

A. Osherenko, *Social Interaction, Globalization and Computer-Aided Analysis*, Human–Computer Interaction Series, DOI 10.1007/978-1-4471-6260-5_4,

Fig. 4.1 Audio-visual SAL
corpus

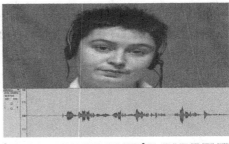

Because, well law of averages man, you know, law of averages. I mean, when so many shit things happen
to you, you know, odds are something nice is bound to happen sometime soon.

SAL was transcribed and annotated by four labelers with FEELTRACE[1] data
(Cowie et al. 2000) that identifies occurring emotions according to the E/A (evalu-
ation/activation) dimensions (Plutchik 1994). Affect annotation of a turn in FEEL-
TRACE contains numeric E/A data supplied continuously on the whole turn. Particularly important is that the annotation considers, besides turn texts, other information as mimics, gestures, or acoustics in the user behavior that plays an important
role in the intercultural processing.

Annotations of turns and their transcriptions can be visualized using ANVIL.
ANVIL is a free video annotation tool allowing frame-accurate, hierarchical multi-
layered annotation that manages an annotation board showing annotation tracks in
time-alignment (Kipp 2005). It was originally developed for annotating gestures,
but it is also suitable for research in many other fields (Fig. 4.2).

Figure 4.2 shows an ANVIL annotation of a SAL turn containing (from left to
right, from top to bottom) the ANVIL system console, the window for a video
(dancer_), the track window (indirect/direct verbal cue) containing the turn text,
e.g., *Oh yes, Oh yes, I do, Yes, Indeed,* and the attribute *calculated-emotion.* There
is the ANVIL annotation board below these windows showing the most significant
tracks in a particular scenario. Time alignment in the dialogue is presented by a
vertical line in the middle.

For simplicity, the FEELTRACE annotations of turns are mapped onto five
emotion segments in the E/A space: high activation/negative evaluation (*high_neg*),
high activation/positive evaluation (*high_pos*), low activation/negative evaluation
(*low_neg*), low activation/positive evaluation (*low_pos*), and *neutral* (Fig. 4.3).

Figure 4.3 shows the chosen E/A segmentation. The *neutral* affect segment represents turns with evaluation and arousal annotated in FEELTRACE within the em-
pirically determined 0.2 circle (Fig. 4.3).

The chosen affect segment of a turn corresponds to the vote of the majority of
the annotators at the turn end where emotionally contradictory long turns are not

---

[1]FEELTRACE is a tool for continuous annotation of perceived emotions as values of the E/A
dimensions.

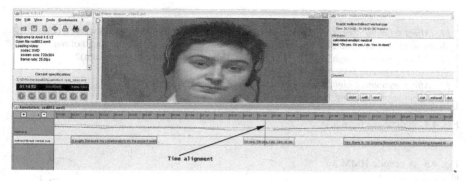

Fig. 4.2   Labeling an emotional corpus

considered in further experiments. Thus, 98 out of 672 turns are discarded due to the missing agreement between annotators or contradictory FEELTRACE data. The inter-annotator agreement is thus 85.42 %.

Figure 4.4 shows an example dialogue from SAL. The affect segment calculated using the segmentation in Fig. 4.3 is shown in square brackets.

4.1.1 Populating the Emotion-Related Model

In the following, this book describes how emotional data in SAL can be used to populate emotion-related models—how to calculate probabilities in the HMM for affective behavior. For simplicity, only population of models for the Spike character and not for other characters, for example, Prudence, are described thoroughly.

An emotion model relies on a Hidden Markov Model (HMM) for affective behavior on the basis of Picard's HMM (Picard 1997) (Fig. 4.5).

Fig. 4.3   Affect segmentation in the E/A space

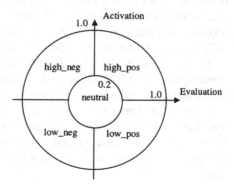

...
[1 - Affect segment: "neutral"] - (Breath intake) Well, I'll be able to have fun when I've done all the work, but you see I have a very, er, heavy, difficult couple of months ahead of me.
[2 - Affect segment: "high_pos"] - (Laugh) I'm damn awful. How are you (laugh)?
[3 - Affect segment: low_pos] - Yup.
[4 - Affect segment: "high_neg"] - Yes, that's not very pleasant, is it?
[5 - Affect segment: "low_neg"] - Erm, that's probably true.

Fig. 4.4   A dialogue from SAL

Fig. 4.5   A generic HMM for affective behavior

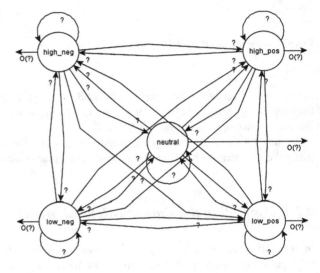

Figure 4.5 shows an HMM for affective behavior, a complete graph, containing five affect-related states (*high_neg, low_neg, neutral, low_pos, high_pos*) connected with arcs characterizing conditional probabilities of emotional transitions.

HMMs for affective behavior can be in a particular affect-related state and exhibit the corresponding behavior. This behavior is manifested through observations occurring with a certain probability. For instance, observations can be interactants' utterances. Observations in Fig. 4.5 are shown using outgoing O arrows from affect-related states (*high_neg, low_neg, neutral, low_pos, high_pos*) that stand numerically for probabilities of corresponding observations.

To implement HMMs for affective behavior, JAHMM (François 2012), a Java implementation of HMMs, is used. To train the HMMs for affective behavior and assess initial probabilities of emotion-related states and transitions' probabilities, different algorithms can be utilized, for example, the *k*-means algorithm (Juang and Rabiner 1990). Training is based on training sequences that can be composed, for instance, from adjacent dialogue turns with Spike such as *low_ pos neutral low_neg neutral low_ pos neutral*, which results from the first, second, ..., sixth turn.

Fig. 4.6 An HMM for
affective behavior of Spike

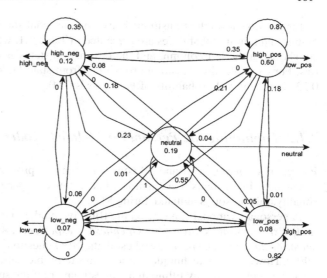

Table 4.1 An HMM for affective behavior for the Spike character

	high_neg	low_neg	neutral	low_pos	high_pos
high_neg	0.35	0.06	0.23	0.01	0.35
low_neg	0	0	1	0	0
neutral	0.18	0	0.55	0.05	0.21
low_pos	0	0	0	0.82	0.18
high_pos	0.08	0	0.04	0.01	0.87
Initial state probabilities:	0.12	0.07	0.19	0.08	0.60
Observations:	*high_neg*	*low_neg*	*neutral*	*high_pos*	*low_pos*

In this book, an HMM for affective behavior is trained statistically using training
sequences consisting of 20 adjacent dialogue turns. The number of resulting training
sequences that could be extracted from SAL is 149. Using 10-fold cross-validation
with stratification, the *Recall* value of 34.83 % averaged over five classes and the
Precision value averaged over five classes of 20.66 % are obtained.

Since available data is too scarce, an approximation of the HMM for affective
behavior is chosen manually based on the fold that represents a person expressing his emotions according to the experienced emotional state (equal labels state-
observation). For example, if Spike is in *low_pos* emotional state, he issues *low_pos*
observations. To detect a fold that can be utilized as a final model for the Spike
character, the folds of the HMM for affective behavior are inspected manually after
calculation of each fold. Consequently, the fold is chosen that calculates the most
concurrences of the same labels "state-observation" (Fig. 4.6 and Table 4.1).

Figure 4.6 shows the transitions between emotional states; the transition probabilities and initial probabilities are presented in Table 4.1, where the source states A
are shown in the left column, and the destination states B are shown in the upper
row. For example, the transition probability from state *high_neg* to state *neutral* is
0.23, and the initial probability of *high_pos* is 0.60.

4.1.2 Populating the Personality-Related Model

Particular scenarios of SI and SS consider cognitive properties of interactants represented by interactants' personalities. For instance, if person A has a neurotic personality, this person is agitated during SI.

A personality model can rely on the Big-Five model that defines five personality
traits *Extroversion, Neuroticism, Openness to experience, Agreeableness*, and *Conscientiousness* and can be assessed using the NEO questionnaire (Costa and McCrae
1991). However, this technique is not always unproblematic since it is static in that
it can be applied only by filling in the questionnaire if the subjects are available and
cooperative. Moreover, the technique of the NEO questionnaire is not suitable for
detection of personality characteristics dynamically, which can be beneficial for the
naturally dynamic SI and SS.

To resolve this problem, the Big-Five model can be evaluated dynamically by
utilizing the HMM for affective behavior in Fig. 4.6. The obtained values of personality traits can be normalized in the range [0 %..100 %].

According to John and colleagues (John et al. 2008) and Robins and colleagues
(Robins et al. 2007), extroverts tend to experience more positive emotions compared
to introverts. Thus, the *extroversion* personality trait PT_E can be assessed by utilizing the transition probabilities for low/high positive affect states from the emotion
model:

$$PT_E = \frac{\sum P(X \rightarrow high\_pos) + \sum P(X \rightarrow low\_pos)}{|\{X \rightarrow high\_pos\}| + |\{X \rightarrow low\_pos\}|}, \qquad (4.1)$$

where $\sum P(X \rightarrow Y)$ is the sum of transition probabilities from the affect state X to
the positive affect states $Y = \{high\_pos, low\_pos\}$. The values of PT_E are normal-
ized by the number of corresponding transitions, $10 = |\{X \rightarrow high\_pos\}| + |\{X \rightarrow low\_pos\}|$.

The *neuroticism* personality trait is assessed similarly to the *extroversion* personality trait from the emotion model of Spike. John and colleagues describe this
trait by the facets *insecurity, emotionality, irritability, anxiety, angry hostility, im-
pulsiveness, vulnerability*, which can be summarized as characteristics of a labile
personality. Hence, the *neuroticism* personality trait can be measured using a formula that considers values of transitions into stable *low_pos* or *low_neg* or *neutral*
states:

$$PT_N = \frac{\sum P(X \rightarrow low\_pos) + \sum P(X \rightarrow low\_neg) + \sum P(X \rightarrow neutral)}{|\{X \rightarrow low\_pos\}| + |\{X \rightarrow low\_neg\}| + |\{X \rightarrow neutral\}|},$$

$$(4.2)$$

where $\sum P(X \to Y)$ is the sum of probabilities of transition from the affect state X to the states $Y = \{low\_pos, low\_neg, neutral\}$. The values of PT_N are normalized by the number of corresponding transitions, $15 = |\{X \to low\_pos\}| + |\{X \to low\_neg\}| + |\{X \to neutral\}|$.

People that are open to experience are characterized as intellectual and insightful in contrast to shallow and unimaginative. John and colleagues describe facets of the *openness to experience* as *imagination/creativity* and *fantasy*. Thus, the *openness to experience* personality trait is assessed by utilizing imagery scores of the words from the Whissell dictionary of affect (Whissell 1989) that show words' difficulty to form a mental picture. The imagery scores of 8,742 verbs, nouns, adjectives, and adverbs from Whissell dictionary participating in Spike's turns are summed, and the sum is normalized by the number of detected Whissell words and the median of the imagery score:

$$PT_O = \frac{\sum w_i}{|W_w| \cdot \overline{ii}}, \tag{4.3}$$

where w_i is the value of the imagery score of the Whissell word, $|W_w|$ is the cardinality of the set of found Whissell words, and $\overline{ii}$ is the median value of the imagery score (2.0).

The *agreeableness* personality trait can be assessed using the ratio of agreeing turns and the overall number of considered turns. In order to measure the *agreeableness* value, Spike's turns were annotated manually according to expressed agreement since the *agreeableness* trait can be calculated as

$$PT_A = \frac{|T_a|}{|T|}, \tag{4.4}$$

where T_a represents a set of agreeing turns, and T is a set of turns in the corresponding dialogues.

If the *agreement* trait of an interlocutor should be analyzed on the basis of information that cannot be annotated, for example, on the basis of a monologue, the trait must be analyzed in other manner. In this case, the *agreement* trait can be calculated through counts of consent words. Moreover, according to Tausczik and Pennebaker (2010), the positive words correlate with agreement. Correspondingly, the *agreement* trait can be calculated using formula (4.4), where T_a represents the set of consent words and positive words, and T is the set of words in an analyzed text.

To assess the *conscientiousness* personality trait, the number of negative words in Spike's turns can be measured taking into account the considerations of Mairesse et al. (2007). Accordingly, conscientious people avoid negations, negative emotion words, and words reflecting discrepancies (e.g., *should* or *would*). Consequently, the occurrences of 2007 negative words and 7 negations from the General Inquirer (GI) database (Stone 1966) are counted:

$$PT_C = \frac{|W_n|}{|W|}, \tag{4.5}$$

Table 4.2 Values of personality traits for the Spike character

Character	PT_E	PT_N	PT_A	PT_O	PT_C
Spike (confront.)	25.0 %	12.46 %	5.23 %	78.85 %	9.13 %
Threshold = 20 %	y	n			

where W_n is the set of occurring negative words, negations, and discrepancy words, and W is the full set of words in Spike's turns.

Table 4.2 shows the values of personality traits calculated using formula in this section.

Note that application of the empirical threshold of, for example, 20 % to the values of personality traits PT_E and PT_N evidences that Spike is an extrovert (y) and not a neurotic person (n). Trait PT_A is calculated using 18 consent words from Linguistic Inquiry and Word Count (LIWC) dictionary (Tausczik and Pennebaker 2010), and 1637 positive words from GI (Stone et al. 1966) for evaluation of the *agreement* personality trait are considered. For more on calculating personality traits, see Sect. 4.2.2.

4.1.3 Populating the Culture-Related Model

Since particular aspects of SI are defined by character's culture, the culture model is indispensable in analysis of SI.

Simplification models such as "synthetic cultures" (Mascarenhas et al. 2009; Hofstede and Pedersen 1999) can be used for modeling cultures in SS. A synthetic culture is an artificial structure that distinguishes five dimensions (Hofstede et al. 2002):

1. *low vs. high power distance* dimension describes the degree to which differences in power, status, privileges are considered by representatives of the culture;
2. *collectivism vs. individualism* dimension distinguishes the primary unit of the culture ("I" vs. "we");
3. *masculinity vs. femininity* dimension defines the orientation of the culture toward achievement and cooperation;
4. *uncertainty avoidance* dimension defines the measure of tolerance to ambiguity;
5. *short-term vs. long-term orientation* dimension indicates to what extent the future has more importance than the past or present.

The SAL corpus that is used in this section to deduce culture-related data was recorded in Ireland. Accordingly, the culture-related dimensions correspond to Irish culture that can be acquired from Hofstede (2001) (Table 4.3).

Table 4.3 shows numerical ranks of the Irish culture and acknowledges, for example, a high power distance and a low individualism. However, culture-related data would be incomplete without consideration of other information about the Irish culture such as empirical facts from Gannon and Pillai (2012), p. 201:

Table 4.3 Acquired cultural values for emotional data

Country	Power distance	Uncertainty avoidance	Individualism/ collectivism	Masculinity/ Femininity	Long-/Short-Term Orientation
Ireland	49	47–48	12	7–8	13

- **Early history and English oppression** The Irish are very concerned about their independence that suffered much in presence of England. Accordingly, SS should issue an alert if independent relationships with the Irish seem to be violated;
- **Identifying links** The Irish tend to value the relationships much and begin every conversation with strangers by identifying common links (common relatives and friends). Correspondingly, an Irish in SS should maintain a network of relationships and consider it in SS.
- **Intersection of Gaelic and English** The Irish enjoy their patterns of pronunciation that can be baffling for outsiders. Thus, SS can define an alert that gives a corresponding hint to an expert. The same curiosities must be taken into account when considering important writers or memorable sounds.
- **Prayer as conversation** Irish conversations and Irish actions are considerably influenced by religious matters. Many Irish begin and end their day with prayer. Accordingly, SS that represents a scenario of Irish life should install an alert that considers religious matters.
- **A Free-Flowing Conversation: Irish Hospitality** Irish conversations can "take many strange turns," and not only the substance, but also the manner in which it is expressed is important. Correspondingly, SS should take into account, for instance, emotions occurring in Irish conversations. Moreover, the flow of conversation can be influenced by the culture—the Irish are famous for their hospitality toward friends and strangers, which can be reflected by SS in the conversation flow.
- **Places of Conversations: Irish Friends and Families** The Irish attach central importance to family dinners. Consequently, SS of an Irish scenario should consider relationships between participants in a dinner simulation. Irish weddings and wakes are special events that can, for example, last two or three days—an alert can be necessary that watches out for correct passing of Irish ceremonies. Pubs are a frequent place for gathering, which should be considered in the simulation context of SS scenarios.
- **Ending a Conversation** The Irish attach great importance to the issues of ending a conversation. Gannon stresses that the Irish culture according to Hofstede (2001) is ranked as seventh in the masculinity trait. Correspondingly, SS should consider this issue in a scenario that simulates the Irish conversation.

4.2 Acquisition on the Basis of Personality-Related Data

This section describes a heuristic that acquires emotion-related data from personality-related data. As personality-related data, the Mairesse corpus is used that provides values for the personality traits based on the Big-Five model (Mairesse et al. 2007).

4.2.1 Populating the Personality-Related Model

The Mairesse corpus contains 2,479 essays, the authors of which assessed their personality by filling in the Big-Five Inventory questionnaire (John et al. 1999). The data contains assessments of personality traits: extraversion (y = extravert, n = shy), emotional stability (y = secure, n = neurotic), agreableness (y = friendly, n = uncooperative), openness (y = insightful, n = unimaginative), conscientiousness (y = precise, n = careless). Note that the *emotional stability* trait is the semantic converse of the *neuroticism* trait in the Big-Five model.

To find an author whose personality can be compared with that of Spike, the dialogue texts of Spike and the essays of students in Mairesse corpus are correlated with each other. For simplicity, the analysis considers texts of certain persons and calculates intersection of tokens using the NLTK toolkit (Bird 2006). Accordingly, student 1310 whose verbal expressions revealed the most intersections with dialogues of Spike (275 words) was chosen as the person with appropriate personality assessed as ["y", "n", "y", "n", "n"].

The revealed personality traits are mapped onto numeric values where the "y" value is mapped onto 20 %, and the "n" value is mapped onto 0 %. Accordingly, the personality ["y", "n", "y", "n", "n"] corresponds to [20 %, 0 %, 20 %, 0 %, 0 %].

4.2.2 Populating the Emotion-Related Model

Student 1310 in the Mairesse corpus is a person that was previously identified as a person that behaves linguistically like Spike. Now, the emotion-related model of student 1310 based on an HMM for affective behavior in Fig. 4.5 can be populated using mathematical means. Accordingly, the initial basis for our exploration is the personality that is assessed as the sequence ["y", "n", "y", "n", "n"]. This sequence corresponds numerically after changing the value of the emotional stability trait to 20 % for conformance with Big-Five values to [20 %, 20 %, 20 %, 0 %, 0 %]. To calculate the HMM for affective behavior exacter and provide a beneficial basis for training, for example, using k-means, the set of Eqs. (4.1) and (4.2) in Sect. 4.1.2 is resolved making empirical assumptions.

Supposing that "y" means that the trait value is higher than 20 %, for example, $PT_E = 30$ % and "n" means that the trait value is lower than 20 %, for instance, $PT_N = 10$ %, formulae (4.1) and (4.2) can be resolved to

$$PT_E = \frac{\sum P(X \rightarrow high\_pos) + \sum P(X \rightarrow low\_pos)}{|\{X \rightarrow high\_pos\}| + |\{X \rightarrow low\_pos\}|} = 30\ \%, \tag{4.6}$$

$$PT_N = \frac{\sum P(X \rightarrow low\_pos) + \sum P(X \rightarrow low\_neg) + \sum P(X \rightarrow neutral)}{|\{X \rightarrow low\_pos\}| + |\{X \rightarrow low\_neg\}| + |\{X \rightarrow neutral\}|} = 10\%$$

(4.7)

$\Rightarrow$

$$\sum P(X \rightarrow high\_pos) + \sum P(X \rightarrow low\_pos) = 10 \cdot 30\% = 3,$$

(4.8)

$$\sum P(X \rightarrow low\_pos) + \sum P(X \rightarrow low\_neg) + \sum P(X \rightarrow neutral)$$

$$= 15 \cdot 10\% = 1.5,$$

(4.9)

where X and Y are unknowns representing an emotional state. Conventionally, the sums of probabilities equal 1:

$$\begin{cases} \sum P(high\_neg \rightarrow Y) = 1, \\ \sum P(low\_neg \rightarrow Y) = 1, \\ \sum P(neutral \rightarrow Y) = 1, \\ \sum P(low\_pos \rightarrow Y) = 1, \\ \sum P(high\_pos \rightarrow Y) = 1. \end{cases}$$

Evidently, there are too many unknowns in these equations to consider an exact analytical solution. That is why a mathematical approximation is calculated. Supposing equal mean values of transition probabilities, for example, $\sum P(X \rightarrow low\_neg) = 0.5$, we have

$$\sum P(X \rightarrow high\_pos) \overset{(4.8)}{=} 3 - 0.5 = 2.5 \Rightarrow P(X \rightarrow high\_pos) = 2.5/5 = 0.5,$$

(4.10)

$$\sum P(X \rightarrow low\_pos) \overset{(4.9)}{=} 0.5 = 1.5/3 \Rightarrow P(X \rightarrow low\_pos) = 0.5/5 = 0.1,$$

(4.11)

where (4.8) and (4.9) are the reference formulas considered in calculating the corresponding transitions.

The transition probabilities from states *high_neg*, *low_neg*, and *neutral* are calculated on the basis of the equation

$$\sum P(high\_pos \rightarrow Y) = 1 \Rightarrow 0.4 = 1 \overset{(4.10)}{-} 0.5 \overset{(4.11)}{-} 0.1 \Rightarrow 0.13(3) = 0.4/3,$$

where $3 = 5 - 1 - 1$ since emotional states *high_pos* and *low_pos* are considered before. The initial probabilities of states *high_neg*, *high_pos*, *low_neg*, *low_pos*, and *neutral* correspond to the majority values calculated from the set $0.13, 0.1, 0.5$.

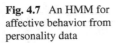

Fig. 4.7 An HMM for
affective behavior from
personality data

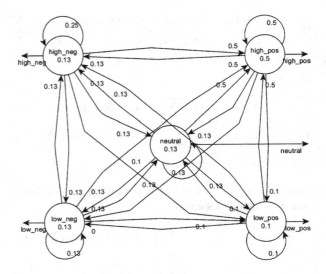

Table 4.4 An HMM for affective behavior from the personality-related data

	high_neg	low_neg	neutral	low_pos	high_pos
high_neg	0.13	0.13	0.13	0.1	0.5
low_neg	0.13	0.13	0.13	0.1	0.5
neutral	0.13	0.13	0.13	0.1	0.5
low_pos	0.13	0.13	0.13	0.1	0.5
high_pos	0.13	0.13	0.13	0.1	0.5
Observations:	high_neg	low_neg	neutral	low_pos	high_pos
Initial probabilities:	0.13	0.13	0.13	0.1	0.5

Figure 4.7 shows the HMM for affective behavior of student 1310 created from
the personality-related data. Table 4.4 shows the HMM in a table form.

4.2.3 Populating the Culture-Related Model

The Mairesse corpus relies on data from students of two American Universities,
Southern Methodist University and University of Texas. Hence, student 1310 is assumed to be a representative of the American culture that is characterized in Hofstede (2001) through the following dimensional values (Table 4.5).

Additionally, the culture-related model can be augmented by the facts from Gannon and Pillai (2012, p. 247), specifying additional information about the American
culture:

Table 4.5   Values for the culture-related model

Country	Power distance	Uncertainty avoidance	Individualism/ collectivism	Masculinity/ Femininity	Long-/Short-Term Orientation
United States	38	43	1	15	27

- **The Tailgate Party** Americans attach special importance to US football. Accordingly, SS should define football as a culturally valuable subject;
- **Pregame and Halftime Entertainment** American football is a ceremony for fans. It is a special experience and a ritual. Correspondingly, SS should distinguish particular temporal phases of American football such as pregame or halftime entertainment, track these phases, and issue appropriate alerts;
- **Strategy and War** American football considers particular strategies. SS can take into consideration strategic planning and issue appropriate alerts;
- **Selection, the Training Camp, and the Playbook** American companies spend much money for selecting and training right people. SS can consider appropriate issues such as the price of an expensive player.

4.3 Acquisition on the Basis of Case-Based Data

This section discusses another heuristic to collecting data for SS that relies on existing cases of intercultural communication and can be reconsidered again to populate cognitive models.

For example, incidents of intercultural communication in Cushner and Brislin (1995) are problematic situations that can be taken into account for data acquisition in SS. Paradoxes of cultural clashes in Gannon (2007) are also descriptions of cases where consideration of intercultural SS is necessary.

In the next step, numerical data from these descriptions can be acquired to perform intercultural SS. For this purpose, descriptions of SI scenarios are analyzed. A description normally begins with a discussion of interactants of the intercultural clash and their cultures that can result in typical settings, traditions, etc. of these cultures from the special literature.

Second, a description typically explains the problematic situation and contains episodes that explain emotions of the interactants that can be used to populate an emotion-related model based on an HMM for affective behavior.

4.3.1 Populating the Culture-Related Model

Assume that an SS system maintains an agent with the same cognitive properties as the Hong Kong student from a well-situated family in the American culture in the incident "The Trip to the Doctor" (see Sect. 3.3).

Table 4.6 Cultural dimensions for chosen incidents

Country	Power distance	Uncertainty avoidance	Individualism/ collectivism	Masculinity/ Femininity	Long-/Short-Term Orientation
Hong Kong	15–16	49–50	37	18–19	2

To analyze the behavior of this student, the numerical values of cultural dimensions from Hofstede (2001) can be acquired (Table 4.6).

Other cultural issues, for example, traditions of the Hong Kong student are necessary. Unfortunately, there is no discussion of Hong Kong traditions in Cushner and Brislin (1995) or Sorrells (2012, p. 448). However, there is an indirect way to define them over the Chinese culture. Indeed, both Cushner and Brislin (1995) and Sorrells (2012) claim the similarity of Hong Kong culture with the Chinese; in the first case, by the statement that 95 % of the Hong Kong population is Chinese, and in the second case, by grouping Hong Kong with China.

Chinese culture distinguishes according to Gannon and Pillai (2012), Chap. 26 the following issues that can be considered in SS:

- **The Importance of Family** The importance of the family in China cannot be overestimated. For example, SS should consider relationships between interactants. Moreover, particular agents representing family members must hold or carry certain valuable objects, for instance, photos of the family. If such valuable objects are not present, SS can issue an alert that an intact relation between family members is threatened;
- **The Expatriate Chinese** Expatriate Chinese are typically very successful no matter in which country they settled in. Nevertheless, all Chinese experience a need for emotions such as roundness, fluidity, and harmony. Correspondingly, a believable SS should issue an alert that watches out for the appropriate emotions if a Chinese does not experience corresponding emotions for a considerable period of time.

4.3.2 Populating the Emotion-Related Model

Maybe unintentionally, incidents in Cushner and Brislin (1995) contain much information on emotional states of interactants. If, however, incidents are intentionally emotional, descriptions of incidents can be used to populate emotion models of SS interactants.

Hence, this section discusses an approach to populating the emotion model of the Hong Kong student relying on the approach described in Sect. 4.1.1. At the beginning of his life in America the student is satisfied. After a while, he feels disappointment and goes to a doctor. What is the best approach to populate his emotion model?

SS can divide the description temporally into different events to construct sequences of emotions that can be used to train the emotion model. Thus, a training

Fig. 4.8 An HMM for
affective behavior from the
case-based data

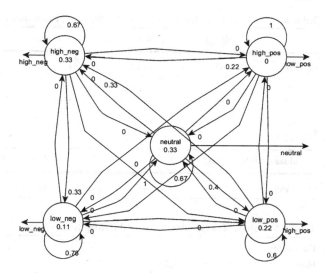

sequence of events for the Hong Kong student can look like <satisfaction>... <dis-
appointment>, where particular events correspond to significant life episodes such
as matriculation, found housing, disappointment in the work, etc.

These life episodes can be mapped onto emotional segments and utilized for
composition of an emotion model based on HMMs for affective behavior. Hence,
satisfaction can correspond to a *low_pos* emotion and embarrassment to a *low_neg*
emotion. To compose training sequences, the happy life in the home country can be
associated with a *high_pos* emotion followed by the journey to the foreign country
with a resulting *low_pos* emotion, colloquial faint with the *neutral* emotion state
concluded by embarrassment with a *low_neg* emotion, and severe headaches with a
high_neg emotion state.

Assuming that these events occurred periodically, a resulting emotional training
sequence can look like

```
high_pos ... low_pos ... neutral ... low_neg ... high_neg
```

and can be used to train the emotional model.

Thus, the training sequence contains 15 observations that can be used to compose
a dataset with instances representing five adjacent observations. To train an HMM
for affective behavior using this dataset, 10-fold cross-validation with stratification
is performed, and the *Recall* value of 26.67 % averaged over five classes and the
Precision value averaged over five classes of 48 % are calculated.

After each fold, a resulting HMM for affective behavior is analyzed according to
concurrences of states-observations. An HMM for affective behavior that calculates
the most account of concurrences of the same labels state-observation is shown in
Fig. 4.8 and Table 4.7.

Table 4.7 An HMM for affective behavior for the Hong Kong student

	high_neg	low_neg	neutral	low_pos	high_pos
high_neg	0.67	0.33	0	0	0
low_neg	0	0.78	0	0	0.22
neutral	0.33	0	0.67	0	0
low_pos	0	0	0.4	0.6	0
high_pos	0	0	0	0	1
Initial state probabilities:	0.33	0.11	0.33	0.22	0
Observations:	high_neg	neutral	low_neg	low_pos	high_pos

Table 4.8 Values of personality traits for the Hong Kong student

Character	PT_E	PT_N	PT_A	PT_O	PT_C
Hong Kong student	18.2 %	17.87 %	N/A	N/A	N/A

4.3.3 Populating the Personality-Related Model

Values of personality-related traits can be calculated on the basis of the HMM for affective behavior using heuristics in Sect. 4.1.2 (Table 4.8).

Table 4.8 shows personality-related dimensions calculated on the basis of probabilities in Fig. 4.8.

4.4 Empirical Cultural Data

Existing numerical data with cultural values can be insufficient to simulate scenarios of SI and SS in Chap. 3 believably. This section presents empirical data collected by different researchers that can be used for augmentation.

Numerical cultural data can be acquired in most cases from Hofstede (2001). Although Hofstede presents a considerable number of cultures (53), some cultures can miss, for example, the culture of Saudi Arabia. If a particular country is not present in the Hofstede's list, its cultural model can be approximated by an appropriate cluster. For example, Hofstede joins cultures in clusters according to historical, linguistic, and economic factors as follows (p. 62):

1. Korea, Peru, Salvador, Chile, Portugal, and Uruguay;
2. (former) Yugoslavia, Turkey, Arabic speaking countries, and Greece, plus Argentina, Spain, and Brazil;
3. Ecuador, Venezuela, Colombia, and Mexico;
4. Pakistan and Iran, Indonesia, Thailand and Taiwan, East and West Africa;
5. Guatemala, Panama, and Costa Rica;

6. Malaysia, Philippines, India, Hong Kong, Singapore, and Jamaica;
7. Denmark, Sweden, Netherlands, Norway, and Finland;
8. Australia, United States, Canada Great Britain. Ireland, and New Zealand;
9. Germany, Switzerland, South Africa, and Italy;
10. Austria and Israel (the state of Israel was founded by Austrian intellectuals);
11. Belgium and France;
12. Japan (all by itself).

Alternatively, Gupta and Hanges (2004) describes 62 countries grouped in 10 clusters that can be utilized to reveal empirical data. For example, Russia that is not present in Hofstede (2001) is listed in Gupta and Hanges (2004) in the cluster with Greece, which in turn is present in Hofstede's study. Moreover, the values of cultural dimensions can be deduced from similar historical, linguistic, and economic factors. If the values of cultural dimensions seem to be misleading (for example, Gannon and Pillai 2012, p. 41) doubts that ranking Japan as 22–23 in the individualism dimension among 53 nations is realistic), empirical data from other sources can be used in intercultural experiments.

In general, dimensional consideration of cultures as in Hofstede (2001) can be inadequate. For instance, short-/long-term dimension in Spanish culture characterizes high respect for traditions in a particular scenario only insufficiently. In certain cases, a high respect for bullfight must be emphasized especially.

Culture facts can be also defined by different organizations, for instance, demographic information from the World Bank.[2] However, such information can be misleading since it provides data for large human populations but not for a concrete situation of intercultural interaction of several persons. Thus, numerical facts about a certain culture are not collected in this book. In contrast, particular facts from Gannon and Pillai (2012) that reveal valuable subjects (traditions) of particular nations can be utilized for understanding SI and SS—an SS system simulating a particular scenario can maintain information on these facts and issue an alert, for example, signal an exceptional value of bullfight in Spain or specific value of tango in Argentine. If more detailed information on a specific issue is required, the SS system can be extended with specific facts on a particular phenomenon.

Table 4.9 presents a summary of empirical data that can be used for setting up experiments on SI and SS.

In Table 4.9, column *Country* lists the countries or geographical areals, e.g., continents the cultures of which are evaluated; column *Hofstede (2001)* (*traits*) refers to data in Exhibit 5.1, Exhibit 5.2, Exhibit 5.3 (pp. 500–502) of Hofstede (2001), where particular ranks' lists correspond to the ranks of the culture traits *Power Distance, Uncertainty Avoidance, Individualism/Collectivism, Masculinity/Femininity, Long-/Short-Term Orientation* in Sect. 4.1.3; column *Hofstede (2001)* (*cluster*) shows a cluster number in Hofstede (2001); column *Gupta and Hanges (2004)* (*cluster*) defines a cultural cluster in Gupta and Hanges (2004).

---

[2]http://data.worldbank.org.

Table 4.9 Empirical cultural data

No.	Country	Hofstede (2001) (traits)	Hofstede (2001) (cluster)	Gupta and Hanges (2004) (cluster)
1.	Albania	–	–	EE
2.	Argentina	[35–36, 10–15, 22–23, 20–21, –]	2	LA
3.	Australia	[41, 37, 2, 16, 22–24]	8	A
4.	Austria	[53, 24–25, 18, 2, 22–24]	10	GE
5.	Bangladesh	[80, 60, 20, 55, 40]*	–	–
6.	Belgium	[20, 5–6, 8, 22, 18]	11	–
7.	Brazil	[14, 21–22, 26–27, 27, 6]	2	LA
8.	Bulgaria	[70, 85, 30, 40, –]*	–	–
9.	Canada	[39, 41–42, 4–5, 24, 30]	8	A
10.	Chile	[24–25, 10–15, 38, 46, –]	1	–
11.	China	[80, 30, 20, 66, 118]*	–	CA
12.	Colombia	[17, 20, 49, 11–12, –]	3	LA
13.	Costa Rica	[42–44, 10–15, 46, 48–49, –]	5	CA
14.	Czechia	[57, 74, 58, 57, 13]*	–	–
15.	Denmark	[51, 51, 9, 50, 10]	7	NE
16.	Ecuador	[8–9, 28, 52, 13–14, –]	3	LA
17.	Egypt	4, 20, 35	–	ME
18.	Estonia	[40, 60, 60, 30, –]*	–	–
19.	Finland	[46, 31–32, 17, 47, 14]	7	NE
20.	France	[15–16, 10–15, 10–11, 35–36, 17]	11	LE
21.	Georgia	–	–	EE
22.	Germany	[42–44, 29, 15, 9–10, 22–24]	9	GE
23.	Great Britain	[42–44, 47–48, 3, 9–10, 28–29]	8	A
24.	Greece	[27–28, 1, 30, 18–19, –]	2	EE
25.	Guatemala	[2–3, 3, 53, 43, –]	5	LA

Table 4.9 (Continued)

No.	Country	Hofstede (2001) (traits)	Hofstede (2001) (cluster)	Gupta and Hanges (2004) (cluster)
26.	Hong Kong	[15–16, 49–50, 37, 18–19, 2]	6	CA
27.	Hungary	[46, 82, 80, 88, 50]*	–	EE
28.	Indonesia	[8–9, 41–42, 47–48, 30–31, –]	4	SA
29.	India	[10–11, 45, 21, 20–21, 7]	6	SA
30.	Iran	[29–30, 31–32, 24, 35–36, –]	4	SA
31.	Ireland	[49, 47–48, 12, 7–8, 13]	8	A
32.	Israel	[52, 19, 19, 29, –]	10	LE
33.	Italy	[34, 23, 7, 4–5, 19]	9	LE
34.	Jamaica	[37, 52, 25, 7–8, –]	6	–
35.	Japan	[33, 7, 22–23, 1, 4]	12	CA
36.	Kazakhstan	–	–	EE
37.	Korea (South)	[27–28, 16–17, 43, 41, 5]	1	CA
38.	Kuwait	–	–	ME
39.	Luxembourg	[40, 70, 60, 50, –]*	–	–
40.	Malaysia	[1, 46, 36, 25–26, –]	6	SA
41.	Malta	[56, 96, 59, 47, –]*	–	–
42.	Mexico	[5–6, 18, 32, 6, –]	3	LA
43.	Morocco	[70, 68, 46, 53, –]*	–	ME
44.	Namibia	–	–	SSA
45.	Netherlands	[40, 35, 4–5, 51, 11–12]	7	GE
46.	New Zealand	[50, 39–40, 6, 17, 25–26]	8	A
47.	Nigeria	–	–	SSA
48.	Norway	[47–48, 38, 13, 52, 11–12]	7	–
49.	Pakistan	[32, 24–25, 47–48, 25–26, 34]	4	–
50.	Panama	[2–3, 10–15, 51, 34]	5	–
51.	Peru	[21–23, 9, 45, 37–38]	1	–
52.	Philippines	[4, 44, 31, 11–12, 31–32]	6	SA
53.	Poland	[68, 93, 60, 64, 32]	–	EE

Table 4.9 (Continued)

No.	Country	Hofstede (2001) (traits)	Hofstede (2001) (cluster)	Gupta and Hanges (2004) (cluster)
54.	Portugal	[24–25, 2, 33–35, 45, 25–26]	1	LE
55.	Qatar	–	–	ME
56.	Romania	[90, 90, 30, 42, –]*	–	–
57.	Russia	[93, 95, 39, 36, –]*	–	EE
58.	Salvador	[18–19, 5–6, 42, 40, –]	1	LA
59.	Saudi Arabia	–	–	–
60.	Samoa	–	–	–
61.	Singapore	[13, 53, 39–41, 28, 9]	6	CA
62.	Slovenia	–	–	EE
63.	Slovakia	[104, 51, 52, 110, 38]*	–	–
64.	South Africa	[35–36, 39–40, 16, 13–14, –]	9	SSA, A
65.	Spain	[31, 10–15, 20, 37–38, 31–32]	2	LE
66.	Surinam	[85, 92, 47, 37, –]*	–	–
67.	Sweden	[47–48, 49–50, 10–11, 53, 20]	7	NE
68.	Switzerland	[45, 33, 14, 4–5, 15–16]	9	LE, GE
69.	Taiwan	[29–30, 26, 44, 32–33, 3]	4	CA
70.	Thailand	[21–23, 30, 39–41, 44, 8]	4	SA
71.	Trinidad	[47, 55, 16, 58, –]*	–	–
72.	Turkey	[18–19, 16–17, 28, 32–33, –]	2	ME
73.	Uruguay	[26, 4, 29, 42, –]	1	–
74.	Vietnam	[70, 30, 20, 40, 80]*	–	–
75.	United States	[38, 43, 1, 15, 27]	8	A
76.	Venezuela	[5–6, 21–22, 50, 3, –]	3	LA
77.	Yugoslavia	[12, 8, 33–35, 48, 49, –]	2	–
78.	Zambia	–	–	SSA
79.	Zimbabwe	35	–	SSA

Table 4.9 (Continued)

No.	Country	Hofstede (2001) (traits)	Hofstede (2001) (cluster)	Gupta and Hanges (2004) (cluster)
Regions:				
80.	Arab countries	[7, 27, 26–27, 23, –]	2	–
81.	East Africa	[21–23, 36, 33–35, 39, 28–29]	4	–
82.	West Africa	[10–11, 34, 39–41, 30–31, 33]	4	–
83.	Australian continent	[36, 51, 90, 61, 31]	–	–
84.	African continent	–	–	–

Legend: Clusters according to the GLOBE study A – Anglo, CA – Confucian Asia, EE – Eastern Europe, GE – Germanic Europe, LA – Latin America, LE – Latin Europe, ME – Middle East, NE – Nordic Europe, SA – Southern Asia, SSA – Sub-Sahara Africa, * – Estimates of personality traits (Hofstede 2001, p. 502)

Some rows of Table 4.9 are incomplete. For example, the *Albania* row contains only information about the cultural cluster (*EE*). To complete the *Albania* row with useful information, other participants of the *EE* cluster can be considered, which results in the list of *EE* countries:

```
 1. Albania ---- ---- EE
21. Georgia ---- ---- EE
24. Greece [27-28,1,30,18-19,-] 2 EE
27. Hungary [46,82,80,88,50]* ---- EE
36. Kazakhstan ---- ---- EE
53. Poland [68,93,60,64,32] ---- EE
57. Russia [93,95,39,36,-]* ---- EE
62. Slovenia ---- ---- EE
```

4.5 Summary and Outlook

This chapter introduced heuristics to acquire data for SS. It studied approaches to data acquisition on the basis of emotional, personality-related data and presented a case-based heuristics to acquire such data. Moreover, this chapter discussed empirical data that can be used in SS.

To collect further intercultural data that contains important information for SS, future work can consider:

1. Switchboard, a large multispeaker corpus of conversational speech and text (Godfrey et al. 1992);
2. MultiMASC, a broad-genre open language data (Ide 2012);

3. Parallel corpora, for example, a corpus with proceedings of the European Parliament including versions in 21 European languages (Koehn 2005) or a corpus with translations in the six official languages of the United Nations (Rafalovitch and Dale 2009) to correlate different translations and their notions with each other;

References

Bird, S. (2006). NLTK: the natural language toolkit. In *Proceedings of the COLING/ACL on interactive presentation sessions, COLING-ACL '06* (pp. 69–72). Stroudsburg: Association for Computational Linguistics. doi:10.3115/1225403.1225421. http://dx.doi.org/10.3115/1225403.1225421.

Costa, P., & McCrae, R. R. (1991). The NEO personality inventory: using the five-factor model in counseling. *Journal of Counseling and Development, 69,* 367–372.

Cowie, R., Douglas-Cowie, E., Savvidou, S., McMahon, E., Sawey, M., & Schröder, M. (2000). 'FEELTRACE': an instrument for recording perceived emotion in real time. In *Proceedings of the ISCA workshop on speech and emotion,* Northern Ireland (pp. 19–24). http://www.qub.ac.uk/en/isca/proceedings.

Cushner, K., & Brislin, R. W. (1995). *Intercultural interactions: a practical guide (cross cultural research and methodology)* (2nd ed.). Thousand Oaks: Sage. ISBN:978-0-803-95991-0. http://amazon.com/o/ASIN/0803959915/.

Douglas-Cowie, E., Cowie, R., Sneddon, I., Cox, C., Lowry, O., McRorie, M., Martin, J. C., Devillers, L., Abrilian, S., Batliner, A., Amir, N., & Karpouzis, K. (2007). The HUMAINE database: addressing the collection and annotation of naturalistic and induced emotional data. In *Proceedings of the 2nd international conference on affective computing and intelligent interaction (ACII),* Lisbon, Portugal (pp. 488–500).

François, J. M. (2012). JAHMM. An implementation of hidden Markov models in Java. https://code.google.com/p/jahmm/.

Gannon, M. J. (2007). *Paradoxes of culture and globalization.* Thousand Oaks: Sage. ISBN:978-1-412-94045-0. http://amazon.com/o/ASIN/1412940451/.

Gannon, M. J., & Pillai, R. R. K. (2012). *Understanding global cultures: metaphorical journeys through 31 nations, clusters of nations, continents, and diversity* (5th ed.). Thousand Oaks: Sage. ISBN:978-1-412-99593-1. http://amazon.com/o/ASIN/1412995930/.

Godfrey, J. J., Holliman, E. C., & McDaniel, J. (1992). Switchboard: telephone speech corpus for research and development. In *IEEE international conference on acoustics, speech, and signal processing, ICASSP-92* (Vol. 1, pp. 517–5201). doi:10.1109/ICASSP.1992.225858.

Gupta, V., & Hanges, P. J. (2004). Regional and climate clustering of societal cultures. In R. J. House, P. J. Hanges, M. Javidan, P. W. Dorfman & V. Gupta (Eds.), *Culture, leadership, and organizations: the globe study of 62 societies* (1st ed., pp. 178–218). Thousand Oaks: Sage. ISBN:978-0-761-92401-2.

Hofstede, G. (2001). *Culture's consequences: comparing values, behaviors, institutions and organizations across nations* (2nd ed.). Thousand Oaks: Sage. ISBN:978-0-803-97324-4. http://amazon.com/o/ASIN/0803973241/.

Hofstede, G. J., & Pedersen, P. (1999). Synthetic cultures: intercultural learning through simulation games. *Simulation & Gaming, 30*(4), 415–440. doi:10.1177/104687819903000402.

Hofstede, G. J., Smith, D. M., & Hofstede, G. (2002). *Exploring culture: exercises, stories and synthetic cultures.* Boston: Nicholas Brealey.

Ide, N. (2012). Multimasc: an open linguistic infrastructure for language research. In *Proceedings of the fifth workshop on building and using comparable corpora.*

John, O. P., Donahue, E. M., & Kentle, R. L. (1999). *The "Big Five" inventory: versions 4a and 5b* (Tech. rep.). Berkeley: University of California, Institute of Personality and Social Research.

John, O., Naumann, L., & Soto, C. (2008). Paradigm shift to the integrative big-five trait taxonomy: history, measurement, and conceptual issues. In O. P. John, R. W. Robins & L. A. Pervin (Eds.), *Handbook of personality: theory and research* (2nd ed., pp. 114–158). New York: Guilford. ISBN:978-1-593-85650-2. http://amazon.com/o/ASIN/1593856504/.

Juang, B. H., & Rabiner, L. R. (1990). The segmental K-means algorithm for estimating parameters of hidden Markov models. *IEEE Transactions on Acoustics, Speech and Signal Processing, 38*(9). doi:10.1109/29.60082. http://dx.doi.org/10.1109/29.60082.

Kipp, M. (2005). *Gesture generation by imitation: from human behavior to computer character animation.* Dissertation.com.

Koehn, P. (2005). Europarl: a parallel corpus for statistical machine translation. In *Conference proceedings: the tenth machine translation summit* (pp. 79–86). Phuket: AAMT. http://mt-archive.info/MTS-2005-Koehn.pdf.

Mairesse, F., Walker, M. A., Mehl, M. R., & Moore, R. K. (2007). Using linguistic cues for the automatic recognition of personality in conversation and text. *Journal of Artificial Intelligence Research, 30,* 457–500.

Mascarenhas, S., Dias, J., Afonso, N., Enz, S., & Paiva, A. (2009). Using rituals to express cultural differences in synthetic characters. In *AAMAS '09: proceedings of the 8th international conference on autonomous agents and multiagent systems,* Richland: International Foundation for Autonomous Agents and Multiagent Systems (pp. 305–312). ISBN:978-0-9817381-6-1.

Picard, R. (1997). *Affective computing.* Cambridge: MIT Press.

Plutchik, R. (1994). *The psychology and biology of emotion.* New York: Harpercollins College. http://amazon.com/o/ASIN/B000OEQ84O/.

Rafalovitch, A., & Dale, R. (2009). United nations general assembly resolutions: a six-language parallel corpus. In *Proceedings of the MT summit XII* (pp. 292–299). Allschwil: International Association of Machine Translation. http://www.uncorpora.org/Rafalovitch_Dale_MT_Summit_2009.pdf.

Robins, R. W., Fraley, R. C., & Krueger, R. F. (Eds.) (2007). *Handbook of research methods in personality psychology* (1st ed.). New York: Guilford. ISBN:978-1-593-85111-8. http://amazon.com/o/ASIN/1593851111/.

Sorrells, K. (2012). *Intercultural communication: globalization and social justice.* Thousand Oaks: Sage. ISBN:978-1-412-92744-4. http://amazon.de/o/ASIN/1412927447/.

Stone, P. J. (1966). *The general inquirer: a computer approach to content analysis.* Cambridge: MIT Press.

Stone, P. J., Dunphy, D. C., Smith, M. S., & Ogilvie, D. M. (1966). *The general inquirer: a computer approach to content analysis.* Cambridge: MIT Press. http://www.webuse.umd.edu:9090/.

Tausczik, Y. R., & Pennebaker, J. W. (2010). The psychological meaning of words: LIWC and computerized text analysis methods. *Journal of Language and Social Psychology, 29,* 24–54. doi:10.1177/0261927X09351676. http://homepage.psy.utexas.edu/homepage/students/Tausczik/Yla/index.html.

Whissell, C. (1989). The dictionary of affect in language. In R. Plutchik & H. Kellerman (Eds.), *Emotion. Theory, research and experience: Vol. 4. The measurement of emotions* (pp. 113–131).

Chapter 5
Framework for Data Processing

Until now, this book formed a basis for an approach to building intercultural SS: it described the purposes of this book (Chap. 1) and the existing approaches (Chap. 2). In Chap. 3, different scenarios of SI and SS were introduced. In Chap. 4, data that can be used in intercultural experiments were discussed. However, something is still missing, namely a robust framework that relies on these findings and implements flexible prototypes of SS systems. Such framework would, for example, compose SS systems that realize required simulation behavior and tackle shortcomings in Sect. 2.13.

This chapter describes the framework for statistical processing and prototyping, SocioFramework. Moreover, it presents additional findings focusing on intercultural processing.

5.1 Introduction

SocioFramework relies on findings in Osherenko (2011) and performs statistical processing of intercultural data and constructs software prototypes that simulate desired interaction scenarios. Additionally, it maintains tools to analyze simulation results allowing one to provide plausible explanations of intercultural problems.

In statistical processing, SocioFramework is designed as modality-, domain-, and language-independent and can be used in different fields of study, for example, in neurobiological processing. SocioFramework relies on a supervised approach meaning that data to be processed is annotated by a human according to the desired meaning.

SocioFramework processes data and generates statistical datasets that can be:

1. evaluated;
2. fused;
3. optimized;
4. defined for composition of software prototypes.

A. Osherenko, *Social Interaction, Globalization and Computer-Aided Analysis*, Human–Computer Interaction Series, DOI 10.1007/978-1-4471-6260-5_5,

Fig. 5.1 Generation of
datasets theoretically

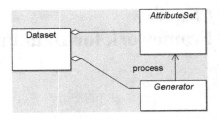

The framework is implemented in Java and Jython and was tested in the emotional domain in particular on the EmoText for long texts. Although the framework needs a final refinement and will be finished in future, it can be used now for numerous experiments in SI and SS.

The framework is controlled by a graphical user interface containing five tabs corresponding to four processing steps of statistical datasets (generation, evaluation, fusion, optimization) and a tab for the prototype creation. The following sections discuss each of them.

5.2 Generation

In the generation step, SocioFramework processes necessary data, for example, texts or neurobiological signals and composes ARFF datasets using WEKA (Witten and Frank 2005, pp. 53–55) for further analysis (Fig. 5.1).

Figure 5.1 shows a class diagram that represents a dataset. The *Dataset* class corresponds to a statistical dataset with the information to be processed; the abstract *AttributeSet* class represents attributes (features) that participate in the dataset and must be defined for processing; the abstract *Generator* class provides the *generator* function used to traverse through the specified custom data and to generate the necessary dataset.

SocioFramework composes statistical datasets in the ARFF format that defines attributes and data for processing (Fig. 5.2).

Figure 5.2 shows the generation tab containing the field *Data* indicating data to be processed and the list *Feature groups* containing feature groups *observation_sequence_spike_10* with features that are extracted using the current data. The button *Generate* starts generation of statistical datasets according to the specified data. Progress of generation is shown in the table below, which specifies the number of generated dataset files and their paths.

The following subsections describe the generation procedure in SocioFramework: a specification of the data to be processed, feature groups that are extracted for processing, and a generation procedure.

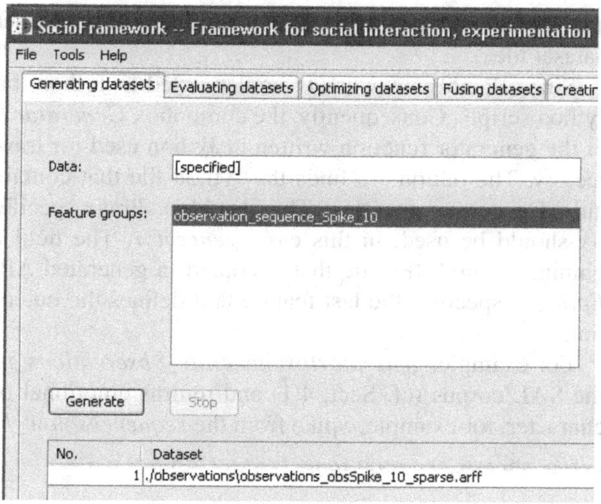

Fig. 5.2 Generation of datasets in SocioFramework

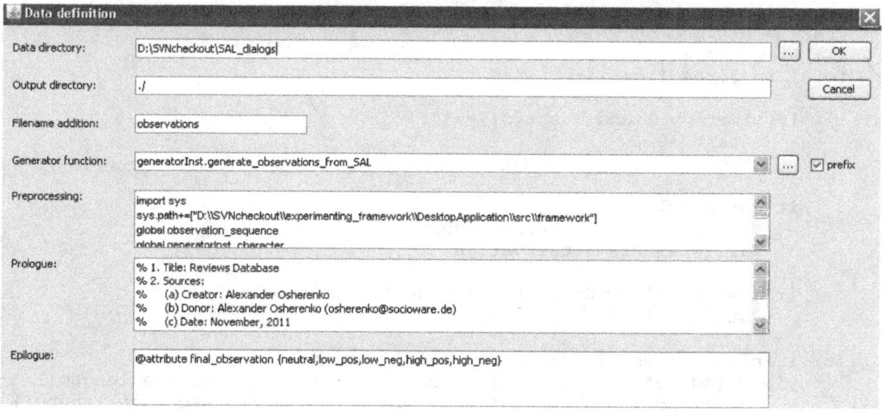

Fig. 5.3 Defining data in SocioFramework

5.2.1 Data Definition

SocioFramework processes custom data, for example, lexical, acoustic, neurobiological that is defined in the *Data definition* window (Fig. 5.3).

Figure 5.3 contains the field *Data directory* that specifies the source of data and the field *Output directory*, where the resulting dataset file is stored after generation. The button ... allows us to specify the required data directory. The field *Filename addition* specifies the text, for example, *observations*, that is added to the resulting dataset filename.

Certain data can need preprocessing. For instance, preprocessing of lexical data can calculate a frequency list of the data that contains words ordered by their fre-

quency and generate a list of features that will be extracted in the generated ARFF
dataset file.

Since SocioFramework is implemented in Jython, preprocessing also relies on
Jython scripts. Consequently, the combobox *Generator function* specifies the name
of the generator function written in Jython used for traversing through the data directory. The button ... finds the Jython file that contains the definition of the required generator function. The checkbox *Prefix* specifies if a function name prefix should be used, in this case, *generator*. The field *Prologue* specifies the beginning of an ARFF file that is copied in generated ARFF files, whereas the field
Epilogue specifies the last feature that defines the outcome of statistical classification.

For example, *generatorInst.generate_observations_from_SAL* traverses through
the SAL corpus (cf. Sect. 4.1) and returns emotional observations of a particular
character, for example, Spike from the *sequences_low_high.txt* file:

```
def generate_observations_from_SAL(self):

    #collect sequence elements
    f = open("D:\\SVNCheckout\\SAL_Dialogs\\sequences_low_high.txt")

    start = 0
    all_elements = []
    for l in f.readlines():

        if start == 1 and l.strip()=="":
            start =0
            break

        if (start==1):
            observation = l.strip().split()
            all_elements+=observation

        if l.startswith("Character " + self.character):
            start = 1

    for i in range(len(all_elements)-self._sequence_length):
        yield {"data": ",".join(all_elements[i:i+self._sequence_length]),
               "line":"", "rating": all_elements[i+self._sequence_length]}

    f.close()
```

The text area *Preprocessing* specifies the Jython code that will be used for initializing processing, for example:

```
...
from feature_groups import observation_sequence
from generator_functions import generator

generatorInst = generator("",10)
generatorInst.character = "Spike"
```

This code instantiates the *generator* class that specifies observations in 10 turns
of Spike's dialogues.

The field *Prologue* specifies the prologue of the ARFF file that is added at the
beginning of the generated ARFF file, for example:

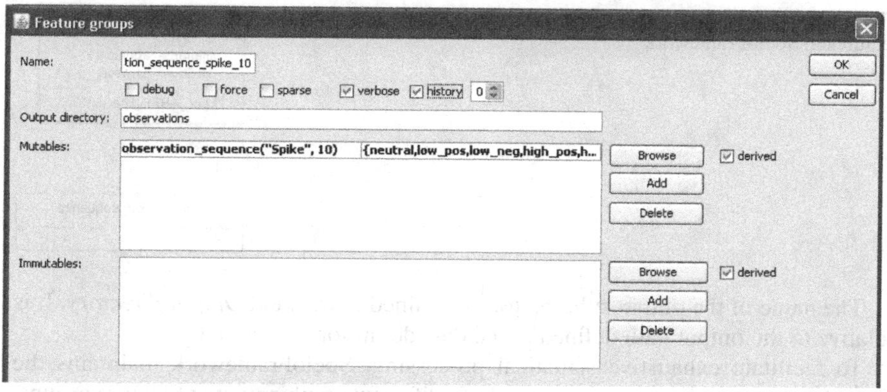

Fig. 5.4 Extracting features in SocioFramework

```
% 1. Title: Observations
% 2. Sources:
%       (a) Creator: Alexander Osherenko
%       (b) Donor: Alexander Osherenko (osherenko@socioware.de)
%       (c) Date: November, 2011
%
%
@relation observations
```

The definition of the outcome feature *final_observation* in the ARFF format is defined in the field *Epilogue*, for example, as the line

  @*attribute final_observation* {*neutral, low_pos, low_neg, high_pos, high_neg*}

This string is also added to the dataset in the definition section of an ARFF file.

5.2.2 Extraction of Feature Groups

The dataset is generated according to extracted features groups (Fig. 5.4).

In Fig. 5.4, the field *Name* defines the name of a feature group, for example, *observation_sequence_spike*_10 that we saw in the list *Feature groups* in Fig. 5.3.

The checkboxes *debug, force, sparse, verbose, history* define processing of the ARFF dataset file. The *debug* checkbox switches the debug mode on and prints debug messages on the system console. To bypass general avoidance of SocioFramework to consider combinations of instances of equal feature classes (see below list *Mutables*), the *force* checkbox is implemented. The *sparse* checkbox defines that the output ARFF dataset file is stored in the sparse ARFF format. The *verbose* checkbox defines the output of messages additional to debug messages. The *history* checkbox sets processing for several data entries the number of which is defined in the next combobox.

Fig. 5.5 New statistical
features in SocioFramework

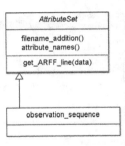

The name of the output subdirectory is defined in the field *Output directory*. It is relative to the output path defined in the data definition in Fig. 5.3.

To facilitate exhaustive statistical processing, SocioFramework maintains the lists *Mutables* and *Immutables* that specify different combinations of feature groups. The list *Mutables* defines variable combinations of feature groups that will be extracted during generation, whereas *Immutables* specifies feature groups that are extracted in the dataset in each generated dataset. Mathematically, the list *Mutables* specifies the list of attribute instances the combinatorial combinations of which are considered by the generator function to compose ARFF dataset files. For example, the list *Mutables* with two instances of attribute classes produces per combinatorics three ARFF datasets ($3 = 2^2 - 1$), where each feature group defines own features and adds its part to the whole dataset name. The list *Immutables* defines only one dataset file, where its name is concatenated from the parts of class instances (see *filename_addition* below).

To define instantiation of features in Fig. 5.4, the first column in the lists *Mutables* and *Immutables* specifies a constructor of the class with the necessary arguments, for example, *observation_sequence("Spike", 10),* and the second column, datatype of the outcome in the ARFF format, specifies, for example, a nominal *neutral, low_pos, low_neg, high_pos, high_neg*. If the second column is empty, the feature is considered as numeric.

Custom features can be developed in Jython. To integrate them in SocioFramework, they must be derived from the abstract class *AttributeSet* and implement the interface in Fig. 5.5.

Figure 5.5 describes custom features in SocioFramework. For example, the custom feature *observation_sequence* can be implemented as follows:

```
class observation_sequence(AttributeSet):

    def __init__(self, character, sequence_length):
        #initializes the instance
        ...

    def filename_addition(self):
        #adds a text to the name of the dataset file
        ...

    def attribute_names(self):
        #returns the list with names of features
        ...
```

```
def get_ARFF_line(self, data):
    #returns the feature instance in the ARFF format
    #and its classification outcome
    ...
```

The *Browse, Add, Delete* buttons change the lists *Mutables* and *Immutables*. The *Browse* button allows one to add feature classes defined in a specified Jython source file. The *Add* and *Delete* buttons add or delete instances of feature classes. If the *Derived* checkbox is defined, only classes derived from the class *AttributeSet* can be added to the lists *Mutables* and *Immutables*.

5.2.3 Generation Procedure

The Jython procedure that generates ARFF dataset files considers custom information specified during data and feature groups' definition. Essentially, it defines two steps of processing:

1. Initializing processing by reading custom arguments and values;
2. Generating ARFF datasets by composing combinations of immutable and immutable feature groups and composing corresponding ARFF files.

Below is the definition of the Jython function that maintains generation of ARFF datasets in SocioFramework:

```
def generate(self, args):
    //initialize variables
    ...

    for length in range(1, len(lstMutable)+1):

        for mutableEngines in
                xuniqueCombinations(lstMutable, length):

            //open the output file
            ...

            for engine in lstMutable:
                //write statistical features
                ...

            for engine in lstImmutable:
                //write statistical features
                ...

            #epilogue
            outputFile.write(epilogue)

            outputFile.write("\n\n@data\n")
```

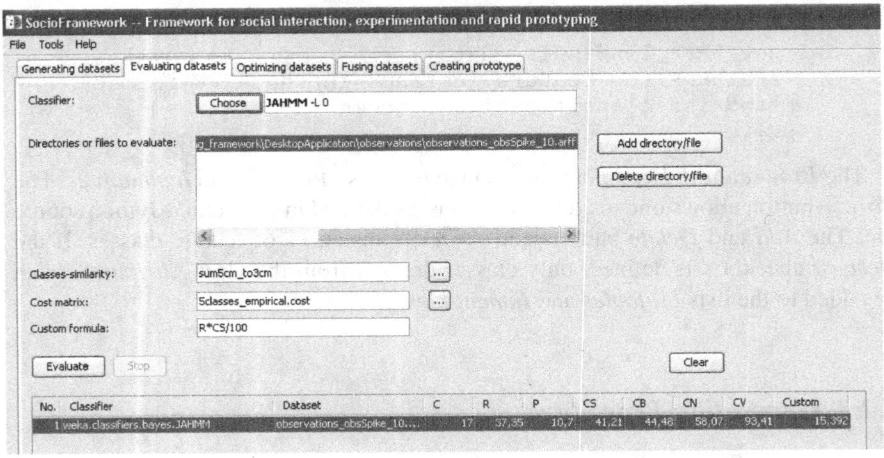

Fig. 5.6 Evaluation of datasets in SocioFramework

```
//write data
for arff_line in generatorRuns:
    ...

    for engine in lstMutable:
        line+=engine.get_ARFF_line(text)["line"]

    for engine in lstImmutable:
        line+=engine.get_ARFF_line(text)["line"]

    line += rating


    ...
```

The necessary parameters such as lists of mutable or immutable features are extracted from the lists *Mutables* and *Immutables* in Fig. 5.4, respectively.

5.3 Evaluation

Evaluation of a dataset represents results of data classification. Figure 5.6 shows the tab *Evaluating datasets* that controls evaluation of statistical datasets in SocioFramework.

Figure 5.6 shows the used classifier (field *Classifier*) and evaluated datasets (the list *Directories or files to evaluate*). The fields *Classes-similarity*, *Cost matrix*, and *Custom formula* define other parameters that can be used for calculating evaluation measures described in Sect. 5.3.2 such as the name of the cost-matrix file used for evaluation of the *CS* measure. The *Evaluate* button starts evaluation and calculates the evaluation measures. The table below shows the results of evaluation containing the utilized classifier, the datasets' names, and the evaluation measures.

5.3.1 Classifier

The cornerstone of statistical processing is a mathematical algorithm, called classifier, that automatically calculates a classification outcome after training.

Most prominent examples of classifiers are Support Vector Machines (SVM) that provide an analytical algorithm to classify information (Joachims 1999) or the probabilistic NaïveBayes algorithm that relies on the Bayes theorem (Witten and Frank 2005).

SocioFramework generates ARFF datasets that represent custom data split in instances. These datasets can be processed in the WEKA toolkit (Witten and Frank 2005). To wrap the ARFF representations and mathematical classifiers, SocioFramework implements a wrapper class that considers classification of ARFF files using a desired mathematical algorithm such as SVM or NaïveBayes (Appendix B). Since our approach is based on HMMs, an HMM classifier is developed that is compatible with the WEKA toolkit and is based on JAHMM (François 2012), a Java library for HMM implementation (Appendix A).

5.3.2 Measures

The results of the supervised classification in data mining are specified in a Confusion Matrix (CM). In the supervised approach, two measures are relevant for estimating results of evaluation, a measure of classification considered by a human supervisor and a measure calculated by an automatic algorithm. To assess statistical evaluation, a CM is used to store correlations of both measures by recording discrepancies between expected and calculated results for all classification outcomes.

This section describes measures that can be used to provide interpretation of these results in SocioFramework. Since comprehensive discussion of data mining issues would go outside the scope of this book, this book limits itself to references to the data mining literature.

5.3.2.1 Recall and Precision

A classifier calculates classification outcomes using statistical datasets. A dataset contains data instances consisting of a class feature that defines, in the supervised approach, an outcome expected by a human supervisor. To assess classification results, most data mining approaches use the *Recall* and *Precision* values, the conventional measures of classification that assess difference between the expected and the calculated outcomes of classification (cf. Witten and Frank 2005, p. 171). The recall and precision values R and P are calculated as

$$R = \frac{I^+}{I},$$

(5.1a)

$$P = \frac{I^t}{I},$$

(5.1b)

where I^+ is the number of correctly classified instances, I^t is the total number of retrieved instances that the classifier considers to be relevant, and I is the total number of classified instances in a dataset.

Classified instances can be grouped into different classes. To calculate classification results independent from the number of classified instances of certain classes, the *Recall* and the *Precision* values can be averaged over classes as follows:

$$R = \frac{\sum_{c=1}^{N} R_c}{N},$$

(5.2a)

$$P = \frac{\sum_{c=1}^{N} P_c}{N},$$

(5.2b)

where N is the number of classes, R_c is the recall value of instances' classification of class c, and P_c is the precision value of instances' classification of class c.

5.3.2.2 Class Similarity Measure

This measure considers classification errors of similar classes. For example, misclassification of an emotion as a high negative emotion is not considerable if it was specified by a human supervisor as a low negative emotion. However, if the same emotion is misclassified as a *high positive* emotion, this is a significant learning error. The Class Similarity (CS) measure considers such similarity and defines · means to transform the original CM into an auxiliary CM. Numerically, the CS measure equals to the recall value of classification using the auxiliary confusion matrix (cf. Osherenko 2011)

$$CS = R(CM^A),$$

(5.3)

where recall R applies to CM^A representing a transformed confusion matrix.

5.3.2.3 Cost-Based Measure

The Cost-Based (CB) measure defines a value of data classification relying on manually specified costs of misclassification of data. Mathematically, CB is defined as

$$CB = \frac{1}{N} \sum_{c=1}^{N} \left(1 - \frac{K_c^{c'}}{I_c \max k_c} \right),$$

(5.4)

where c is a class number, $K_c^{c'}$ is the cost of misclassification of an instance of class c as an instance of class c', $\max k_c$ is the maximal cost value of class c, I_c is the number of instances of class c, and N is the number of classes in classification (cf. Osherenko 2011).

5.3.2.4 Class Number Measure

The Classes Number (CN) measure provides a classification interpretation corresponding to the number of classified classes. CN is defined mathematically as

$$CN = \frac{N}{N-1} - \frac{1}{(N-1)R},\tag{5.5}$$

where R is the recall value of data classification, and N is the number of classes in classification (cf. Osherenko 2011).

5.3.2.5 Classification-Variety Measure

To solve the problem of sparse data, the cross-validation technique can be used that reuses the same data several times but in different constellations. In SocioFramework, the 10-fold cross-validation is used that splits data into 10 parts: nine parts are used for learning, and one part for testing. Classification of different folds can differ significantly, and Classification-Variety (CV) measure shows the homogeneity of fold classification. The closer this measure is to 0 %, the more reliable is the cross-validation. On the contrary, if the measure goes to 100 %, the cross-validation results are too different and more likely to be unreliable.

To calculate the CV measure, a sequence S consisting of 10 classification results (ratio success/total) for each fold is composed, and its standard deviation is calculated:

$$CV = \sqrt{\frac{1}{N-1} \sum_{i=0}^{N-1} (r_i - \mu)^2}\tag{5.6}$$

where r_i is the ratio of successful and total outcomes in the fold i, μ is the mean of values in S, and N is the number of folds in classification, 10.

5.3.2.6 Custom Evaluation Measures

Since statistical experimentation can require other evaluation measures than that discussed in this section, SocioFramework considers the possibility to specify custom evaluation measures. For this purpose, a custom evaluation measure represented through a mathematical formula can be defined in SocioFramework and contain evaluation variables described above such as R, P, CS, CB, CN, CV and also the number of correct outcomes C. For example, the value of the custom evaluation *Custom* can be calculated as

$$Custom = R \cdot CV,\tag{5.7}$$

where R is the recall value of classification, CV is the value of the CV measure.

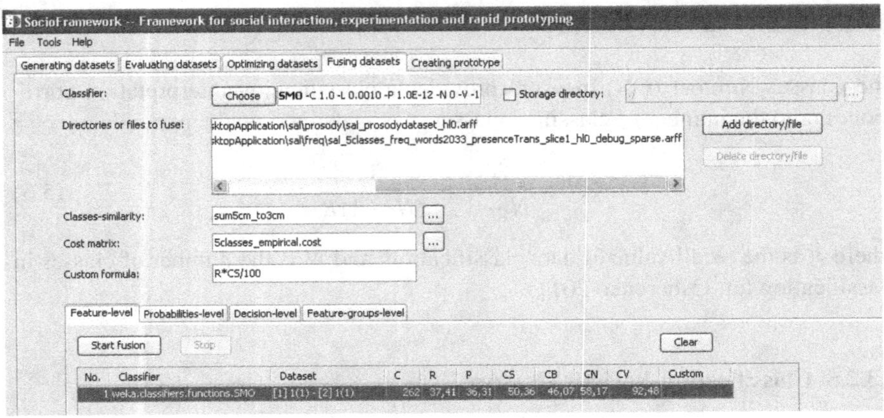

Fig. 5.7 Fusion of datasets in SocioFramework

Since the custom evaluation formula is evaluated by the Jython interpreter in SocioFramework, the formula can contain other mathematical operations, for example, standard function *sqrt*.

5.4 Fusion

Statistical datasets can be fused and combine information from different sources in order to improve results of statistical processing. For example, multimodal data such as the SAL data can be fused using the SVM classifier. In this case, a dataset composed on the basis of lexical information is fused with a dataset composed on the basis of acoustic information.

SocioFramework maintains the tab *Fusing datasets* that controls statistical fusion (Fig. 5.7).

In Fig. 5.7, the field *Classifier* specifies the used classifier. The result dataset can be stored in the directory specified in the field *Storage directory*. The list *Directories or files to fuse* defines datasets to be fused and can be changed by clicking the button *Add directory/file* or *Delete directory/file*. The fields *Classes-similarity*, *Cost matrix*, *Custom formula* define other parameters used for calculating evaluation measures from Sect. 5.3.2 such as the name of the cost-matrix file used for evaluation of the *CS* measure. The button *Start fusion* starts the feature-level fusion calculating the evaluation measures from Sect. 5.3.2 for the fused dataset shown in the table below.

There are different ways to perform fusion: feature level, decision level, probability level, decision-integration level. Feature-level fusion is implemented in SocioFramework; other fusion types are considered for future implementation.

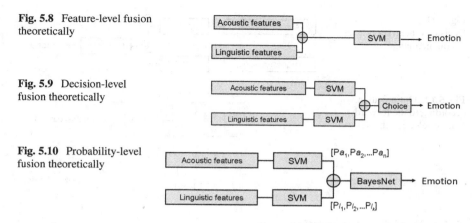

Fig. 5.8 Feature-level fusion theoretically

Fig. 5.9 Decision-level fusion theoretically

Fig. 5.10 Probability-level fusion theoretically

5.4.1 Feature Level

The conventional approach of fusion is fusion at the feature-level fusion that joins features of different data sources. Figure 5.8 shows an example of fusion of acoustic and linguistic datasets theoretically.

In Fig. 5.8, acoustic features and lexical information are used, for example, to analyze emotions using the SVM classifier.

5.4.2 Decision Level

Fusion can be performed at the decision level. In this case, statistical processing is performed independently in each information type, and only final decisions (outcomes) of analysis are fused (Fig. 5.9).

Figure 5.9 shows a decision-level fusion theoretically using an example of emotional fusion.

5.4.3 Probability Level

Probability-level fusion defines a two-phase approach to classification of information. In the first phase, information (for example, acoustic and linguistic) is analyzed independently for each modality and classifiers; for instance, SVM calculates probabilities of outcomes for each classification class. In the second phase, these probabilities are used to train the second classifier, for instance, BayesNet to calculate the final classification result, e.g., *Emotion*. More formally, the probabilities of n acoustic outcomes $P_{a_1}, \ldots, P_{a_n}$ and the probabilities of k linguistic outcomes $P_{l_1}, \ldots, P_{l_k}$ are calculated using SVM. These probabilities are joined, and a BayesNet classifier is used to calculate the final result *Emotion* (Fig. 5.10).

Fig. 5.11
Decisions-integration-level
fusion theoretically

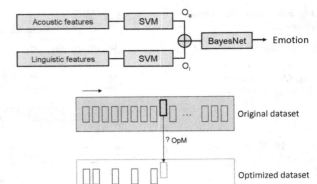

Fig. 5.12 Optimization
according to the forward
feature selection theoretically

5.4.4 Decision-Integration Level

Similarly to the probability-level fusion, fusion at the decision-integration level also considers a two-phase approach to classification of information. First, the information (for example, acoustic or linguistic) is analyzed by the SVM classifiers to calculate decisions of classification, for example, an acoustic outcome O_a and a linguistic outcome O_l. In the second phase, an additional classifier, for instance, BayesNet, integrates these decisions by making a choice and calculating the final result *Emotion* (Fig. 5.11).

5.5 Optimization

Optimization of statistical datasets allows improvement of classification by optimizing the feature space and filtering undesirable features. The idea is to find a subset of features of the original feature set that improves classification by searching in the space of features.

For example, a simple sequential algorithm of optimization, Forward Feature Selection (FFS) (Witten and Frank 2005, p. 292; Hall 1999, p. 27), can be used to optimize a dataset (Fig. 5.12).

Figure 5.12 shows the theoretical foundation of FFS. FFS goes through the set of statistical features in the original dataset and proves its addition in the initially empty result dataset. If the feature addition increases the Optimization Measure (OpM), the extracted feature is permanently added to the optimized dataset. OpM can be, for example, the *R* or *CV* measure. Otherwise, the feature is rejected, and the algorithm extracts the next feature in the original dataset. For simplicity, this book abstains from the problem of overfitting in learning (Mitchell 1997, p. 67) and a problem of the local maxima that accompany optimization (Elidan et al. 2002).

Datasets that were generated previously, for example, using the approach in Sect. 5.2, can be optimized according to different optimization measures, for instance, the values of *Recall* or *Custom*. For this purpose, SocioFramework maintains the *Optimizing datasets* tab (Fig. 5.13).

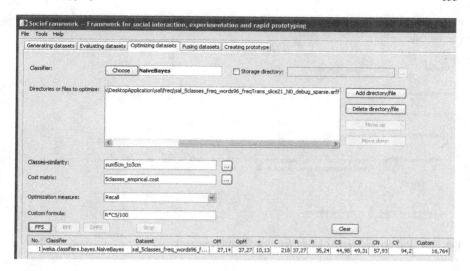

Fig. 5.13 Optimization of datasets in SocioFramework

In Fig. 5.13, the tab *Optimizing datasets* defines the utilized classifier in the field *Classifier* (for example, NaiveBayes) and the directory to store the optimized dataset (the field *Storage directory*). The list *Directories or files to optimize* contains file(s) to optimize. The fields *Classes-similarity*, *Cost matrix*, *Custom formula* define other parameters that can be used for calculating evaluation measures from Sect. 5.3.2 such as the name of the cost-matrix file used for evaluation of the *CS* measure. The button *FFS* starts the FFS optimization procedure and calculates the optimized measures (Fig. 5.12).

The optimization table shows current optimization results in the corresponding columns: the original recall value 27.14 % in the OM column, the *OpM* column shows the optimized value 37.27 %, the optimization improvement is specified in the column "+", which in this case is 10.13 %, and evaluation measures such as *R*, *P*, or *CS*. Additionally, the table specifies other evaluation measures from Sect. 5.3.2 such as the *CS* measure.

5.6 Prototyping

SocioFramework composes and reviews software prototypes that can be either an NL ECA (a simple classification sample) based on a Java servlet or an SS system relying on a MAS.

SocioFramework can compose NL avatars (classification samples) based on Java servlets (Fig. 5.14).

Figure 5.14 shows the tab *Creating prototype* for prototyping NL ECAs or classification samples. It contains the used classifier (JAHMM), the root directory for

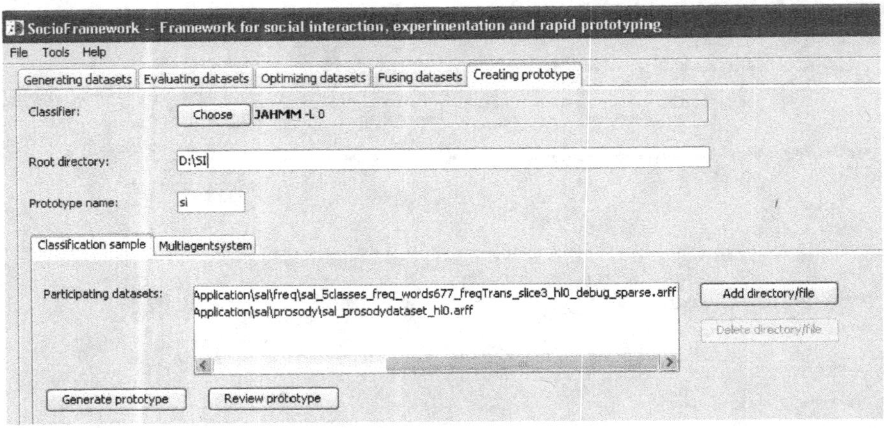

Fig. 5.14 Prototyping servlet-based agents in SocioFramework

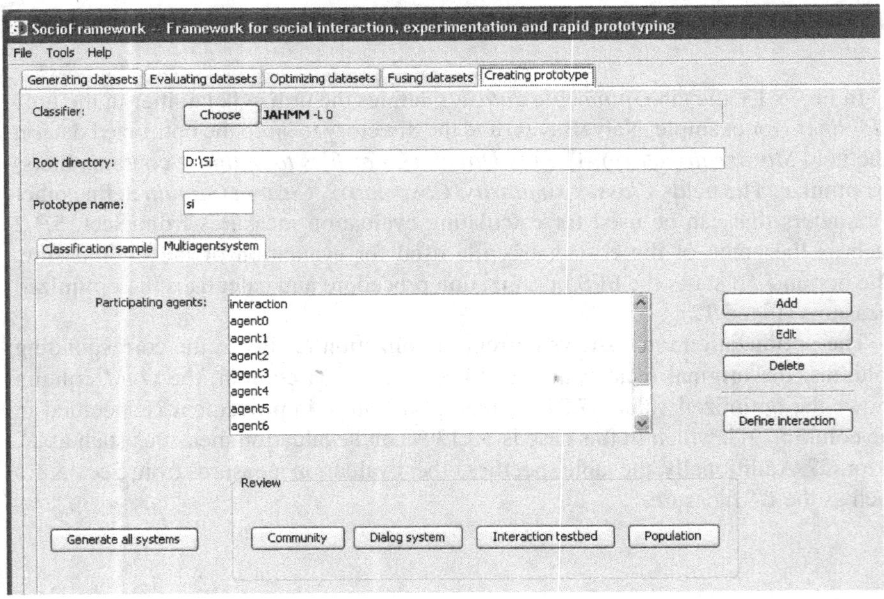

Fig. 5.15 Prototyping multiagent systems in SocioFramework

the destination project (D:\SI), the prototype name (si), and participating datasets for statistical processing (the ARFF files). the button *Generate prototype* creates the prototype (Sect. 6.3.1). The button *Review prototype* reviews the prototype by running it in an Internet browser.

SS systems relying on MAS maintain different agents, for example, NL ECAs and can be composed according to a custom interaction specification (Fig. 5.15).

Fig. 5.16 Swing hierarchy

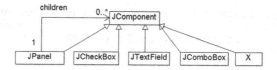

Figure 5.15 shows the tab *Creating prototype* with a meta *interaction* agent and several ECAs (*agentN*) on the SocioFramework GUI. It defines the basis classifier that will be used in the new simulation program (JAHMM), the root directory for the destination NetBeans project that can be adjusted in your favorite IDE and Java sources (D:\SI), and the prototype name (si). The button *Define interaction* defines interaction specification for the new SS system (cf. Sect. 6.5.1). The button *Generate all systems* generates SS prototypes and create Java projects, for example, for processing in NetBeans (Petri 2010). the buttons *Review* start the JADE environment and the generated SS system: the button *Community* starts a content-synchronized community (Sect. 6.3.2), the button *Dialog system* starts a sequential dialog system (Sect. 6.3.3), the button *Interaction testbed* starts a testbed synchronized through interaction exchanges (Sect. 6.3.4), and the button *Population* starts a GUI-less population (Sect. 6.3.5). To facilitate statistical processing, each agent can wrap statistical datasets using a specific classifier (cf. Appendix B).

For further information about prototyping, see Chap. 6.

5.7 Auxiliary

This section describes auxiliary means used in SocioFramework to facilitate processing and to analyze processing results.

5.7.1 Storing Configuration

To avoid time-consuming operations such as defining on GUI values, for example, names and options of chosen classifiers or datasets' lists every time from scratch, SocioFramework maintains means to store and restore configuration in an XML file (Ray 2003).

To read and write configuration files, the hierarchy of visual elements on the SocioFramework GUI based on Java Swing library (Elliott et al. 2002) is utilized (Fig. 5.16).

Figure 5.16 illustrates processing of configuration files relying on the SocioFramework GUI. To read configuration, SocioFramework traverses the GUI beginning from the root element and fills the values of specified visual (Swing) elements with names beginning with a certain prefix (*EXPORT_PREFIX*) using a recursive function *readCompChildren(Document doc, Element root, JComponent comp)*:

```
private void readCompChildren(Document doc, Element root,
                             JComponent comp) {
    if (root == null) {
        ...
    }
    if (comp.getName() != null) {
        if (comp.getName().startsWith(EXPORT_PREFIX)) {
            if (comp instanceof JPanel) {
                ...
            }
            if (comp instanceof JCheckBox) {
                ...
            }
            if (comp instanceof JTextField) {
                ...
            }
            if (comp instanceof JComboBox) {
                ...
            }
            //if (comp instanceof X)
            ...
        }
    }
    for (int ind = 0; ind < comp.getComponentCount(); ind++) {
        if (comp.getComponent(ind) instanceof JComponent) {
            readCompChildren(doc, xmlRoot, (JComponent)
            comp.getComponent(ind));
        }
    }
}
```

To write an XML configuration, SocioFramework traverses GUI beginning from the root element and writes the values of specified visual (Swing) elements with names beginning with a certain prefix (*EXPORT_PREFIX*) using a recursive function *writeCompChildren(Document doc, Element root, JComponent comp)*:

```
private void writeCompChildren(Document doc, Element root,
                              JComponent comp) {
    if (root == null) {
        ...
    }
    if (comp.getName() != null) {
        if (comp.getName().startsWith(EXPORT_PREFIX)) {
            if (comp instanceof JPanel) {
                ...
            }
            if (comp instanceof JCheckBox) {
                ...
            }
            if (comp instanceof JTextField) {
                ...
            }
```

```
                if (comp instanceof JComboBox) {
                   ...
                }
                //if (comp instanceof X)
                   ...
            }
        }
        for (int ind = 0; ind < comp.getComponentCount(); ind++) {
            if (comp.getComponent(ind) instanceof JComponent) {
                writeCompChildren(doc, localRoot, (JComponent)
                  comp.getComponent(ind));
            }
        }
    }
}
```

A configuration file consists of the definitions of all tabs and all visual elements within them. For example, a configuration file in Appendix C defines a population prototype shown in Fig. 5.19.

5.7.2 Visualizing Classification Results

SocioFramework allows one to show many classification results graphically that are calculated in the tab *Evaluating datasets*. For this purpose, SocioFramework visualizes a function that transforms a dataset name (cf. Fig. 5.6) into the dataset number and maps this number onto a specified evaluation measure. For mapping, regular expressions (Friedl 2006) are utilized that represent a certain bit in the dataset name (Fig. 5.17).

In Fig. 5.17, the list *Bitwise visualization patterns* shows a list of patterns used to calculate a number of a classification result for the dataset name. A pattern is a regular expression containing a number representing power of 2 and a regular expression that is searched for in the file name of a dataset name. For instance, the pattern *(?P<4>sdsl)(?P<3>sdwl)...* calculates 1 as the 4th bit of a dataset number if *sdsl* text is found in the file name of a dataset and 0 otherwise; 1 as the 3th bit of a dataset number if *sdwl* text is found in the file name of a dataset and 0 otherwise, and so on.

The combobox *Visualization measure* shows a measure that represents a result of classification, for example, *Recall*. The button *Visualize* shows results graphically in the result field *Graph*. The button *Close* closes the dialog window.

Given that the dataset *sal_sdsl_words_sdwl.arff* was evaluated with a recall value 55 %, SocioFramework visualizes this result in the graph as a point $(2^4 + 2^3, 55\ \%)$ since the dataset name contains the pattern *sdsl* and the pattern *sdwl*.

For more information on mapping, see Osherenko (2011), Sect. 5.2.3 *Plotting classification results*.

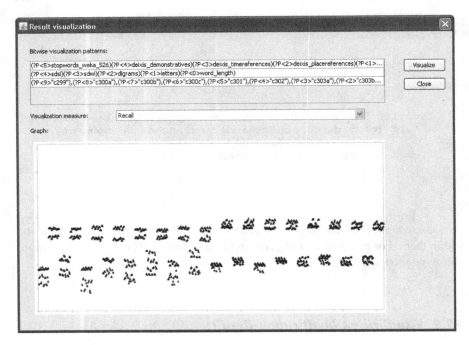

Fig. 5.17 Visualizing results

5.7.3 Interaction Analysis of Affective Behavior

The proposed emotion model relies on HMMs for affective behavior that can be used to analyze patterns of SI. For example, certain emotional observations can be used to compose an HMM for affective behavior, whereas its probabilities can change during an emotional dialogue. To assess this change numerically, HMMs for affective behavior of interactants can be compared using the Kullback–Leibler measure D (Juang and Rabiner 1985) as follows:

$$D(\lambda_1, \lambda_2) = \log Pr(O_\tau | \lambda_1) - \log Pr(O_\tau | \lambda_2), \tag{5.8}$$

where O_τ are observations in HMMs λ_1, λ_2.

SocioFramework uses JAHMM, a Java library for HMM processing. In JAHMM, the textual format of an HMM (François 2012, p. 8) defines the version of the HMM format, for example, 1.0; the number of states as NbStates, for instance, 5; the states with their initial probabilities (P_i); the state-to-state transitions (A); a description of the observation distribution function (*IntegerOPDF*). Summarizing, an HMM for affective behavior similar to Fig. 4.6 can be defined textually as

```
Hmm v1.0
NbStates 5
```

Fig. 5.18 Comparing HMMs

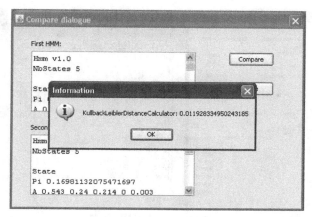

```
State
Pi 0.16981132075471697
A 0.543 0.2 0.214 0 0.043
IntegerOPDF [1 0 0 0 0]

State
Pi 0.11949685534591195
A 0.238 0.344 0.354 0.048 0.016
IntegerOPDF [0 1 0 0 0]

State
Pi 0.6352201257861635
A 0.039 0.092 0.859 0 0.01
IntegerOPDF [0 0 1 0 0]

State
Pi 0.006289308176100629
A 1 0 0 0 0
IntegerOPDF [0 0 0 1 0]

State
Pi 0.06918238993710692
A 0 0 0.176 0 0.824
IntegerOPDF [0 0 0 0 1]
```

Given, during a dialogue with Spike, an HMM for affective behavior changes and probabilities of transitions from the first state *A 0.543 0.2 0.214 0 0.043* become *A 0.543 **0.24** 0.214 0 **0.003*** (Fig. 5.18).

Figure 5.18 shows a proposal for a comparison dialogue in SocioFramework that measures the similarity of HMMs for affective behavior using the Kullback–Leibler measure implementation in JAHMM. The HMMs for affective behavior are defined as texts in the textboxes *First HMM* and *Second HMM*. The comparison results in the Kullback–Leibler measure of 0.012.

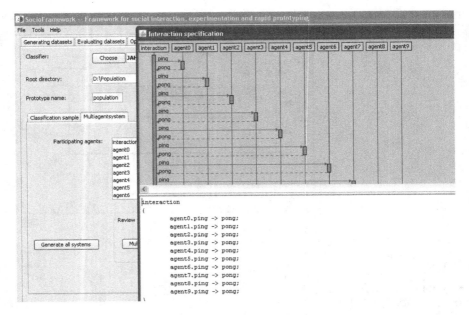

Fig. 5.19 Prototyping a population

5.7.4 Populations

SocioFramework can compose a prototype behaving according to a certain inter-action specification. For example, the prototype can be a MAS that represents a population of 10 agents behaving according to a ping-pong scheme: the avatars get a ping message from the *interaction* meta-agent and respond with a pong message (Fig. 5.19).

Figure 5.19 shows an interaction specification for a population of agents in So-cioFramework. To create such a specification, the dialog window *Population settings* can be used that composes an interaction specification with repetitive SI patterns (Fig. 5.20).

Fig. 5.20 Creating a
population specification

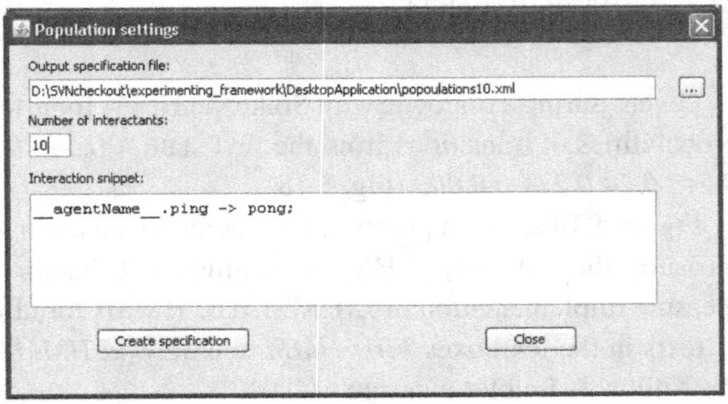

In Fig. 5.20, the field *Output specification file* defines the name of the composed XML file with the population specification, for example, ... \populations10.xml; the text field *Number of interactants* shows the number of interactants participating in SI, for instance, 10; the text field *Interaction snippet* shows a repetitive pattern that will be used to compose the interaction specification. Note that the example snippet _ _agentName_ _.ping ->pong; contains the pattern _ _agentName_ _ that will be resolved into the current agent name during composition of the interaction specification (cf. the field *Name* in Fig. 6.5). The button *Create specification* creates the specification, an XML text file, that can be used as a configuration file and modified later in a common text editor.

5.7.5 Interface to Jython Editor

As already mentioned, SocioFramework relies on the Jython programming language that combines Java and Python. To facilitate editing code, for example, classes in Fig. 5.4, SocioFramework can use the Python editor, Idle, available in the Python distribution.

5.7.6 Statistical Case-Based Expert System

The incidents' descriptions and possible answers can be used as a basis for an expert system for Case-Based Reasoning (CBR). For example, the incident "Social Ease" in Sect. 3.3 presents the best explanation and three improbable explanation variants. The idea of case-based expert systems relies on analogy: if a CBR (statistical) engine is trained to discriminate intercultural problems, it can analyze new cases by analogy. For example, a CBR engine trained on the basis of verbal descriptions of scenarios and their solutions can classify new cases using the trained engine by similarity, and a human expert chooses the best answer among probable answers (Fig. 5.21).

In Fig. 5.21, a case represented colloquially in the field *Colloquial description* can be analyzed by a CBR engine and show possible explanations in the field *Explanations*.

5.8 Summary and Outlook

This chapter discussed SocioFramework, the framework for statistical processing and prototyping, used to process intercultural data and implement prototypes of SS systems relying on certain interaction specifications.

In future, SocioFramework will implement a CBR system to assist an expert in finding possible explanations of scenarios' outcomes. For example, this CBR

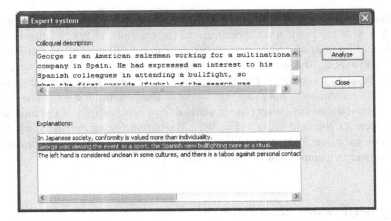

Fig. 5.21 The expert system

system will use the ontology-based Java approach in Diaz-Agudo et al. (2007) to integrate an expert system in SocioFramework. Alternatively, this system would estimate the probabilities of outcomes using statistical means, for example, a system that maintains a multivariate classifier (cf. Sect. 3.3).

Appendix A: The HMM Classifier

This appendix shows an implementation of an HMM Classifier that relies on JAHMM and is compatible with WEKA:

```java
public class JAHMM extends AbstractClassifier {

    //number of observations in case of emotional E/A
    //space - 5
    protected int m_NumClasses;

    //number of states in case of emotional E/A space - 5
    protected int m_States;

    //the number of the sequence attribute
    protected int m_SeqAttr = -1;

    //0 - k-means, 1 - Baum-Welch, 2 - scaled Baum-Welch
    protected int m_LearningMethod = 0;

    //Builds the current classifier. m_SeqAttr specifies
    //the sequential attribute.
    @Override
    public void buildClassifier(Instances data) throws
```

```
Exception {

    ...

    //build HMM
    OpdfIntegerFactory factory =
      new OpdfIntegerFactory(m_NumClasses);
    Hmm<ObservationInteger> hmm =
      new Hmm<ObservationInteger>(m_States, factory);
    hmm.getOpdf(0).fit(new ObservationInteger(4));

    List<List<ObservationInteger>> sequences;
    sequences = extractSequences(data);

    switch (m_LearningMethod) {
        case 0:
            // KMeans learning
            KMeansLearner<ObservationInteger> kml =
                new KMeansLearner<ObservationInteger>
                (m_NumClasses, factory, sequences);

            learntHmm_ = kml.learn();

            break;
        case 1:
            /* Baum-Welch learning */
            BaumWelchLearner bwl = new BaumWelchLearner();

            learntHmm_ = bwl.learn(hmm, sequences);

            break;

        case 2:
            BaumWelchScaledLearner bwsl =
              new BaumWelchScaledLearner();

            learntHmm_ = bwsl.learn(hmm, sequences);

            break;
    }
}

//Classifies the given test instance
@Override
public double classifyInstance(Instance instance) throws
Exception {

    Instances seq = instance.relationalValue(m_SeqAttr);

    //extracts a training sequence from the given instance
    List<ObservationInteger> sequence =
      extractSequenceFromInstance(seq.instance(0));
```

```
        int[] states =
          learntHmm_.mostLikelyStateSequence(sequence);

        double bestClass = states[states.length - 1];

        return bestClass;
    }
} //endclass
```

Appendix B: The ARFF Wrapper

This appendix presents the Java source of a wrapper that maintains a WEKA-compatible classifier and ARFF data in the prototypes of SS systems. Note that the wrapper uses names of the dataset files to extract and evaluate statistical features for identifying necessary POS processing and lemmatization done by TreeTagger (Schmid 1994). For example, TreeTagger assumes that POS tagging is necessary for evaluating features in a dataset with the name containing string _grammar_:

```
package coreEmotionalEngine.emotext;

//imports emotext
//import TreeTagger
//imports java
//imports WEKA

public class ARFFWrapper {

    //a base classifier used for analyzing texts
    private Classifier c_ = null;

    //name of the dataset file
    private String datasetName_ = null;

    //WEKA instances used for training and testing
    protected Instances instances_ = null;

    //interface to evaluate statistical features
    private IFeatureEvaluation fe_ = null;

    public Classifier buildClassifier(Classifier clsr,
      String datasetName) throws Exception {
        ...
        return classifier;
    }

    public ARFFWrapper(Classifier c, TreeTagger tagger,
      String datasetName) {
        treetagger_ = tagger;

        try {
```

```
          if (datasetName.contains("fusion") &&
            (datasetName.endsWith(".spec"))) {
          //build a fusion classifier
          ...
        else {
          c_ = buildClassifier(c, datasetName);
          datasetName_ = datasetName;
        }
    } catch (Exception e) {
      e.printStackTrace();
    }
}

public double classifyInstance(Instance instance) throws
  Exception {
    return c_.classifyInstance(instance);
}

public Instance buildInstance(String text) {
    Instance i = null;
    if (datasetName_.contains("_fusion")) {
        //a spec is found that identifies part datasets
        //used for fusion
        i = buildFusedInstance(text);
    } else if (datasetName_.contains("_lexical_")) {
        //build a lexical instance of processed data
        i = buildLexicalInstance(text);
    } else if (datasetName_.contains("_stylometry_")) {
        //build a stylometric instance of processed data
        i = buildStylometricInstance(text);
    } else if (datasetName_.contains("_grammar_")) {
        //build a grammatical instance of processed data
        i = buildGrammarInstance(text);
    } else if (datasetName_.contains("_deixis_")) {
        //build a deictic instance of processed data
        i = buildDeixisInstance(text);
    } else {
        assert (false);
    }
    return i;
}


    private Instance buildFusedInstance(String text) {
    ...
    return instance;
    }

private Instance buildDeixisInstance(String text) {
    ...
    return instance;
}
```

```
private Instance buildGrammarInstance(String text) {
   ...
   return instance;
}

private Instance buildLexicalInstance(String text) {
   ...
   return instance;
}

private Instance buildStylometricInstance(String text) {
   ...
   return instance;
}
}
```

To build statistical instances, the *ARFFWrapper* class references variable *fe_* that refers to the *IFeatureEvaluation* interface maintaining feature evaluation:

```
package coreEmotionalEngine.emotext;

public interface IFeatureEvaluation {
    public abstract double value(double original);
}
```

Three implementations of this interface are available: the presence evaluation that evaluates features according to their presence in the analyzed text as 1 or 0 (*PresenceFeatureEvaluation*), the inverse evaluation that evaluates a feature as a reciprocal frequency value (*InverseFeatureEvaluation*), or the frequency evaluation that evaluates a feature as a frequency value (*FrequencyFeatureEvaluation*). See (Osherenko 2011, p. 80) for details of feature evaluation.

Appendix C: Storing Configuration

This appendix shows a configuration file used to store the parameters of SocioFramework (	 is interpreted by the XML engine in Java as a tab character;
 as a linebreak; " as a quotation mark):

```
<?xml version="1.0" encoding="UTF-8"?>
<SocioFramework>
    <GeneratingPanel>
        <!- Values of visual elements of the Generation panel
        in Fig. 5.2 ->
        <DataDefinition>
            <PreprocessingTextArea value="import sys&#xa;
            sys.path+=[&quot;D:\\SVNcheckout\\
            experimenting_framework\\DesktopApplication\\
            src\\framework&quot;]&#xa;
            global observation_sequence&#xa;
            global generatorInst, character&#xa;
            from feature_groups import
```

```
                    observation_sequence&#xa;
                    from generator_functions import generator&#xa;
                    &#xa;
                    generatorInst = generator(&quot;&quot;, 1)&#xa;
                    generatorInst.character = &quot;Obadiah&quot;
                    &#xa;"/>
                <EpilogueTextArea value="@attribute
                    evaluation_class {zero,zerofive,one,onefive,
                    two,twofive,three,threefive,four}"/>
                <PrologueTextArea value=
                    "% 1. Title: Reviews Database&#xa;
                    % 2. Sources:&#xa;%
                    (a) Creator: Alexander Osherenko&#xa;%
                    (b) Donor: Alexander Osherenko
                    (osherenko@informatik.uni-augsburg.de)&#xa;%
                    (c) Date: November, 2011&#xa;%&#xa;%&#xa;
                    @relation Berardinelli"/>
                <GeneratorFunctionComboBox value=
                    "generatorInst.generate_observations_from_SAL"/>
                <OutputDirTextField value="./"/>
                <DataDirTextField value=""/>
                <GeneratorFunctionCheckBox value="true"/>
                <FilenameAdditionTextField value="SAL"/>
            </DataDefinition>
            <FeatureGroups>
                <FeatureGroup>
                    <NameTextField value="observation_sequence"/>
                    <DebugCheckbox value="false"/>
                    <ForceCheckbox value="false"/>
                    <SparseCheckbox value="true"/>
                    <VerboseCheckbox value="true"/>
                    <HistoryCheckbox value="false"/>
                    <HistoryLengthSpinner value="0"/>
                    <ImmutablesTable value="ImmutablesTable">
                        <Item value=""/>
                    </ImmutablesTable>
                    <OutputGroupDirTextField value=
                     "observations"/>
                    <DerivedImmutablesCheckBox value="true"/>
                    <MutablesTable value="MutablesTable">
                        <Item value="observation_sequence(&quot;
                        Obadiah&quot;, 1)"/>
                        <Item value="{neutral,low_pos,low_neg,
                        high_pos,high_neg}"/>
                    </MutablesTable>
                    <DerivedMutablesCheckBox value="true"/>
                </FeatureGroup>
            </FeatureGroups>
        </GeneratingPanel>
        <EvaluatingPanel>
            <!- Values of visual elements of the Evaluation
            panel in Fig. 5.6 ->
            <ClassesSimilarityTextField value="sum9cm_to5cm"/>
            <ClassifierPanel value=
```

```xml
              "weka.classifiers.functions.SMO
              -C 1.0 -L 0.0010 -P 1.0E-12 -N 0 -V -1 -W 1 -K &quot;
              weka.classifiers.functions.supportVector.PolyKernel
              -C 250007 -E 1.0&quot;"/>
          <EvaluateDFList value="EvaluateDFList">
              <Item value="./observations\
                  SAL_obsObadiah_1_sparse.arff"/>
          </EvaluateDFList>
          <EvaluatingCustomFormulaTextField value="R*CV"/>
          <CostMatrixTextField value="9classes_empirical.cost"/>
      </EvaluatingPanel>
      <OptimizingPanel>
          <!- Values of visual elements of the Optimization
          panel in Fig. 5.13 ->
          <ClassifierOptimizingPanel value=
          "weka.classifiers.functions.SMO -C 1.0 -L 0.0010 -P
          1.0E-12 -N 0 -V -1 -W 1 -K &quot;
          weka.classifiers.functions.supportVector.PolyKernel
          -C 250007 -E 1.0&quot;"/>
          <OptimizingStorageCheckBox value="false"/>
          <OptimizingStorageDirectoryTextField value=""/>
          <OptimizingDFList value="OptimizingDFList"/>
          <OptimizingComboBox value=""/>
          <OptimizingCustomFormulaTextField value="R*CV"/>
          <ClassesSimilarityOptimizingTextField value=
          "sum9cm_to5cm"/>
          <CostMatrixOptimizingTextField value=
          "9classes_empirical.cost"/>
      </OptimizingPanel>
      <FusingEvaluatingPanel>
          <!- Values of visual elements of Fusion panel
          in Fig. 5.7 ->
          <ClassifierProbabilitiesFusionPanel value=
          "weka.classifiers.functions.SMO -C 1.0 -L 0.0010 -P
          1.0E-12 -N 0 -V -1 -W 1 -K &quot;
          weka.classifiers.functions.supportVector.PolyKernel
          -C 250007 -E 1.0&quot;"/>
          <ClassifierFusionPanel value=
          "weka.classifiers.functions.SMO -C 1.0 -L 0.0010 -P
          1.0E-12 -N 0 -V -1 -W 1 -K &quot;
          weka.classifiers.functions.supportVector.PolyKernel
          -C 250007 -E 1.0&quot;"/>
          <FusionStorageCheckBox value="false"/>
          <FusionStorageDirectoryTextField value="./"/>
          <FuseDFList value="FuseDFList"/>
          <ClassesSimilarityFusionTextField value=
          "sum9cm_to5cm"/>
          <FusingCustomFormulaTextField value="R*CV"/>
          <CostMatrixFusionTextField value=
          "9classes_empirical.cost"/>
      </FusingEvaluatingPanel>
      <CreatingPrototypePanel>
          <!- Values of visual elements of Prototyping panel
```

```
        in Fig. 5.15 ->
      <PrototypeDFList value="PrototypeDFList"/>
      <Agents>
          <Agent>
              <AgentNameTextField value="interaction"/>
              <AgentClassTextField value="jade.core.Agent"/>
              <AgentOntologyTextField value=""/>
              <AgentDatasetsTable value=
                "AgentDatasetsTable">
                  <Item value="D:\SVNcheckout\
                  experimenting_framework\
                  DesktopApplication\observations\
                  observations_obsSpike_1.arff"/>
              </AgentDatasetsTable>
          </Agent>
          <Agent>
              <AgentNameTextField value="agent0"/>
              <AgentClassTextField value="jade.core.Agent"/>
              <AgentOntologyTextField value=""/>
              <AgentDatasetsTable value=
                "AgentDatasetsTable">
                  <Item value="D:\SVNcheckout\
                  experimenting_framework\
                  DesktopApplication\observations\
                  observations_obsSpike_1.arff"/>
              </AgentDatasetsTable>
          </Agent>
          <!-other population agents->
      </Agents>
      <DefineInteractionPanel>
          <SequencePanel value="interaction&#xa;
          {&#xa;&#x9;agent0.ping -> pong;&#xa;&#x9;
          agent1.ping -> pong;&#xa;&#x9;
          agent2.ping -> pong;&#xa;&#x9;
          agent3.ping -> pong;&#xa;&#x9;
          agent4.ping -> pong;&#xa;&#x9;
          agent5.ping -> pong;&#xa;&#x9;
          agent6.ping -> pong;&#xa;&#x9;
          agent7.ping -> pong;&#xa;&#x9;
          agent8.ping -> pong;&#xa;&#x9;
          agent9.ping -> pong;&#xa;}"/>
      </DefineInteractionPanel>
      <PrototypeNameTextField value="population"/>
      <RootDirTextField value="D:\Population"/>
      <ClassifierCreatingPrototypePanel value=
        "weka.classifiers.bayes.JAHMM -C 1.0 -L 0.0010 -P
        1.0E-12 -N 0 -V -1 -W 1 -K &quot;
        weka.classifiers.functions.supportVector.PolyKernel
        -C 250007 -E 1.0&quot;"/>
  </CreatingPrototypePanel>
</SocioFramework>
```

References

Diaz-Agudo, B., Recio-García, J. A., & Gonzalez-Calero, P. A. (2007). Natural language queries in CBR systems. In *19th IEEE international conference on tools with artificial intelligence, ICTAI 2007* (Vol. 2, pp. 468–472). doi:10.1109/ICTAI.2007.27.

Elidan, G., Ninio, M., Friedman, N., & Schuurmans, D. (2002). Data perturbation for escaping local maxima in learning. In *Eighteenth national conference on artificial intelligence* (pp. 132–139). Menlo Park: American Association for Artificial Intelligence. ISBN:978-0-262-51129-0. http://dl.acm.org/citation.cfm?id=777092.777116.

Elliott, J., Eckstein, R., Loy, M., Wood, D., & Cole, B. (2002). *Java swing, second edition* (2nd ed.). New York: O'Reilly Media. ISBN:978-0-596-00408-8. http://amazon.com/o/ASIN/0596004087/.

François, J. M. (2012). JAHMM. An implementation of hidden Markov models in Java. https://code.google.com/p/jahmm/.

Friedl, J. E. F. (2006). *Mastering regular expressions* (3rd ed.). New York: O'Reilly Media. ISBN:978-0-596-52812-6. http://amazon.com/o/ASIN/0596528124/.

Hall, M. A. (1999). *Correlation-based feature selection for machine learning*. PhD thesis, Department of Computer Science, The University of Waikato.

Joachims, T. (1999). Making large-scale support vector machine learning practical. In B. Schölkopf, C. J. C. Burges & A. J. Smola (Eds.), *Advances in kernel methods.* (pp. 169–184). Cambridge: MIT Press. 0-262-19416-3. http://dl.acm.org/citation.cfm?id=299094.299104.

Juang, B. H., & Rabiner, L. R. (1985). A probabilistic distance measure for hidden Markov models. *AT&T Technical Journal, 64*(2), 391–408. http://citeseer.ist.psu.edu/context/244209/0.

Mitchell, T. M. (1997). *Machine learning* (1st ed.). New York: McGraw-Hill Science/Engineering/Math. ISBN:978-0-070-42807-2. http://amazon.com/o/ASIN/0070428077/.

Osherenko, A. (2011). *Opinion mining and lexical affect sensing: computer-aided analysis of opinions and emotions in texts*. Berlin: Südwestdeutscher Verlag für Hochschulschriften. ISBN:978-3-838-12488-9. http://amazon.de/o/ASIN/383812488X/.

Petri, J. (2010). *Netbeans platform 6.9 developer's guide*. New York: Packt. ISBN:978-1-849-51176-6. http://amazon.com/o/ASIN/1849511764/.

Ray, E. T. (2003). *Learning XML* (2nd ed.). New York: O'Reilly Media. ISBN:978-0-596-00420-0. http://amazon.com/o/ASIN/0596004206/.

Schmid, H. (1994). Probabilistic part-of-speech tagging using decision trees. In *Proceedings of the international conference on new methods in language processing*, Manchester, UK.

Witten, I., & Frank, E. (2005). *Data mining: practical machine learning tools and techniques* (2nd ed.). San Francisco: Morgan Kaufmann.

Chapter 6
Prototypes of Social Simulation

This chapter continues the description of SocioFramework from Chap. 5 with discussion how SocioFramework composes prototypes of SS systems and how implementations of necessary modeling dimensions are realized. Moreover, it presents programmatic templates of the proposed prototypes and goes into a discussion of software execution issues such as the runtime behavior.

6.1 Prototype Architecture

SocioFramework implements two types of architecture in prototypes of intercultural SS systems: a prototype based on a standalone NL ECA (classification sample) embedded in a Java servlet and a MAS.

A servlet prototype in SocioFramework is an NL ECA (Hunter and Crawford 2001). A servlet is a Java class commonly used to extend capabilities of an Internet server that runs in a Java browser.

The prototype of an SS system based on MAS relies on the JADE multiagent environment (Bellifemine et al. 2007). In this case, an SS prototype maintains agents each containing two components: the core component and the custom component. The core component communicates with other system components, for example, NL ECAs using JADE infrastructure (see Appendix A); the custom component maintains specific behaviors defined by the scenario simulated in the current prototype and encapsulates means for modeling agent-specific dimensions described in Sect. 6.4.

To prototype an SS system and realize simulation-wide modeling dimensions (cf. implementations in Sect. 6.5), SocioFramework realizes the prototyping principle in Sect. 6.2.

A. Osherenko, *Social Interaction, Globalization and Computer-Aided Analysis*,
Human–Computer Interaction Series, DOI 10.1007/978-1-4471-6260-5_6,
© Springer-Verlag London 2014

Fig. 6.1 Template for a
servlet-based agent

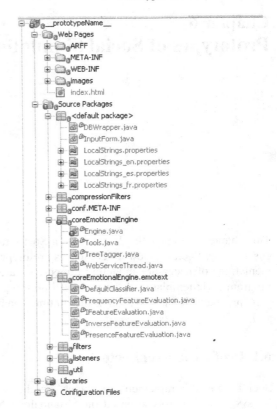

6.2 Prototyping Principle

This section describes the principle of software composition that underlies SocioFramework and explains what resources are used insofar.

SocioFramework uses a jar-archive as a template of a prototype containing project files, Java source files, and auxiliary files that can be adjusted according to specific patterns defined on the SocioFramework GUI. To create a prototype, files from the predefined template jar-file are copied into the destination directory, whereas particular patterns of file contents and file names are replaced with a user-defined contents. For example, the file __agentName__DialogueAgent.java in the jar-archive is replaced with the agent name "A" specified on the SocioFramework GUI resulting in "ADialogueAgent.java." The pattern __agentName__ is also replaced in the text of the file "ADialogueAgent.java."

Figure 6.1 shows the directory structure of the template jar file for a servlet-based agent.

The file context.xml in the directory META-INF

```
<?xml version="1.0" encoding="UTF-8"?>
<Context path="/__prototypeName__"/>
```

Fig. 6.2 A prototype project
with resolved file names

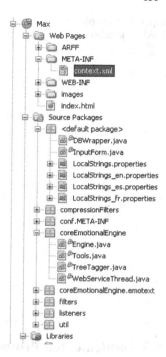

becomes

```
<?xml version="1.0" encoding="UTF-8"?>
<Context path="/Max"/>
```

after replacement of the pattern _ _*prototypeName*_ _ with, for example, the agent
name *Max*. The resulting project structure is shown in Fig. 6.2.

The described principle can be applied to building a MAS (Fig. 6.3).

Figure 6.3 shows a template structure for a MAS simulation. Accordingly,
this project contains the directory _ _*prototypeMASAppl*_ _ that will be renamed
as the name of the SS prototype after prototype generation or file
_ _*agentName* _ _*GUIAgent.java* that is renamed as *MaxGUIAgent.java* if the agent
name is Max.

Figure 6.4 shows the structure of the SI project in Fig. 6.3 with resolved file
names.

SocioFramework can define ECAs of particular classes, an ontology of processed
messages and maintained statistical datasets (Fig. 6.5).

Figure 6.5 shows a dialog window that specifies the name of the agent (for example, *agent0*), its class (for instance, *jade.core.Agent*), Java class of the ontology
of messages sent by the agent (for example, *AgentOntology.java*), and the statistical
datasets (for instance, *observations_Spike_1.arff*).

To specify interaction between iteractants, an interaction specification based on
the UML sequence diagram is used (cf. Sect. 6.5.1).

Fig. 6.3 A template for a
MAS simulation

6.3 Implemented Prototypes

A servlet prototype in SocioFramework is an NL ECA that maintains an engine for statistical and semantic NL processing (Fig. 6.6).

Figure 6.8 shows a UML composite structure diagram of a servlet prototype with class *InteractionAgent* maintaining a GUI as a frame of the class *AgentFrame*, the variable *StatisticalNLClassifiers* containing a map with statistical classifiers processing NL input information, and a semantic engine *SemanticNLEngine* that processes user input, for example, using a WebService.

In some scenarios, a standalone (servlet-based) system cannot sufficiently implement certain requirements of SS. In such cases, an SS system can be realized as a MAS—as a testbed that behaves according to a certain interaction specification, as a dialog system that implements a conversation, or as a GUI-less population (Fig. 6.7).

Figure 6.7 shows a UML composite structure diagram with a user through its *InputForm*, the *Engine* with a map *StatisticalNLClassifiers* containing statistical classifiers processing NL input information, and a semantic engine *SemanticNLEngine* that processes user input, for example, using a WebService.

6.3.1 Servlet-Based Prototypes

The most trivial case of SS does not require several ECAs but can be applied for classification of information, for example, NL texts in a standalone NL ECA. In

Fig. 6.4 A prototype project of a MAS SS system with resolved file names

SocioFramework, such an SS system is based on a standalone servlet-based agent (Fig. 6.8).

A servlet-based ECA in Fig. 6.8 shows an example of a servlet prototype that maintains cognitive models, for example, an HMM for affective behavior (cf. Fig. 4.5).

See Appendix B for details of the Java implementation.

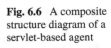

Fig. 6.5 Defining the agent representing an interactant

Fig. 6.6 A composite
structure diagram of a
servlet-based agent

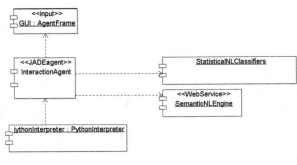

Fig. 6.7 A composite
structure diagram of MAS
prototypes

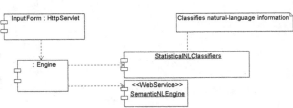

6.3.2 Content-Synchronized Communities

SocioFramework can create prototypes of communities of NL ECAs, for example,
a prototype of a community of three characters (Spike, Obadiah, Poppy) that carry
on a conversation (Fig. 6.9).

Figure 6.9 shows a community of NL ECAs that conduct a conversation such as
the following imaginary NL dialogue:

```
Obadiah to Spike: -Do I detect a note of sarcasm?

Spike to Obadiah and Poppy: -Are you kidding me?
This lady is off the charts.

Poppy: - uhhh, sacrasm detector, this is really a
cool invention!
```

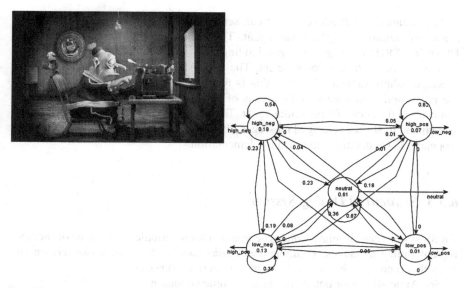

Fig. 6.8 Prototyping a servlet-based agent (*Left*: courtesy of Melodrama Pictures)

Each ECA in SocioFramework maintains a statistical dataset representing an emotion model of SAL characters shown in Sect. 4.1. Besides maintaining statistical datasets, the created agents (Poppy, Spike, Prudence, Obadiah) can communicate with each other by means of JADE.

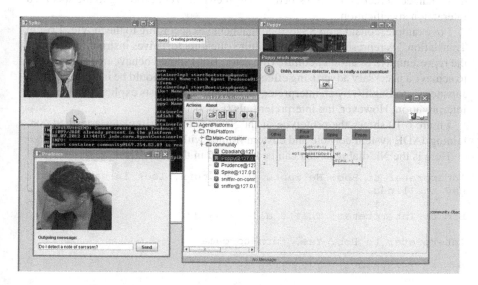

Fig. 6.9 Prototyping communities using SocioFramework

For instance, the Prudence agent can send a QUERY-IF message "Do I detect a note of sarcasm?" to the Spike agent. The Spike agent replies with the NOT-UNDERSTOOD message "Are you kidding me? This lady is off the charts" that is also forwarded to the Poppy agent. The Poppy agent agrees using the AGREE message "uhhh, sacrasm detector, this is really a cool invention." The messages are not supplied interactively by means of an interaction specification but rather statically in the code of a particular agent. To review the created prototype of the SS system and to show exchanged messages, the JADE Sniffer agent can be used. See Appendix C for details of the Java implementation.

6.3.3 Sequential Dialog Systems

An SS system can simulate a dialogue that defines a periodical exchange of incoming/outcoming messages. To implement a dialogue, the SS system can rely on an array that represents NL turns, its interlocutors (receivers), etc.

See Appendix D for details of the Java implementation.

6.3.4 Interaction-Synchronized Experimentation Testbeds

An SS system is more believable if an interrogative behavior of an interactant is replied with an appropriate behavior of another interactant. To implement such systems (named hereafter an SS testbed), SS testbeds can act according to the specified interaction specification.

For example, consider an SS testbed that behaves according to the movie "Lost in Translation." A representative of one culture (the director) gives instructions on how the representative of another culture (the actor, Bob) should behave in a commercial to achieve a necessary advertising effect. The instructions should be interpreted from Japanese into English by an interpreter, and the director insists explicitly on an exact interpretation. However, the interpreter fails (Fig. 6.10).

Figure 6.10 shows the prototype of the SS system that simulates a testbed containing JADE system console and custom frames with ECAs.

Here is the NL dialogue that can be simulated in the SS testbed:

```
Interpreter to Bob: He wants you to turn, look in camera and
say the lines.

Bob to Interpreter: That's all he said?

Interpreter to Bob: Yes, turn to camera!

Bob to Interpreter: Turn left or right?

Interpreter to Bob: Right side. And with intensity.
```

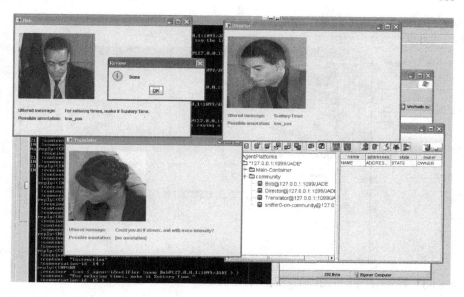

Fig. 6.10 A dialogue of the testbed characters: interpreter, director, Bob

```
Bob to Interpreter: Is that everything? It seemed like he was
saying a lot more.

Interpreter to Bob: Like an old friend, and into the camera.

Director to Bob: Suntory Time!

Bob to Director: For relaxing times, make it Suntory Time.

Interpreter to Bob: Could you do it slower, and with more
intensity?

Bob to Interpreter: Okay.

Bob: For relaxing times, make it Suntory Time.
```

SocioFramework creates the prototype of the SS testbed as a MAS that maintains NL ECAs representing the interpreter, the director, and the actor (Bob). The fourth interaction agent is a meta-agent that does not maintain any models and only coordinates processing (Fig. 6.11).

Figure 6.11 shows the prototyping panel of SocioFramework and the interaction specification coordinating SS.

A textual representation of interaction specification can be defined as follows:

```
interaction {
  //initialization
  Interpreter.init -> finish {
    Interpreter.readModels -> models {
```

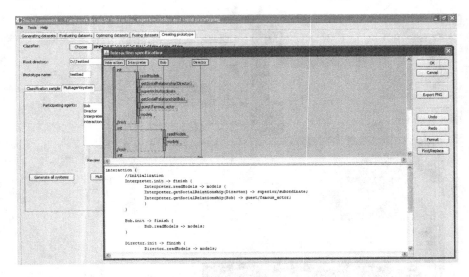

Fig. 6.11 Prototyping testbeds using SocioFramework

```
    Interpreter.getSocialRelationship(Director)
    -> superior/subordinate;
    Interpreter.getSocialRelationship(Bob)
    -> guest/famous_actor;
  }
}

Bob.init -> finish {
  Bob.readModels -> models;
}

Director.init -> finish {
  Director.readModels -> models;
}

  //shooting
Director.shooting -> finish {
Bob.japaneseMessage -> not_understood;
  Interpreter.interpret(japaneseMessage){
    Interpreter.modulateInterpretation(personality,
    socialRelationship)
    -> shortInterpretedMessage;
    Bob.act -> embarrassed;
  }
}
}
```

To observe interaction in the new SS system, the JADE Sniffer can be used
(Fig. 6.12).

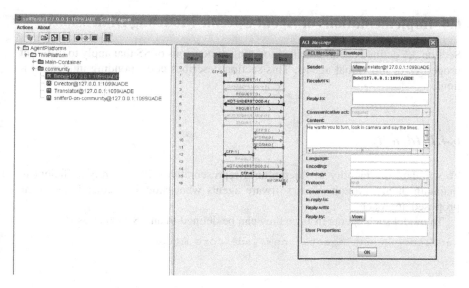

Fig. 6.12 The messages exchange in the constructed testbed

Figure 6.12 shows messages in the prototype of the SS testbed resulting from the specified interaction specification. Hence, an *interaction* agent initializes processing by sending the *init* message to the individual agents (interpreter, director, Bob). Individual agents read their models (emotion, personality, culture, context), for example, from the local storage modulated by the parameter *socialRelationship*. For the *Interpreter* agent, this could mean that the parameters change the emotion model of the *Interpreter* agent in the manner that carrying out the duties is not possible. Afterwards, the *interaction* agent initializes shooting and forwards control to the *Director* agent. The *Director* gives instructions in Japanese to *Bob*. *Bob* does not understand and is embarrassed. The *Interpreter* agent should interpret the utterances. However, the *Interpreter* agent does not have an explainable interpretation.

See Appendix E for details of the Java implementation.

6.3.5 GUI-less Populations

Some SS systems do not need a GUI since visual input/output is obsolete. This can be the case, for example, if all simulation information is supplied automatically. Hence, an SS system can be based on a population that specifies interaction specification of fully automatic agents. To develop such SS populations, SocioFramework uses an interaction specification that defines GUI-less agents (cf. Sect. 5.7.4).

See Appendix F for the Java implementation.

6.4 Implementations of Agent-Specific Modeling Dimensions

Section 3.5 defined agent-specific modeling dimensions of SS that apply to different properties of individual agents. This section describes corresponding implementations.

6.4.1 Identity

To simulate the identity of intercultural representatives, it is merely sufficient to maintain them as autonomous software agents what should be considered in the proposed approach.

To model such agents in Java, they can be defined in an SS system as

```
jade.core.Agent agent = new jade.core.Agent();
```

6.4.2 Emotions

Depending on the scenarios of SI and SS, emotions can be implemented as discrete or continuous values. In case of discrete categories, emotions can be represented as string values:

```
String emotion = "love";
```

Alternatively, emotions can be modeled in continuous E/A space (cf. Fig. 4.3) and represented as an array, for example:

```
Double[] love = {HIGH_POSITIVE, HIGH_ACTIVE};
```

where *HIGH_POSITIVE* and *HIGH_ACTIVE* are constants representing a high positive evaluation value and a high activation value, respectively.

To abstain from defining particular discrete/continuous emotions, an emotional classifier can be trained. For example, this classifier can be used in SS for analyzing emotions based on HMMs for affective behavior:

```
weka.classifiers.bayes.JAHMM hmmClassifier =
              new weka.classifiers.bayes.JAHMM();
```

6.4.3 Personality

A personality model can be defined by five personality traits: *Extroversion*, *Neuroticism*, *Openness to experience*, *Agreeableness*, and *Conscientiousness* (cf. Sect. 4.1.2). Accordingly, a programmatic implementation can based on an array, for example:

```
Double[] personality = {HIGH_EXTROVERSION,
 HIGH_NEUROTICISM, HIGH_OPENNESS_TO_EXPERIENCE,
 HIGH_AGREEABLENESS, HIGH_CONSCIENTIOUSNESS};
```

where the constants *HIGH_EXTROVERSION*, *HIGH_NEUROTICISM*, *HIGH_OPENNESS_TO_EXPERIENCE*, *HIGH_AGREEABLENESS*, *HIGH_CONSCIENTIOUSNESS* define high values of the corresponding personality traits.

6.4.4 Culture

A culture model can be defined by five culture traits: *Power distance, Uncertainty avoidance, Individualism/collectivism, Masculinity/Femininity, Long-/Short-Term Orientation* (cf. Sect. 4.1.3). Consequently, cultural dimensions can be implemented as an array, for example:

```
Double[] culture  = {HIGH_POWER_DISTANCE,
 HIGH_UNCERTAINTY_AVOIDANCE,
 HIGH_INDIVIDUALISM_COLLECTIVISM,
 HIGH_MASCULINITY_FEMININITY,
 HIGH_LONG_SHORT_TERM_ORIENTATION};
```

where the constants *HIGH_POWER_DISTANCE*, *HIGH_UNCERTAINTY_AVOIDANCE*, *HIGH_INDIVIDUALISM_COLLECTIVISM*, *HIGH_MASCULINITY_FEMININITY*, *HIGH_LONG_SHORT_TERM_ORIENTATION* define high values of the corresponding culture traits.

6.4.5 Input/Output

Input/output of experimental information in the SS system can be supplied in different ways depending on the simulated scenario. For example, output can be presented as graphics with neurobiological information, whereas input can be provided by a sensor of physiological data.

For simple experiments, however, input/output using textual means is satisfactory. In this case, input/output can be organized as a single window with an input and an output text field (Fig. 6.13).

Figure 6.13 shows a frame window with an output for dialogue utterances and their annotations realized using the Java Swing library (Elliott et al. 2002):

```
JFrame in_output = javax.swing.JFrame("Input/output");
```

For more believable interaction, NL ECAs can output information reacting to interactant's utterances by generating NL utterances, for example, relying on SimpleNLG (Gatt and Reiter 2009).

Fig. 6.13 Input/Output of information in social simulation

6.4.6 Statistical Engines

Different scenarios need several statistical engines that calculate the probabilities of different outcomes. To maintain multiple statistical outcomes programmatically, the calculating classifiers can be stored in a map that is defined in Java as

```
Map<Integer,ARFFWrapper> classifiersMap =
    new HashMap<Integer,ARFFWrapper>();
```

where the map stores different wrappers to WEKA classifiers trained using ARFF datasets indexed by their number.

6.4.7 Natural-Language Processing

SI and SS consider different sources of information, for example, NL texts. As an example, this section briefly describes approaches to NL processing based on opinion mining and lexical affect sensing in Osherenko (2011). Since intercultural setting implies discussion of language-independence, this section elaborates on adoption of proposed approaches in various languages of intercultural interactants.

6.4.7.1 Opinion Mining

Opinion mining can be performed statistically using different features: lexical, deictic, grammatical, and stylometric.

Lexical features represent words occurring in analyzed texts (typically "bag-of-words"). An SS system can extract three sources of lexical features: (1) the frequency list of studied texts; (2) the frequency list of the British National Corpus (BNC) (Kilgarriff 2010); (3) words of Whissell Dictionary of Affect (DAL) (Whissell 1989). Furthermore, it can lemmatize[1] the words in every source of lexi-

---

[1] *Lemmatization* refers to a process of extraction of the base form of a word.

cal features and, thus, extract additionally three lists containing lemmata using Tree-Tagger (Schmid 1994). Overall, six sources of lexical features can be extracted.

The frequency list of a corpus contains words ordered by the number of occurrences in the analyzed texts. The BNC frequency list, freely available on the Internet, lists occurrences of words in BNC. BNC (Kilgarriff 1997) is a 100 million word collection of samples of written and spoken language from a wide range of sources, representing current British English, both spoken and written.

The Whissell dictionary of affect, also called Dictionary of Affect Language (DAL), consists of 8,742 words of different inflection. DAL words are scored along three dimensions: *evaluation*, *activation*, and *imagery*, which are determined by human judgement. The *evaluation* dimension range describes words from 1 (unpleasant) to 3 (pleasant), the *activation* dimension range from 1 (passive) to 3 (active), for *imagery* dimension range from 1 (difficult to form a mental picture of this word) to 3 (easy to form a mental picture). SS can evaluate lexical features differently: as binary values (1/0) representing that a particular word is found in the analyzed text or according to the frequency or a reciprocal frequency.

An SS system can maintain the following deictic features: demonstratives as determiners, demonstratives as pronouns, place references, time references, and forms of the third person. Since deictic words are per se stopwords, they can be extracted together with stopwords. For this purpose, SocioFramework extracts 526 stopwords from the WEKA toolkit (Witten and Frank 2005) in deictic datasets.

Deictic features can be evaluated as a frequency vector. An SS system can perform opinion mining using grammatical information (Leech and Svartvik 2003), for example, interjections evaluated as a frequency vector. Grammatical features in an SS system can be evaluated as a frequency vector where necessary tagging/lemmatization is performed using TreeTagger. The following stylometric features can be extracted for emotional analysis in NL processing: the standard deviation of sentence lengths evaluated as corresponding standard deviation, the standard deviation of word lengths evaluated as corresponding standard deviation, the digrams (letter pairs) evaluated as a frequency vector, and the letters evaluated as a frequency vector.

6.4.7.2 Semantic Affect Sensing

The lexical affect sensing in an SS system can rely on an approach that uses the SPIN parser (Engel 2006), a semantic parser for spoken dialog systems, to detect predefined patterns of words. The SPIN parser is used in combination with the probabilistic Stanford parser to automatically detect the sentence structure (Klein and Manning 2003).

For instance, the approach defines the SPIN rule

$$<negation> <intensifier> <emotionword+> \rightarrow <result-> \qquad (6.1)$$

that can be utilized for analysis of the phrase *I am not very happy*. In the first analysis phase, the emotion word *happy*, the intensifier *very*, and the negation *not* are extracted, and the string *not very happy* is composed; in the second analysis phase, this string is analyzed by rule (6.1) calculating the negative emotional meaning *<result—>*.

SocioFramework relies on an approach to semantic affect sensing that maintains 1049 negations, 264 intensifiers, 6819 emotion words from Levin verbs (Levin 1993), WordNet-Affect (Valitutti et al. 2004), GI (Stone et al. 1966), EQI (Myrick and Erney 1984). Moreover, this approach considers special grammatical SPIN rules: 19 empirical SPIN rules for linking grammatical clauses, 18 SPIN rules from literature (Leech and Svartvik 2003), and 20 SPIN rules from empirical examples.

6.4.7.3 Natural-Language WebService

An SS system can perform NL processing using a WebService (WS). This is useful in case the interactants are situated distantly but want to utilize the same analysis engine.

A WS engine can be used to analyze emotional meaning of English sentences relying on the semantic approach in Osherenko (2011). The emotional WS engine in SocioFramework implies following restrictions on the analysis of the texts:

- Analyzed texts are assumed to be grammatically correct sentences;
- The engine does not consider emotional meaning of emoticons;
- The text context is not considered in the semantic approach;
- Anaphora resolution is not taken into account.

The WS engine evaluates the 5-class affect sensing result. A WS call has the following syntax:

```
http://www.socioware.de/SemanticEmoText/servlet/AciiForm?text=
<text>
```

For example, the command

```
http://www.socioware.de/SemanticEmoText/servlet/AciiForm?text=
I%20am%20very%20concerned%20about%20it
```

processes the text *I am very concerned about it* and calculates the emotional meaning *high_neg* using the rule (6.1).

6.4.7.4 Language-Independence

This section introduced above an approach to statistical opinion mining and an approach to semantic affect sensing. Since interactants of intercultural SI and SS can represent different cultures, flexible processing of NL information means most of all language-independent processing. Hence, the utterances of interactants that participate in an intercultural communication should be analyzed by language-independent NL engines.

In statistical opinion mining, language-independence means consideration of features that can represent different languages. Having datasets that extract lexical, deictic, grammatical, stylometric features in English language, it is necessary to formulate an approach that transforms the existing features in English language into features of other languages.

Such a transformation is fairly straightforward in case of lexical features since they are extracted on the basis of a frequency list of a big corpus (such as BNC) and extraction of lexical features of other languages means extraction of features from a frequency-list of the other languages. Consequently, it is only necessary to find a frequency list of a destination language to adapt the proposed opinion mining approach to a required language. Useful resources containing frequency lists of many languages provide Wiktionary[2] or a blog of Hermit Dave.[3]

Deictic and stylometric features are mostly equal for many languages, and only their evaluation should be corrected to consider peculiarities of other languages. Quite another matter are grammatical features because they are extracted on the basis of grammatical information of a particular language that is different in every language. Due to a close linguistic relationship between English and German, it is possible to find German equivalents of English emotional rules in Leech and Svartvik (2003) that were used to analyze grammatical interdependencies. For example, the fronted negation rule that defines a negation at the beginning of a sentence can be unproblematically carried over in the German–English text *Not every film is so good!* becomes the German text *Nicht jeder Film ist so gut!*, but this coincidence is more a lucky accident than a rule. That is why in semantic affect sensing, a direct transformation in the form of translation is possible only if the source language (English) and destination language are similar. A general transformation recommendation is therefore not possible.

6.4.8 Social Relationships

Interactants in an SS system maintain relationships. In some cultures, these relationships can be manifold, for example, a mother is a relative and a friend; in some cultures, for instance, Filipino culture, it is impossible (incident "The proposal process," item 16 on p. 75).

A social relationship can be implemented as

```
List<Relationship> relationships =
    new Vector<Relationship>();
```

where the variable *relationships* represents a vector of relationships maintained by an agent.

To represent a single relationship, the Java implementation can be defined as follows:

```
Relationship relationship =
    new Relationship("Max");
```

---

[2]http://en.wiktionary.org/wiki/Wiktionary:Frequency_lists.

[3]http://invokeit.wordpress.com/frequency-word-lists/.

where the instance of class *Relationship* represents a relationship to other person, for example, Max.

6.4.9 Context (Agent-Specific)

Situational context considers social relationships between interactants in an interactional situation. The context can define the race, age, education, marital status, social class, religion, etc.

The context can be stored rule-based or as a blank data. The rule-based storage can be based on SPIN rules (Engel 2006), for instance, the rule

$$mice \rightarrow scary \tag{6.2}$$

means that the person represented by a certain agent consider mice as scary.

In Java, an engine that defines a rule-based context can be maintained using the class *Spin* as

```
Spin context = new Spin(ruleFiles, spinTypeSystem,
                        lexFiles, initOptions);
```

where the argument *ruleFiles* specifies files with SPIN rules, the argument *spinTypeSystem* defines SPIN types used by the engine, the argument *lexFiles* defines a list of files containing entries of the lexicon used by the engine, and the argument *initOptions* defines the initial options for the engine.

Blank data considers facts about the agent. For example, the age represented by an agent can be coded as

```
Double age = 39.5;
```

6.4.10 Knowledge (Agent-Specific)

The agent-specific knowledge refers to thenknowledge held by a particular agent. For example, this knowledge can define particular abilities of an agent and be implemented rule-based as the following SPIN rule:

```
knowledge(actor:interactant) ->
    ability(name:joinery, actor:interactant)
```

where this rule describes an ability of the actor *interactant* for joinery.

6.4.11 Time (Agent-Specific)

An SS system can maintain an agent-specific simulation time to implement temporal issues in SS, for example, remedying jet lag. The local time can be realized using a system clock of the local computer.

Alternatively, to maintain the local time, an agent can utilize means of the JADE's *TickerBehaviour* that uses an overloaded method *onTick* to count time.

Fig. 6.14 Interpreting an interaction specification

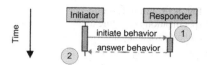

6.5 Implementations of Simulation-Wide Modeling Dimensions

An SS system simulates interaction of several interactants that act independently from each other. However, some actions should be performed centralized, for example, setting up the system time. In such cases, an agent, for example, an ECA should delegate some tasks to a more "competent" agent without loss of independence or autonomy that would accomplish the tasks more efficiently in the simulation-wide mode.

6.5.1 Explicit Specifications

SocioFramework maintains interactive means to define specifications of interaction scenarios termed hereafter *interaction specification*.

6.5.1.1 Overview

Interaction specifications are used for defining interaction in SS prototypes. An interaction specification is visually a sequence diagram known from UML (Miles and Hamilton 2006). In terms of UML, an interaction specification contains agents as lifelines and interaction events as messages.

An interaction specification is implemented in SocioFramework using a sequence diagram package (Moffat 2012) that provides a very simple sequence diagram editor (Fig. 6.14).

Figure 6.14 explains how interaction specification is interpreted by the SocioFramework and integrated in an SS prototype in more detail. It shows an interaction specification with two agents that interact with each other, the agent *Initiator* and the agent *Responder*. The interaction is initialized by the temporally ordered event *initiate_behavior* and the event *answer_behavior*. As (Moffat 2012) identifies, the event *initiate_behavior* occurs at the moment 1 before the event *answer_behavior* at the moment 2. From this specification, SocioFramework composes two JADE-behaviors with the names containing the name of the initiator, the name of the responder, the name of the transaction, and the number of initiator–responder combination. Accordingly, the names of two JADE behaviors are 1) *Initiator_Responder_initiate_behavior_0* and 2) *Responder_Initiator_answer_behavior_0*. The number is necessary to avoid ambiguity in naming behavior names if the same agents interact several times with each other.

A more comprehensive example of an interaction specification is defined by the diagram in Fig. 6.15.

Fig. 6.15 An interaction
specification according to the
coincidence analysis

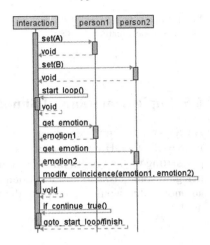

The interaction specification in Fig. 6.15 corresponds to Algorithm 3.6 on p. 61.
The meta-agent *interaction* communicates with two agents *person1* and *person2*
that interact with each other and analyze coincidence of occurring emotions in an
interaction. Note that such an interaction specification has low readability: it contains repetitive actions such as the statements *start_loop* and *goto_start_loop/finish*)
and conditions such as the statement *if_continue_true*.

Although the proposed interaction specification works out in this case, it is un-
suitable for specifying simulation of realistic scenarios of SI with more agents due to
low readability. To increase readability, an interaction specification should encapsu-
late a formalism that allows more flexibility, for example, loops or conditional statements. For this purpose, SocioFramework defines additional elements in traditional
sequence diagrams by adding special conventions in processing of interaction specifications. Such conventions define means as passing arguments in message calls,
returning values, loops, or conditional statements. To specify these conventions, interaction specifications use an extended syntax.

6.5.1.2 Jython Interpreter

For processing additional elements, every agent holds an instance of the Jython interpreter that defines required data, for example, variables and constants. The Jython
interpreter can be used additionally for processing other information, for example,
a text.

6.5.1.3 Variables and Constants

Interaction specifications can define particular information that is read from
the Jython interpreter. For example, in the behavior call *repository.initCulture
(initInstance, culture, 'German')*, the variables *initInstance, culture* and the constant *'German'* are read from the Jython interpreter of the agent *repository*.

6.5.1.4 Sending Values

To send a variable value to another agent, an interaction specification should define
an individual behavior. For instance, the interaction specification

```
interaction {
  destination.sendValue(source);
}
```

sends the value of variable *source* of the agent *interaction* to the agent *destination*
using the behavior *interaction_destination_sendValue_0* of the agent *destination*.

6.5.1.5 Passing Arguments

Interaction specifications can define a behavior call that contains arguments. To interpret these arguments, the Jython interpreter of the destination agent is used. The
format of a behavior call is

```
interaction {
  destination.behavior(<list of arguments>);
}
```

where the agent *interaction* sends a message to the agent *destination* using the behavior *interaction_destination_behavior_0* of the agent *destination*. The list of supplied arguments is defined in the content of the message that starts the behavior.
  In the example

```
interaction {
  repository.initCulture(culture, 'German');
}
```

the behavior *interaction_repository_initCulture_culture___German___0* of the
repository agent intercepts the *initCulture* message of the agent *repository* with two
arguments in the content: the variable *culture* and *'German'*, a constant value that
must be defined in the Jython interpreter of the agent *repository*. To pass a list in a
behavior, the argument should be defined in brackets, for instance,

```
interaction {
  group.setSize(['dyads', 'quads']);
}
```

where the list *['dyads', 'quads']* is passed in the content of the message *interac-
tion_group_setSize___dyads____quads___0* of the agent *group*.
  Note that special characters in the names of generated behaviors such as apostrophes are substituted through underscores for compatibility with name conventions
for Windows files and Java classes (cf. Chap. 7).

6.5.1.6 Returning Values

Every behavior call returns a reply to the caller behavior as a message with the
corresponding content. A return value can be a scalar value or an object encapsulated
in the content of the reply message.

Fig. 6.16 An interaction
specification for assigning
values

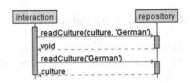

Figure 6.16 illustrates two approaches to returning values in an interaction specification.

Textually, interaction specification of two approaches can be defined as follows:

```
interaction {
    repository.readCulture(culture, 'German');
    repository.readCulture('German') -> culture;
}
```

In Fig. 6.16, the statement *repository.readCulture(culture, 'German')* generates two behaviors: the behavior *behavior_interaction_repository_readCulture_culture ___German___0* that assigns the variable *culture* in the Jython interpreter of the agent *repository* an object corresponding to the German culture and returning the behavior *behavior_repository_interaction_void_0* that returns control to the agent *interaction*. In contrast, the statement *repository.readCulture('German') ->culture* creates also two behaviors, but with other meaning regarding the variable assignment. The behavior *behavior_interaction_repository_readCulture__German___0* initiates a return of a value corresponding to the German culture, and the behavior *behavior_repository_interaction_culture_0* finishes this return by responding to the agent *interaction* with the content of a *reply* message that is assigned after the return to the value of variable *culture* of the agent *interaction*.

Note that special characters in the names of generated behaviors such as apostrophes are substituted through underscores for compatibility with name conventions for Windows files and Java classes (cf. Chap. 7).

The first behavior class *behavior_interaction_repository_readCulture_culture ___German___0* can be implemented in Java as

```
...
public class behavior_interaction_repository_readCulture_
  culture___German___0 extends Behaviour {
    ...
    public behavior_interaction_repository_readCulture_
      culture___German___0(Agent a) {
        ...
    }

    public void action() {
        ACLMessage msg = myAgent.blockingReceive();
        if ((msg!=null) && msg.getContent().
          equals("readCulture(culture, 'German')")) {
            ACLMessage reply = new
                ACLMessage(ACLMessage.INFORM);
```

```
        AID receiver = new AID("interaction",
          AID.ISLOCALNAME);
        reply.addReceiver(receiver);
        reply.setContent("void");
        a_.send(reply);
      }
  }
  ...
}
```

where   *behavior_interaction_repository_readCulture_culture___German___0*
blocks until receipt of the *readCulture* message.

The second behavior class *behavior_interaction_repository_readCulture__*
German___0 in realized in Java as follows:

```
...
public class behavior_repository_interaction_culture_0
  extends Behaviour {
  ...
  public behavior_repository_interaction_culture_0(Agent a) {
  ...
  }

  public void action() {
      ACLMessage msg = myAgent.blockingReceive();
      if ((msg!=null) && msg.getContent().
          equals("readCulture('German')")) {
          ACLMessage reply =
            new ACLMessage(ACLMessage.INFORM);
          AID receiver =
            new AID("repository", AID.ISLOCALNAME);
          reply.addReceiver(receiver);
          reply.setContent("<pickle-object>");
          a_.send(reply);
      }
  }
  ...
}
```

To return an object from a behavior, the object can be transformed in its textual
form. The textual representation of an object is calculated by the Jython module
pickle (Baker et al. 2010). In the following example, the value of object *SN* is stored
as textual representation calculated by *pickle* in the file *data_SN.txt*. Afterwards, this
textual representation can be read as the value of variable *serObject*:

```
from pickle import *

if __name__=='__main__':
    SN = {"friends": ["John","Lea", "Mary"],
    "relatives":["Papa", "Mama"]}

    output = open('data_CN.txt', 'wb')
    dump(SN, output)
```

```
output.close()

pkl_file = open('data_CN.txt', 'rb')

serObject = load(pkl_file)
print "Restored serialized object:", serObject

pkl_file.close()
```

The textual representation of the object *SN* is stored in file *data_CN.txt* as follows:

```
{}
(dp0
S'relatives'
p1
(lp2
S'Papa'
p3
aS'Mama'
p4
asS'friends'
p5
(lp6
S'John'
p7
aS'Lea'
p8
aS'Mary'
p9
as.
```

This representation can be sent to other agents of the SS system (Fig. 6.17).

Figure 6.17 shows JADE's RMA, Sniffer GUI with two tracked agents (*interaction* and *person1*), as well as the content of the reply message received by the *interaction* agent. Note that the content slot of the JADE message contains a textual representation of the *SN* object.

6.5.1.7 Loops

Interaction specifications can define loops using a special syntax, for example, that traverses through turns in the dialogue

```
interaction {
  managingAgent.~condition() -> ~ {
    agent.repetitiveProcedure();
  }
}
```

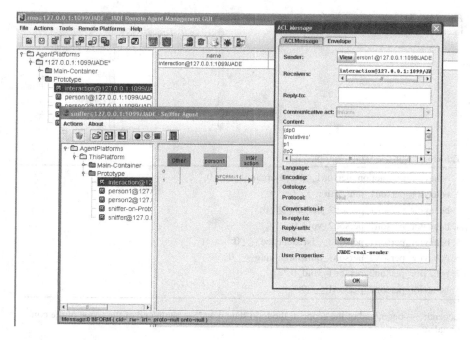

Fig. 6.17 Sending objects in JADE

where the behavior *managingAgent_agent_repetitiveProcedure_0* of the agent *agent* is called so long till the reply of the behavior *interaction_managingAgent__condition_0* received by the agent *managingAgent* evaluates to *true*. A behavior call is said to evaluate to *true* if the content of its reply is not empty. Otherwise, the behavior call evaluates to *false*. To define the scope of the loop statement, *behavior_managingAgent_interaction___0* is used.

6.5.1.8 Conditions

Interaction specifications can define conditional statements. The proposed syntax for such statements is defined as

```
interaction {
  managingAgent.$condition() -> $ {
    agent.procedure();
  }
}
```

Similar to the loop processing, processing of conditional statements defines that if the reply of behavior *interaction_managingAgent_condition_0* received by the agent *managingAgent* evaluates to *true*, the behavior *managingAgent_agent_procedure_0* of the agent *agent* is initiated. To define the scope of the conditional statement, *behavior managingAgent_interaction__* is used.

Fig. 6.18 Example of an
interaction specification

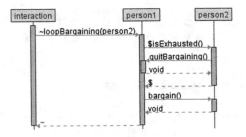

Table 6.1 Summarizing example

1. behavior_interaction_person1__loopBargaining___0;~

2. behavior_person1_interaction___0;

3. behavior_person1_person2_bargain___0;

4. behavior_person1_person2_void_0;

5. behavior_person1_person2__isExhausted___0;$

6. behavior_person2_person1_quitBargaining___0;

7. behavior_person2_person1_void_0;$

8. behavior_person2_person1___0;~

Legend: ~—begin/end of the scope of the loop statement; $—begin/end of the scope of the conditional statement

6.5.1.9 Summarizing Example

This section concludes a discussion of processing of interaction specifications. In the following example, two interacting ECAs *person1* and *person2* participate in the bargaining scenario. If *person2* is exhausted, it signals exhaustion to *person1* by sending the message *quitBargaining* to *person1* that quits bargaining (Fig. 6.18).

The interaction specification in textual form is defined as follows:

```
interaction {
  person1.~loopBargaining(person2) -> ~ {
    person2.$isExhausted() -> $ {
      person1.quitBargaining();
    }
    person2.bargain();
  }
}
```

Table 6.1 provides a list of behaviors in a summarizing example created by SocioFramework:

6.5.2 History

The history dimension represents previous situations that can be considered in a believable SS system. A Java implementation of a history can be defined as

OxBlue08 4   goal_l 5629   WE2007 1

Fig. 6.19 Conventional RoboCup

```
List<Situation> history = new Vector<Situation>();
```

where the variable *history* holds a list of previous situations in the SS system, for example, previous emotions.

6.5.3 Space

Space dimension can be realized using the infrastructure of RoboCup (Simulation League) (Chen et al. 2013). This infrastructure was already utilized to simulate interaction in André et al. (2000), Binsted et al. (1998).

A RoboCup system is a MAS that maintains individual autonomous clients (players). The players on a soccer field have physical positions and are shown using their numbers. The players can move and perceive (hear, see) objects in their vision cone depending on their head position. RoboCup players communicate with each other through unreliable UDP-messages (Fig. 6.19).

Figure 6.19 shows the conventional RoboCup field with two teams consisting of 11 players that can be identified by their numbers (Fig. 6.20).

Figure 6.20 shows RoboCup players on the soccer field that can be interpreted in terms of SS as interactants of SI. The arrows show movement directions: players run on the field and influence the cognitive state of other players by sending messages. The current states of cognitive models of individual players can be represented visually (Fig. 6.21).

Fig. 6.20 The soccer field in
RoboCup

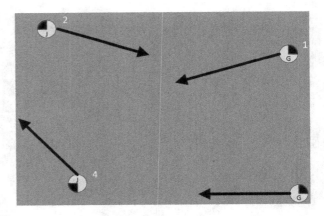

Fig. 6.21 A representation of
an ECA in RoboCup

Figure 6.21 shows a cognitive RoboCup player that shows its emotional state
(*low_neg*) as a black sector in the E/A space; the letter *J* refers to the first letter of
culture's name: (*J*) for the Japanese culture and *G* for the German culture.

To download a server of the RoboCup simulation with C++ source files and docu-
mentation, visit   http://sourceforge.net/apps/mediawiki/sserver/index.php?title=
Download.

6.5.4 Context (Simulation-Wide)

The global (simulation-wide) context results from commonsense facts. For example,
the context can be defined by common real-world facts (Liu et al. 2003) such as
"People find ghosts scary." Second, the context can be cultural. This means, for
instance, that Americans traditionally eat turkeys to Thanksgiving.

Following (Gannon and Pillai 2012, p. 15), the context of SI can focus on "cultural metaphors": religion, small-group behavior, holidays and ceremonies, educational system, etc.

Traditions can be considered as a context of a certain culture. For example, the
notion *tango* in the Argentinian context can be modeled as the SPIN rule

$$tango \rightarrow tradition(culture : Argentina, value : high) \qquad (6.3)$$

where the tradition *tango* is instantiated as an instance of class *tradition* with a *high*
value typical for the Argentinian culture.

Fig. 6.22 A two-agent
solution of the global time

6.5.5 Knowledge (Simulation-Wide)

The simulation-wide knowledge refers to facts that relate to the whole SS system.
For example, a meta-agent that maintains knowledge of an international stock exchange can send new facts such as breaking news to SS agents as soon as these facts
are published on the Internet. A possible Java implementation can be as follows:

```
jade.core.Agent agent = new jade.core.Agent();
ACLMessage msg = new ACLMessage(ACLMessage.INFORM);
msg.addReceiver(new
AID("StockManager@169.254.82.89:1099/JADE", true));
msg.setContent("New Fact from Stock Exchange");

agent.send(msg);
```

6.5.6 Time (Simulation-Wide)

An SS system can maintain simulation-wide time to implement temporal issues in
SS, for example, remedying jet lag. Such a system can read the global time using a
global meta-agent *timeServer* (Fig. 6.22).

Figure 6.22 shows the interaction specification for the *timeServer* scenario in a
jet lag scenario. Consequently, in the loop that counts time zones, the agent *agent*
obtains the global time from the meta-agent *timeServer* using the call *getGlobalTime*
and compares it with an internal clock *getLocalTime()* to calculate the remaining
recover time.

The interaction specification in textual form is defined as follows:

```
interaction
{
  timeServer.~nextZone() -> ~ {
    agent.getGlobalTime(timeServer)->globalTime;
    agent.getLocalTime()->localTime;
    agent.remedyJetLag(globalTime, localTime);
  }
}
```

Fig. 6.23 A directed labeled
multigraph

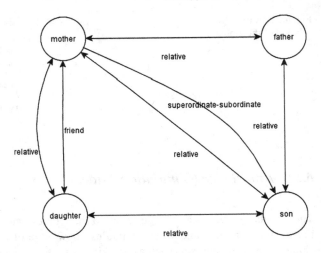

6.5.7 Social Network, Topological Issues

SN is a map representing pairs of agents (persons) and their relationships. Following
(Combe et al. 2010), SN is defined mathematically as a directed labeled multigraph

$$G = (V, E, L), \qquad\qquad (6.4)$$

where V represents the set of nodes, for example, the agent nodes *manager*, *mother*;
E is the set of edges or connections between agents, for example, *mother–son*,
superordinate–subordinate; and L is the set of labels characterizing the edges,
for example, $L(v_i, v_j)|L(v_i, v_j)_{\neq 0}$ that express (asymmetric) relationships between
agents v_i, v_j and cannot be null.

Figure 6.23 presents a directed labeled multigraph that shows a graph representation of a family. This family has a mother, a father, a son, and a daughter modeled
as agents and two-directional edges *relative* modeled as relationships. Additional
edges represent friendship between the mother and daughter. The mother participates in the relationship *superordinate–subordinate* between the mother and son.

Since an SN incorporates relationships of different persons, a programmatical
implementation considers the implementation in Sect. 6.4.8. Hence, an SN in Java:

```
Map<Agent, List<Relationship> SN
 = new HashMap<Agent, Vector<Relationship>;
```

To visualize a comprehensive topology of SS systems, the graphviz software can
be used (Ellson et al. 2004).

6.5.8 Alerts

Alerts that correspond to conditions that should be asserted in the SS system can be
implemented as follows:

1. Using JADE kernel level service that intercepts a particular condition in the SS system (Bellifemine et al. 2007, p. 136). See *examples.service.MessageTracing-Service* and *jade.core.messaging.TopicManagementService* in the JADE distribution for examples of level services;
2. Using a meta-agent that instantiates *jade.tools.sniffer.Sniffer*;
3. Using an instance of the JADE agent (*jade.core.Agent*) that holds an instance of the jade.tools.sniffer.Sniffer class and exemplifies custom behaviors using an interaction specification. Note that the *setup* method of *jade.tools.ToolAgent* is *final* in JADE, and that is why a direct derivation from the class *jade.tools.sniffer. Sniffer* is not possible.

6.5.9 Statistical Processing

Statistical processing of information was already discussed in Chap. 5.

6.6 Maintaining Prototypes

Developing SS systems on the basis of MAS requires consideration of software engineering issues. This section discusses means to facilitate development and execution of SS systems taking into special consideration peculiarities of intercultural simulation, for example, the geographical distance of its interactants. Moreover, it presents recommendations concerning the development process.

Hence, this section discusses thoroughly such issues as:

1. Governing scalability;
2. Dynamic adaptation;
3. Debugging simulation;
4. Simulation mode;
5. Recommendations on the prototype development.

6.6.1 Governing Scalability

A significant task of distributed systems such as SS systems is made up of issues of scalability. According to Tanenbaum and van Steen (2002, p. 10), the scalability can be measured along at least three dimensions with respect to:

1. Size;
2. Geography;
3. Administration.

In the following, this section discusses the corresponding dimensions thoroughly.

6.6.1.1 Size

The proposed approach to developing SS systems relies on JADE. Thus, the size scalability concerns consideration of the number of agents in a JADE system.

It was possible to implement SS systems using the proposed approach with a significant number of ECAs (10,000) that can exchange a big number of interaction events (20,000). Regarding computational complexity, it is possible to build and test an SS system with only 1,000 agents and 2,000 interaction events. Taking into account the utilized development approach, the number of agents and interaction events in the SS system can be even higher, which is also consistent with the information in a JADE forum.[4]

6.6.1.2 Geography

The peculiarity of SS systems that performs intercultural experiments lies in significant geographical distance of participating interactants. Of course, it is not problematic if the administrative JADE agents such as RMA, Sniffer, or Introspector are at hand and can be started locally. However, if the RMA GUI is not available, other means are necessary.

JADE agents (Sniffer and Introspector) can be started remotely from the command console. Given that jade.jar is in the current JAVA path, a JADE agent from a remote host can be run using the command

```
java -cp jade.jar jade.Boot -host <TCP address>
 -agents <semicolon separated list of
   <agent name>:<agent class» -container
```

which starts an instance *<agent name>* of the agent *<agent class>*, where the text *<TCP address>* specifies the TCP address numerically (for example, 93....) or as a name (for instance, localhost). The option *-container* specifies creation of a subordinate container within the main container with the specified agent. Recall that there is only one main container in JADE.

For example, the commands

```
java -cp jade.jar jade.Boot -host 93.135.248.211
 -agents sniffer:jade.tools.sniffer.Sniffer -container
```

```
java -cp jade.jar jade.Boot -host 93.135.248.211
 -agents introspector:jade.tools.introspector.Introspector
 -container
```

start instances of a Sniffer agent or an Introspector agent, respectively, on the host *93.135.248.211*.

---

[4]http://avalon.tilab.com/pipermail/jade-develop/2011q2/016940.html.

6.6.1.3 Administration

For administration of an SS system, a remote copy of system agents (AMS, DF, RMA) can be started.

The following command starts the system AMS agent in an own container:

```
java -cp jade.jar jade.Boot -host 93.135.248.211
 -agents ams1:jade.domain.ams -container
```

The following command starts a DF agent in an own container:

```
java -cp jade.jar jade.Boot -host 93.135.248.211
 -agents df1:jade.domain.df -container
```

The following command starts a RMA agent in an own container:

```
java -cp jade.jar jade.Boot -host 93.135.248.211
 -agents rma1:jade.tools.rma.rma -container
```

6.6.2 Dynamic Adaptation

Some SS systems, for example, in Sun (2005b), introduce systems that can dynamically adapt to particular aspects. For instance, an SN can acquire new members represented through new agents with particular behaviors. Sometimes existing members of an SS system change or get new properties.

Addressing such dynamic adaptation, SS systems based on JADE introduce the following means:

1. **New agents** New agents derived from the class *jade.core.Agent* can be started from JADE GUI or from the system console so that an SS system adapts to the necessary requirements.
2. **New ontologies** JADE agents can exchange messages with new ontologies. JADE maintains means to adjust ontologies dynamically, for example, to add new concepts (cf. Fig. 6.5);
3. **New behaviors** JADE implements the behavior *jade.core.behaviours.Loader Behaviour* that enables a new agent to load new behaviors and adjust them, for example, by passing parameters to them.

6.6.3 Debugging Simulation

To provide helpful assistance for an expert, a reliable SS system should maintain transparency of prototypes' messages. For example, problems of intercultural communication could be made obvious if experimenters can view messages that convey emotions experienced by their interactants. Moreover, observable messages can transmit information about the cognitive states of interactants.

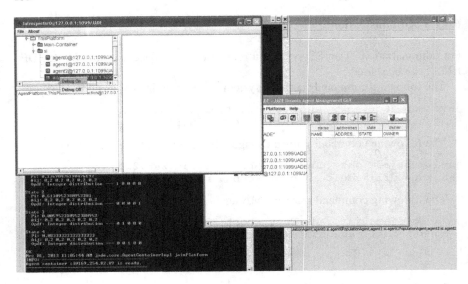

Fig. 6.24   Starting Introspector in JADE

JADE maintains different tool agents for this purpose: *Sniffer*, *Introspector*, *Log Manager*.

The first, Sniffer, introduced in Sect. 6.3.3 allows viewing incoming/outcoming JADE messages (cf. Fig. 6.12).

The second, Introspector, allows observing incoming and outcoming messages as well as viewing the list of installed behaviors. Introspector provides more debugging means, for example, allows tracking behaviors. It can be started from the JADE GUI and initialized to debug JADE agents in the SS system (Fig. 6.24).

Figure 6.24 shows an Introspector agent maintaining a population of agents in the *si* container the messages of which can be tracked by choosing the *Debug On* command from the context menu.

Figure 6.25 shows the Introspector GUI with agents of the SS population.

Note that Fig. 6.25 shows, besides agents and their behaviors, the incoming and outcoming messages. To view a message, JADE maintains the *View Message* command in the context menu.

The Log Manager can be used to save system messages. The specification of the logging can be defined statically and dynamically: statically by specifying the specification file at the start of the JADE environment and dynamically from the GUI.

For example, adopting an example from (Bellifemine et al. 2007), p. 46, logging can be defined statically from the system console:

```
java -Djava.util.logging.config.file=
    SI.properties jade.Boot -container
```

where the file *SI.properties* defines properties of logging in an SS system, for example:

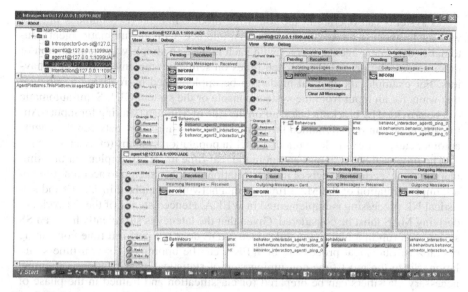

Fig. 6.25 Introspector with population agents

```
handlers = java.util.logging.ConsoleHandler
.level = OFF
jade.core.messaging.level = FINEST
```

A dynamic instantiation of a log manager can be performed from console, for instance:

```
java jade.Boot -container -container-name Log
    Log:jade.tools.logging.LogManagerAgent
```

More information on Log Manager and the specification file can be found in the tutorial on the JADE Logging Service.[5] Detailed information on distributed monitoring, logging, and debugging in JADE systems can be found in Bellifemine et al. (2007, p. 222).

6.6.4 Simulation Mode

The proposed approach differentiates different modes of simulation:

1. **Operation** (manual, semi-automatic, automatic);
2. **Performance** (realtime, simulation-time);
3. **Synchronization** (content, periodical, interaction).

---

[5]http://jade.tilab.com/doc/tutorials/logging/JADELoggingService.html.

SS systems can operate in the following modes: manual (two humans interact with each other), semi-automatic (a human interacts with an automatic agent), automatic (automatic agents interact with each other). To simplify implementation of these modes, the proposed approach relies on semantic implementation of behaviors. For example, the manual mode can be implemented by realizing a behavior that waits for an input from the system console or the system GUI. Semi-automatic can be provided by blocking behavior on the side of a human (waiting for input). Automatic node can be maintained through exchanging messages between the agents automatically, for example, without a GUI in population systems (cf. Sect. 6.3.5).

The proposed SS systems can run in the real-time mode. To implement this simulation mode, certain aspects of implementation must be taken into account. First of all, implementation of the MAS running in a network is realized in JADE, and statistical NL processing is implemented in WEKA. Hence, latency of the network underlying MAS must be considered. Given that the latency is sufficiently high, an SS system can run in a real-time mode since JADE does not perform time-consuming operations. Statistical processing in WEKA can be optimized for real-time simulation. Since the most time-consuming step of statistical classification is training, necessary classifiers can be prepared for classification and trained in the phase of system booting. Afterwards, the classification time can be performed in linear time $O(n)$, where n is the number of statistical features. A positive side effect of real-time mode is that SS systems can run reactive agents (Brooks 1986).

SS systems can be synchronized according to different schemata (cf. Sect. 6.3). Consequently, SS systems can exchange periodically particular messages with a necessary content. Some SS systems can realize a fixed schema of communication, for example, where a query was replied by a particular message such as not understood message. Other SS systems can implement interaction using reaction to particular behaviors.

6.6.5 Recommendations on the Prototype Development

Undoubtedly, every software developer wishes to prototype a qualitative SS system that has a reliable implementation developed in short time. This section describes aspects of SS implementation to bear in mind.

For example, imagine an SS system that maintains an agent representing a repository of SS. Such an agent can maintain cognitive models such as:

1. Emotional models;
2. Personality models;
3. Cultural models.

A repository agent can contain besides the cognitive models, for example, interaction specifications of scenarios in Chap. 3. To transfer these representations to other system parts, a repository agent can use JADE messages or database access. What are the benefits of communication using JADE messages?

Abstaining from problems of database administration since it would go outside the scope of this book and focusing on benefits of JADE-based processing, this book concludes that:

1. **Management advantage** Means of JADE can be utilized both for management of the agents in the developed SS system and also for the management of the repository agent. No other mechanism is necessary. Additionally, the repository agent can be redesigned to be a JADE agent that is endowed with a support of a database.
2. **Development advantage** New behaviors in the repository agent can be easily implemented by adding corresponding statements in the underlying interaction specification. For example, an interaction specification can be extended with the statement *repositoryAgent.getScenario('SocialEase')* that will be transformed by SocioFramework in a corresponding JADE behavior to extract an interaction specification for the *'Social Ease'* scenario in Sect. 3.3.
3. **Homogeneity advantage** An SS system maintains agents that rely on JADE messages. Consequently, maintaining different mechanisms of data access can have negative consequences on system development. To handle this data uniformly and improve reliability, the repository agent should rely on JADE behaviors, for example, on those that handle data exchange.

6.7 Summary and Outlook

This chapter described the composition of a simple servlet-based prototype and comprehensive prototypes of SS systems based on MAS (dialog, testbeds, and population systems) using the prototyping principle in Sect. 6.2. Using the statistical and prototyping apparatus examined in Chap. 5, this chapter showed how to build SS systems that model scenarios in Chap. 3. Since SS systems can maintain NL ECAs under consideration of certain cognitive models, software prototypes of SS systems and the corresponding implementations of modeling dimensions were discussed.

Technical issues were examined that consider different modes of execution such as automatic. Since simulations can use synchronization or run in the real-time mode, this chapter discussed the corresponding considerations and restrictions of implementations.

In future, the prototyping principle can be applied to developing further prototypes of SS systems with desired architecture and topology. For example, this principle can be used to compose systems for social media monitoring (Sponder 2011) or web survey systems (Poynter 2010, p. 16).

Appendix A: The JADE Infrastructure

This appendix describes the architecture of JADE systems that is used for composition of SS systems (Fig. 6.26).

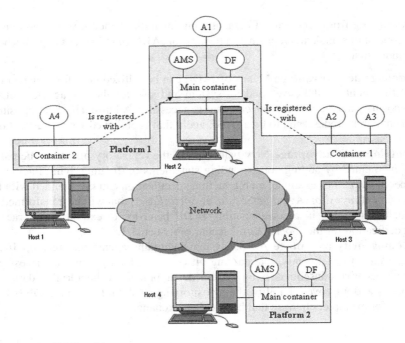

Fig. 6.26 The JADE architecture

Figure 6.26 shows the architecture of JADE (Bellifemine et al. 2007). The minimal component of execution is an agent (here *A1*, *A2*, *A3*, *A4*). One or more agents can be assigned to a particular container (here *Main Container*, *Container 1*, *Container 2*).

A JADE platform is composed of agent containers that can be distributed over the network (here *Platform 1*, *Platform 2*). Agents that participate in a JADE system can be executed on different hosts (here *Host 1*, *Host 2*, *Host 3*, *Host 4*) and communicate with each other using messages.

A special container, *Main Container*, must be the first container in a JADE system. It holds other containers and is unique in a JADE system. *Main Container* maintains JADE infrastructure agents:

1. Agent Management System (AMS), an agent managing other agents in the system, for example, starts or kills them;
2. Directory Facilitator (DF), an agent that manages a list of agent services and facilitates agent search;
3. Remote Management Agent (RMA), a JADE agent that shows running agents and their containers (Fig. 6.27);

Figure 6.27 shows the GUI of the RMA agent with agent platforms, agent containers, and agent names.

JADE agents communicate with each other using messages (Fig. 6.28).

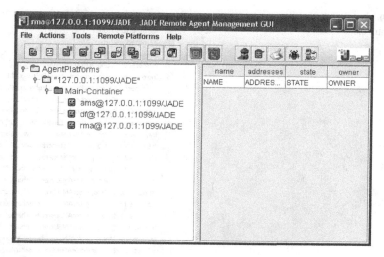

Fig. 6.27 The RMA agent

Fig. 6.28 Components of a
JADE message

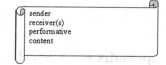

Figure 6.28 shows the structure of a JADE message. Accordingly, the message contains a sender, for example, *interaction@169.254.82.89:1099/JADE*; a receiver or receivers, *Obadiah@169.254.82.89:1099/JADE*; a communicative act (or performative), i.e., the semantic type of the current message, for instance, *INFORM*; and the content, for example, *"This is a content of an interaction message."*

JADE agents maintain different behaviors that handle particular events. For example, a behavior can react to a message with a FIPA[6] performative or response to messages of a particular type.

There is a comprehensive JAVA jade.jar library that allows development of MAS and adjustment of agent's behavior. For example, the *jade* package contains 12 subpackages where the *jade.tools* consist of the *sniffer* subpackage and the *introspector* subpackage (Fig. 6.29).

Figure 6.29 shows an abstract of the JADE Java library with the JADE introspector.

For more information on administration and the JADE library, see Bellifemine et al. (2007).

---

[6]Foundation of Intelligent Physical Agents—www.fipa.org.

Fig. 6.29 Classes of the
JADE Introspector

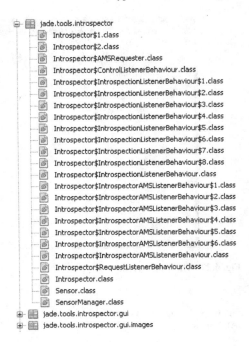

Appendix B: A Servlet-Based Template

This appendix presents Java templates that are used by SocioFramework for composing Java sources of an NL agent (classification sample) implemented as a servlet.

```
//imports java
//import emotext

public class InputForm extends HttpServlet {

    public void doGet(HttpServletRequest request,
            HttpServletResponse response)
            throws IOException, ServletException {
        ...
    }
    public void doPost(HttpServletRequest request,
            HttpServletResponse response)
            throws IOException, ServletException {
        ...
    }
}
```

The servlet processes NL texts using TreeTagger for POS tagging and lemmatization (Schmid 1994). To build statistical instances, prototype datasets extract lexical, stylometric, deictic, grammatical features.

Table 6.2 Prototype patterns

Pattern	Source
__classifierShortName__	Classifier (simple name of the class), Fig. 5.14
__datasetsStringArray__	Participating datasets, Fig. 5.14
__qualifiedSourceName__	Classifier (long name of the class), Fig. 5.15

The servlet can be customized according to user data. Table 6.2 shows the patterns used for customization of a servlet-based prototype.

In the template of a servlet-based prototype, the patterns are marked in bold:

```
package coreEmotionalEngine;

import __qualifiedSourceName__;
//imports emotext
//imports java
//imports WEKA
import coreEmotionalEngine.TreeTagger;

public class Engine {

    //skeleton pattern
    ...

    // Here come implementations of agent-specific dimensions
    // from Sect. 6.4,
    // for example, Hofstede dimensions
    Double[] culture = {0.0, 0.0, 0.0, 0.0, 0.0};
    //or statistical engines
    Map<Integer,ARFFWrapper> classifiersMap =
        new HashMap<Integer,ARFFWrapper>();

    //Here come implementations of simulation-wide dimensions
    //from Sect. 6.5,
    //for example, implementation of a SN
    Map<Agent, List<Relationship>> SN =
        new HashMap<Agent, Vector<Relationship>>;

    private TreeTagger tagger = new TreeTagger(null);

    ...

    private String[] getLemmata(String[][] input) {
        ...
    }

    private String[] getWords(String[][] input) {
        ...
    }

    private String[] getPOS(String[][] input) {
        ...
    }
```

```
private Instance buildLmWordsInstance() {
    ...
}

private Instance buildLmWordsPresenceInstance() {
    ...
}

private Instance buildWordsPresenceInstance() {
    ...
}

private Instance
 buildLmWordsAndPOSInstance(int posLength) {
    ...
}

...

//enumeration with a list of datasets
String[] datasetsArray = __datasetsStringArray__;

static {
    try {
        TreeTagger tagger = new TreeTagger(null);
        for (String dataset : datasetsArray) {
            ARFFWrapper classifier = new
             ARFFWrapper(new __classifierShortName__(),
                    tagger, dataset);
            classifiersMap.put(new
                Integer(classifiersMap.size()), classifier);
        }
    } catch (Exception e) {
        e.printStackTrace();
    }

}

}
```

Appendix C: A Content-Synchronized Community Template

This appendix presents Java templates that are used by SocioFramework for composing Java sources of a community prototype. Agents of the the community prototype are derived from class *jade.gui.GuiAgent* that handles GUI events in a JADE system.

Table 6.3 shows patterns used for customizing community agents.

Patterns in Table 6.3 are marked in bold in the Java template of a community agent:

Table 6.3 Community patterns

Pattern	Source
__agentName__	Name, Fig. 6.5
__classifierShortName__	Classifier (simple name of the class), Fig. 5.15
__datasetsStringArray__	Participating datasets, Fig. 6.5
__prototypeMASAppl__	Prototype name, Fig. 5.15
__qualifiedSourceName__	Classifier (long name of the class), Fig. 5.15

```
/*
 * __agentName__GuiAgent.java
 */

package __prototypeMASAppl__;

//imports emotext
//imports java
import gui.__agentName__Frame;
//imports java
//imports WEKA
import __qualifiedSourceName__;
//imports JADE
import coreEmotionalEngine.TreeTagger;

import org.python.util.PythonInterpreter;

public class __agentName__GuiAgent extends GuiAgent {

    protected __agentName__Frame mf;
    //pointer to the main frame

    // Here come implementations of agent-specific dimensions
    //from Sect. 6.4,
    // for example, Hofstede dimensions
    Double[] culture = {0.0, 0.0, 0.0, 0.0, 0.0};
    //or statistical engines
    Map<Integer,ARFFWrapper> classifiersMap =
        new HashMap<Integer,ARFFWrapper>();

    //Here come implementations of simulation-wide dimensions
    //from Sect. 6.5,
    //for example, implementation of a SN
    Map<Agent, List<Relationship>> SN =
        new HashMap<Agent, Vector<Relationship>>;

    //to hold variables and constants
    protected PythonInterpreter jythonInterpreter = null;

    protected void setup() {
```

```java
    // Registration with the DF
    ...
    try {
        DFService.register(this, dfd);
        WaitReplyOffChartsBehaviour offChartsBehaviour =
         new WaitReplyOffChartsBehaviour(this);
        addBehaviour(offChartsBehaviour);
        mf = new __agentName__Frame(this,
         this.getLocalName());
        mf.setVisible(true);
    } catch (Exception e) {
        doDelete();
    }
}

protected void onGuiEvent(GuiEvent ge) {
    ...
}

private class WaitReplyOffChartsBehaviour extends
 Behaviour {

    ...

    public void action() {
        ACLMessage msg = myAgent.receive();
        if ((msg != null) && !finished_) {
                if (myAgent.getLocalName().
                 equals("Spike")) {
                    ACLMessage reply = msg.createReply();

                    if (msg.getPerformative() ==
                        ACLMessage.QUERY_IF) {
                        reply.setPerformative(
                        ACLMessage.NOT_UNDERSTOOD);
                        reply.setContent("Are you
                         kidding me? This lady is off
                         the charts!");
                    } else {
                        reply.setPerformative(
                        ACLMessage.NOT_UNDERSTOOD);
                        reply.setContent(
                        "( (Unexpected-act " +
                        ACLMessage.getPerformative(
                        msg.getPerformative()) + ") )");
                    }
                    JOptionPane.showMessageDialog(mf,
                     reply.getContent(),
                     myAgent.getLocalName() +
                     " sends message",
                     JOptionPane.INFORMATION_MESSAGE);
                    send(reply);
                    msg = new
```

```
                    ACLMessage(ACLMessage.INFORM);
                msg.setContent(reply.getContent());
                msg.addReceiver( new AID(
                  "Poppy", AID.ISLOCALNAME ) );
                send(msg);

                finished_ = true;
            } else if (myAgent.getLocalName().
              equals("Poppy")) {
                ACLMessage reply = msg.createReply();

                if (msg.getPerformative() ==
                  ACLMessage.INFORM) {
                    reply.setPerformative(
                    ACLMessage.AGREE);
                    reply.setContent("Uhhh," +
                      " sacrasm detector, this is" +
                      " really a cool invention!");
                } else {
                    reply.setPerformative(
                    ACLMessage.NOT_UNDERSTOOD);
                    reply.setContent(
                      "((Unexpected-act " +
                    ACLMessage.getPerformative(
                      msg.getPerformative()) + ") )");
                }
                JOptionPane.showMessageDialog(mf,
                  reply.getContent(),
                  myAgent.getLocalName() +
                  " sends message",
                  JOptionPane.INFORMATION_MESSAGE);
                send(reply);
                finished_ = true;
            } else {
                block();
            }
        }
    }
    ...
} // END of inner class WaitReplyOffChartsBehaviour

//enumeration with a list of datasets
String[] datasetsArray = __datasetsStringArray__;

static {

    try {
        TreeTagger tagger = new TreeTagger(null);
        for (String dataset : datasetsArray) {
            ARFFWrapper classifier = new ARFFWrapper(new
                __classifierShortName__(), tagger,
                    dataset);
            classifiersMap.put(new
```

```
                Integer(classifiersMap.size()), classifier);
            }

        } catch (Exception e) {
            e.printStackTrace();
        }
    }
}
```

Here is the template of a frame instantiated through the above agent that maintains community agents:

```
package gui;

import __prototypeMASAppl__.__agentName__GuiAgent;
//imports java
//imports JADE

public class __agentName__Frame extends javax.swing.JFrame {
    private final Agent agent_;

    public __agentName__Frame(Agent a, String title) {
      initComponents();
      agent_ = a;
      this.setTitle(title);
      ...
    }


    private void initComponents() {

        jImageLabel = new javax.swing.JLabel();
        jOutgoingMessageTextField =
         new javax.swing.JTextField();
        jSendButton = new javax.swing.JButton();


        ...

        jOutgoingMessageTextField.setText("Do I detect" +
         " a note of sarcasm?");
        jOutgoingMessageTextField.addActionListener(new
         java.awt.event.ActionListener() {
            public void actionPerformed(java.awt.event.
             ActionEvent evt)
                jOutgoingMessageTextFieldActionPerformed(evt);
            }
        );
        ...
    }

    private void jSendButtonActionPerformed(java.awt.event.
     ActionEvent evt) {
        ACLMessage msg = new ACLMessage(ACLMessage.QUERY_IF);
        msg.setContent(jOutgoingMessageTextField.getText());
```

Table 6.4 Dialog patterns

Pattern	Source
__agentClass__	Class, Fig. 6.5
__agentName__	Name, Fig. 6.5
__classifierShortName__	Classifier (simple name of the class), Fig. 5.15
__datasetsStringArray__	Participating datasets, Fig. 6.5
__prototypeMASAppl__	Prototype name, Fig. 5.15
__qualifiedSourceName__	Classifier (long name of the class), Fig. 5.15

```
        msg.addReceiver( new AID( "Spike",
         AID.ISLOCALNAME ) );
        agent_.send(msg);
    }

    public static void main(String args[]) {
        java.awt.EventQueue.invokeLater(new Runnable() {
            public void run()
                new __agentName__Frame(new
                  __agentName__GuiAgent(),
                  "__agentName__").setVisible(true);

        });
    }

    // Declarations of GUI variables
    ...
}
```

Appendix D: A Sequential Dialog System Template

This appendix presents Java templates that are used by SocioFramework for composing Java sources of a dialogue. Note that a dialog ECA maintains only one instance of the behavior class *WaitReplyOffChartsBehaviour*.

Patterns in Table 6.4 are marked in bold in the Java template of a dialogue agent:

```
package __prototypeMASAppl__;

import gui.__agentName__DialogueFrame;
//imports emotext
//imports Java
//imports WEKA
import __qualifiedSourceName__;
import __agentClass__;
```

```
//imports JADE
import coreEmotionalEngine.TreeTagger;

import org.python.util.PythonInterpreter;

...

public class __agentName__DialogueAgent extends
 __agentClass__ {

    //pointer to the main frame
    protected __agentName__DialogueFrame mf;

    // Here come implementations of agent-specific dimensions
    //from Sect. 6.4,
    // for example, Hofstede dimensions
    Double[] culture = {0.0, 0.0, 0.0, 0.0, 0.0};
    //or statistical engines
    Map<Integer,ARFFWrapper> classifiersMap =
        new HashMap<Integer,ARFFWrapper>();

    //Here come implementations of simulation-wide dimensions
    //from Sect. 6.5,
    //for example, implementation of a SN
    Map<Agent, List<Relationship>> SN =
        new HashMap<Agent, Vector<Relationship>>;

    //to hold variables and constants
    protected PythonInterpreter jythonInterpreter = null;

    protected void setup() {
        // Registration with the DF
        ...
        try {
            DFService.register(this, dfd);
            WaitReplyOffChartsBehaviour offChartsBehaviour
                = new WaitReplyOffChartsBehaviour(this);
            addBehaviour(offChartsBehaviour);
            mf = new __agentName__DialogueFrame(this,
             this.getLocalName());
            mf.setVisible(true);
        } catch (Exception e) {
            doDelete();
        }
    }

    private class Utterance {

        private String sender_;
        private String receiver_;
        private int performative_;
        private String senderMsg_;
        private String senderIntention_;
```

```java
    public Utterance(String sender, String receiver,
     int performative, String senderMsg,
     String senderIntention) {
        this.sender_ = sender;
        this.receiver_ = receiver;
        this.performative_ = performative;
        this.senderMsg_ = senderMsg;
        this.senderIntention_ = senderIntention;
    }

// Declaration of get-member functions
...


}

private class WaitReplyOffChartsBehaviour extends
 Behaviour {

    private boolean finished_ = false;
    final static int TIME = 500;

    //a dialogue numbered utterances and
    Map utterances_ = new HashMap<Integer, Utterance>();

    public WaitReplyOffChartsBehaviour(Agent a) {
        super(a);
        finished_ = false;
        utterances_.put(utterances_.size(),
         new Utterance("Interpreter", "Bob",
         ACLMessage.REQUEST, "He wants you to turn," +
         " look in camera and say the lines.",
         "[no annotation]"));
        utterances_.put(utterances_.size(),
         new Utterance("Bob", "Interpreter",
         ACLMessage.NOT_UNDERSTOOD,
         "That's all he said?", "?"));
        utterances_.put(utterances_.size(),
         new Utterance("Interpreter", "Bob",
         ACLMessage.REQUEST, "Yes, turn to camera!",
         "[no annotation]"));
        utterances_.put(utterances_.size(),
         new Utterance("Bob", "Interpreter",
         ACLMessage.NOT_UNDERSTOOD,
         "Turn left or right?", "?"));
        utterances_.put(utterances_.size(),
         new Utterance("Interpreter", "Bob",
         ACLMessage.REQUEST, "Right side." +
         " And with intensity.", "[no annotation]"));
        utterances_.put(utterances_.size(),
         new Utterance("Bob", "Interpreter",
         ACLMessage.NOT_UNDERSTOOD,
         "Is that everything? It seemed like" +
         " he was saying a lot more.", "?"));
```

```
    utterances_.put(utterances_.size(),
     new Utterance("Interpreter", "Bob",
     ACLMessage.REQUEST, "Like an old friend," +
     " and into the camera.", "[no annotation]"));
    utterances.put(utterances_.size(),
     new Utterance("Bob", "Director",
     ACLMessage.CFP, "Instruction", "[special]"));
    utterances_.put(utterances_.size(),
     new Utterance("Director", "Bob",
     ACLMessage.INFORM, "Suntory Time!", "low_pos"));
    utterances_.put(utterances_.size(),
     new Utterance("Bob", "Director",
     ACLMessage.INFORM, "For relaxing times," +
     " make it Suntory Time.", "low_pos"));
    utterances_.put(utterances_.size(),
     new Utterance("Director", "Interpreter",
     ACLMessage.CFP, "Instruction", "[special]"));
    utterances_.put(utterances_.size(),
     new Utterance("Interpreter", "Bob",
     ACLMessage.REQUEST, "Could you do it slower," +
     " and with more intensity?", "[no annotation]"));
    utterances_.put(utterances_.size(),
     new Utterance("Bob", "Interpreter",
     ACLMessage.NOT_UNDERSTOOD, "Okay.", "?"));
    utterances_.put(utterances_.size(),
     new Utterance("Interpreter", "Bob",
     ACLMessage.CFP, "Instruction", "[special]"));
    utterances_.put(utterances_.size(),
     new Utterance("Bob", "Bob", ACLMessage.INFORM,
     "For relaxing times, make it Suntory Time.",
     "low_pos"));
}

public void action() {
    ACLMessage msg = myAgent.receive();

    if ((msg != null) && !finished_) {
        mf.toFront();

        Integer reqId =
         new Integer(msg.getConversationId());

        Utterance u = (Utterance)
         utterances_.get(reqId);

        if (u!=null) {

            if (u.getSender().equals(
             myAgent.getLocalName())) {

                if (u.getPerformative()
                 !=ACLMessage.CFP) {
                    mf.setVisibility(false);
```

```
                           mf.setActualColor(Color.BLACK);

                           mf.setUtteredMessage(
                            u.getActualMsg());
                           mf.analyzeText();
                           mf.blink(1);

                           mf.setUtteredReaction(
                            u.getIntention());
                           mf.blink(1);
                       }

                       if (u.getPerformative()==
                        ACLMessage.NOT_UNDERSTOOD) {
                           mf.setNotUnderstood(true);
                           try {
                               Thread.sleep(
                                WaitReplyOffChartsBehaviour
                                .TIME);
                           } catch (InterruptedException ex)
                            {
                               Logger.getLogger(
                               this.getClass().getName())
                               .log(Level.SEVERE,
                               null, ex);
                           }
                           mf.setNotUnderstood(false);
                       }

                       ACLMessage reply = new
                        ACLMessage(u.getPerformative());
                       Integer nextId = new
                        Integer(reqId.intValue() + 1);

                       reply.addReceiver(new
                        AID(u.getReceiver(),
                        AID.ISLOCALNAME));
                       reply.setConversationId(
                        nextId.toString());
                       reply.setContent(u.getActualMsg());

                       send(reply);
                       mf.setActualColor(Color.GRAY);

                   } else {
                       finished_ = true;
                       block();
                   }
               } else {
                   mf.setActualColor(Color.BLUE);
                   JOptionPane.showMessageDialog(mf,
                   "Done", "Review",
                   JOptionPane.INFORMATION_MESSAGE, null);
```

```
                    }
                }
            }
            ...
    } // END of inner class WaitReplyOffChartsBehaviour

    ...

    //enumeration with a list of datasets
    String[] datasetsArray = __datasetsStringArray__;

    static {

        try {
            TreeTagger tagger = new TreeTagger(null);
            for (String dataset : datasetsArray) {
                ARFFWrapper classifier =
                    new ARFFWrapper(new
                        __classifierShortName__(), tagger,
                            dataset);
                classifiersMap.put(new
                    Integer(classifiersMap.size()), classifier);
            }

        } catch (Exception e) {
            e.printStackTrace();
        }

    }
}
```

Here is the template of a dialog frame instantiated by the above agent:

```
/*
 * __agentName__DialogueFrame.java
 *
 */
package gui;

import __prototypeMASAppl__.__agentName__DialogueAgent;
//imports JADE
//imports Java

public class __agentName__DialogueFrame extends
  javax.swing.JFrame {

    private final Agent agent_;

    public __agentName__DialogueFrame(Agent a, String title)
      {
        initComponents();
```

```
        ...
    }

    private void initComponents() {
        ...
    }

    private void jStartDialogueButtonActionPerformed(
      java.awt.event.ActionEvent evt) {
        jStartDialogueButton.setVisible(false);

      Thread th = new Thread() {

          @Override
          public void run() {
              ...
              //semantic analysis of an emotional meaning
              //of an utterance
              analyzeText();

              ACLMessage msg = new
                ACLMessage(ACLMessage.CFP);
              msg.setContent(jMessage.getText());
              msg.addReceiver(new AID("Interpreter",
                AID.ISLOCALNAME));
              msg.setConversationId(
                new Integer(0).toString());
              agent_.send(msg);
          }
      };
      th.start();
    }

    public void analyzeText() {
        {
            if (true) {
                jMessage.setText("neutral");
            } else {
                jMessage.setText("");

                ...

                // run the EmoText webservice
                String str = "[unrecognized]";
                BufferedReader in = null;
                try {
                    URI uri = new URI("http",
                      "www.socioware.de",
                      "/SemanticEmoText/servlet/AciiForm",
                      "text=" + jMessage.getText(), null);
                    URL url = uri.toURL();
                    in = new BufferedReader(new
                      InputStreamReader(url.openStream()));
```

Table 6.5 Testbed patterns

Pattern	Source
__agentClass__	Class, Fig. 6.5
__agentName__	Name, Fig. 6.5
__classifierShortName__	Classifier (simple name of the class), Fig. 5.15
__datasetsStringArray__	Participating datasets, Fig. 6.5
__prototypeMASAppl__	Prototype name, Fig. 5.15
__qualifiedSourceName__	Classifier (long name of the class), Fig. 5.15
__behavioursNameArray__	Behavior names in interaction specification in Fig. 6.11

```
            while ((str = in.readLine()) != null) {
                jMessage.setText(str);
            }
            in.close();
        } catch (Exception ex) {
            Logger.getLogger(this.getClass().
            getName()).log(Level.SEVERE, null, ex);
        }
        ...
        }
    }
}

public static void main(String args[]) {
    java.awt.EventQueue.invokeLater(new Runnable() {

        public void run() {
            new __agentName__DialogueFrame(
            new __agentName__DialogueAgent(),
             "__agentName__").setVisible(true);
        }
    });
}

// Declarations of GUI variables
...

}
```

Appendix E: An Interaction-Synchronized Testbed Template

This appendix presents Java templates that are used by SocioFramework for composing Java sources of a testbed system with certain behaviors.

The testbed agent *__agentName__TestbedAgent.java* maintains behaviors according to the defined interaction specification. Patterns of a testbed in Table 6.5 are marked in bold in the following Java template:

```
package __prototypeMASApp1__;

//imports emotext
//imports Java
//imports WEKA

import __qualifiedSourceName__; import __agentClass__;
 import gui.__agentName__TestbedAgentFrame;
//imports JADE
import coreEmotionalEngine.TreeTagger;

import org.python.util.PythonInterpreter;

/** This example shows a testbed agent that participates in
 simulation of SI.
 */
public class __agentName__TestbedAgent extends
 __agentClass__ {

    protected __agentName__TestbedAgentFrame mf;
      //pointer to the main frame

    // Here come implementations of agent-specific dimensions
    //from Sect. 6.4,
    // for example, Hofstede dimensions
    Double[] culture = {0.0, 0.0, 0.0, 0.0, 0.0};
    //or statistical engines
    Map<Integer,ARFFWrapper> classifiersMap =
        new HashMap<Integer,ARFFWrapper>();

    //Here come implementations of simulation-wide dimensions
    //from Sect. 6.5,
    //for example, implementation of a SN
    Map<Agent, List<Relationship>> SN =
        new HashMap<Agent, Vector<Relationship>>;

    //to hold variables and constants
    protected PythonInterpreter jythonInterpreter = null;

    protected void setup() {
        // Registration with the DF
        ...
        try {
            DFService.register(this, dfd);

            mf = new __agentName__TestbedAgentFrame(this,
             this.getLocalName());
            mf.setVisible(true);

            String[] behavioursNameArray =
             __behavioursNameArray__;
            for (String behaviourName : behavioursNameArray) {
                Class c = Class.forName(behaviourName);
```

```
                    // get the constructor with one parameter
                    java.lang.reflect.Constructor
                            constructor = c.getConstructor(new
                            Class[]{jade.core.Agent.class,
                            __agentName__TestbedAgentFrame
                            .class});

                    // create an instance
                    Behaviour invoker = (Behaviour)
                            constructor.newInstance(new
                            Object[]{this, mf});

                    addBehaviour(invoker);
                }
        } catch (Exception e) {
            e.printStackTrace();
            doDelete();
        }
    }

...

//enumeration with a list of datasets
String[] datasetsArray = __datasetsStringArray__;

static {

    try {
        TreeTagger tagger = new TreeTagger(null);
        for (String dataset : datasetsArray) {
            ARFFWrapper classifier =
                new ARFFWrapper(new
                __classifierShortName__(), tagger,
                    dataset);
            classifiersMap.put(new
              Integer(classifiersMap.size()), classifier);
        }

    } catch (Exception e) {
        e.printStackTrace();
    }

}

public static void main(String[] args) {
    try {
        ...
        AgentController ac = cc.createNewAgent(
          "__agentName__",
          "__prototypeMASApp1__.__agentName__TestbedAgent",
          new Object[0]);
        // Fire up the agent
        ac.start();
```

Table 6.6 Specific patterns of a testbed behavior

Pattern	Source
__behaviourName__	Behavior name, e.g. initiator_responder_initiate_behavior_0, Fig. 6.14
__frameName__	Frame name, e.g., Initiator in Fig. 6.14
__interactionMsg__	Message, e.g., initiate_behavior in Fig. 6.14
__receiverMsg__	Receiver message, e.g., answer_behavior in Fig. 6.14
__receiverName__	Responder name, e.g., Responder in Fig. 6.14
__skipSend__	auxiliary

```
        } catch (Exception ex) {
            Logger.getLogger(__agentName__TestbedAgent.class.
            getName()).log(Level.SEVERE, null, ex);
        }
    }
}
```

Here is the template of a testbed behavior instantiated through the above agent
(specific patterns of a testbed behavior (shown in bold) are listed in Table 6.6):

```
package __prototypeMASAppl__.behaviours;

import gui.__frameName__TestbedAgentFrame;
//imports JADE
//imports java

public class __behaviourName__ extends Behaviour {
        ...
        Agent a_ = null;
        protected __frameName__TestbedAgentFrame mf_;
        //pointer to the main frame

        public __behaviourName__(Agent a,
        __frameName__TestbedAgentFrame mf) {
            super(a);
            a_=a;
            mf_=mf;
            finished_ = false;
        }

        public void action() {
            //waits for an incoming message
            ACLMessage msg = myAgent.blockingReceive();
            if ((msg!=null) && msg.getContent().
             equals("__interactionMsg__")) {
                mf_.toFront();

                mf_.setSentVisibility(false);
                mf_.setReceivedVisibility(false);

                if (!DEBUG) {
                    mf_.setReceivedVisibility(true);
```

```
                        mf_.setReceivedMessage(msg.getContent(),
                         msg.getSender().getLocalName());
                        mf.analyzeText();
                        mf_.blink(1);
                    }
                    if ("__skipSend__".isEmpty()) {
                        ACLMessage reply = new
                         ACLMessage(ACLMessage.INFORM);
                        AID receiver = new AID("__receiverName__",
                         AID.ISLOCALNAME);
                        reply.addReceiver(receiver);
                        reply.setContent("__receiverMsg__");
                        mf_.setSentMessage(reply.getContent(),
                         receiver.getLocalName());
                        mf_.setSentVisibility(true);
                        mf.analyzeText();
                        mf_.blink(1);
                        a_.send(reply);
                    } else {
                        JOptionPane.showMessageDialog(null,
                         "Done", "Interaction",
                         JOptionPane.INFORMATION_MESSAGE, null);
                    }

                }
            }

            ...


}
```

Here is the Java code of the frame that shows agents' messages and blinks in interval 500 milliseconds (TIME) (specific patterns of a testbed behavior, shown in bold, are listed in Table 6.6):

```
/*
 * __agentName__TestbedAgentFrame.java
 *
 */
package gui;

import __prototypeMASAppl__.__agentName__TestbedAgent;
//imports JADE
//imports java

public class __agentName__TestbedAgentFrame extends
 javax.swing.JFrame {

    final static int TIME = 500;

    private final Agent agent_;

    public __agentName__TestbedAgentFrame(Agent a,
```

```
      String title) {
         initComponents();
         agent_ = a;
         this.setTitle(title);
         URL url = this.getClass().
          getResource("/images/logo50x50.png");
         ...

         if (!agent_.getLocalName().equals("interaction")) {
             jStartDialogueButton.setVisible(false);
         }
         setSentVisibility(false);
         setReceivedVisibility(false);
      }

   private void initComponents() {
      ...
   }// </editor-fold>

   ...

   private void jStartDialogueButtonActionPerformed(java.awt.
    event.ActionEvent evt) {
       jStartDialogueButton.setVisible(false);

       Thread th = new Thread() {

           @Override
           public void run() {
               try {
                   ...
                   analyzeText();
                   ACLMessage msg = new
                    ACLMessage(ACLMessage.INFORM);
                   AID receiver = new
                    AID("__initReceiverName__",
                     AID.ISLOCALNAME);
                   msg.addReceiver(receiver);
                   msg.setContent("__initReceiverMsg__");
                   setSentVisibility(true);
                   setReceivedVisibility(false);
                   setSentColor(Color.BLUE);
                   setSentMessage(msg.getContent(),
                    receiver.getLocalName());
                   Thread.sleep(
                    __agentName__TestbedAgentFrame.
                     TIME);
                   setSentColor(Color.GRAY);
                   setReceivedColor(Color.GRAY);
                   agent_.send(msg);
               } catch (InterruptedException ex) {
                   Logger.getLogger(
                    __agentName__TestbedAgentFrame.
```

```
                                class.getName()).log(Level.SEVERE,
                                null, ex);
                        }
                    }
                };
                th.start();
        }

        //run the EmoText webservice
        public void analyzeText() {
            {
                if (true) {
                    jSentMessage.setText("neutral");
                } else {
                    jSentMessage.setText("");

                    ...

                    String str = "[unrecognized]";
                    BufferedReader in = null;
                    try {
                        URI uri = new URI("http",
                         "www.socioware.de",
                         "/SemanticEmoText/servlet/AciiForm",
                         "text=" + jSentMessage.getText(), null);
                        URL url = uri.toURL();
                        in = new BufferedReader(new
                         InputStreamReader(url.openStream()));
                        while ((str = in.readLine()) != null) {
                            jSentMessage.setText(str);
                        }
                        in.close();
                    } catch (Exception ex) {
                        Logger.getLogger(
                          this.getClass().getName())
                          .log(Level.SEVERE, null, ex);
                    }
                    ...
                }
            }
        }


        //Declarations of GUI variables
        ...

        //define visibility set-member-functions

        public void blink(int repetitions) {
           //show interaction using blinking
           ...
        }
```

Table 6.7 Population patterns

Pattern	Source
__agentClass__	Class, Fig. 6.5
__agentName__	Name, Fig. 6.5
__classifierShortName__	Classifier (simple name of the class), Fig. 5.15
__datasetsStringArray__	Participating datasets, Fig. 6.5
__prototypeMASAppl__	Prototype name, Fig. 5.15
__qualifiedSourceName__	Classifier (long name of the class), Fig. 5.15
__behavioursNamePopulationArray__	Behavior names in interaction specification in Fig. 5.19

```java
/**
 * @param args the command line arguments
 */
public static void main(String args[]) {
    java.awt.EventQueue.invokeLater(new Runnable() {

        public void run() {
            new __agentName__TestbedAgentFrame(new
                __agentName__TestbedAgent(),
                "__agentName__").setVisible(true);
        }
    });
}
}
```

Appendix F: A GUI-less Population Template

This appendix presents Java templates that are used by SocioFramework for composing Java sources of a GUI-less population. The patterns used for customization are shown in Table 6.7.

The patterns in Table 6.7 are marked in bold in the Java source code:

```java
package __prototypeMASAppl__;

/*
 * __agentName__PopulationAgent.java
 *
 */
//imports emotext
//imports java
//imports java
//imports WEKA
//imports JADE
import coreEmotionalEngine.TreeTagger; import gui.
```

```java
__agentName__Frame; import __qualifiedSourceName__;
import __agentClass__;

import org.python.util.PythonInterpreter;

public class __agentName__PopulationAgent extends
 __agentClass__ {

    // Here come implementations of agent-specific dimensions
    //from Sect. 6.4,
    // for example, Hofstede dimensions
    Double[] culture = {0.0, 0.0, 0.0, 0.0, 0.0};
    //or statistical engines
    Map<Integer,ARFFWrapper> classifiersMap =
        new HashMap<Integer,ARFFWrapper>();

    //Here come implementations of simulation-wide dimensions
    //from Sect. 6.5,
    //for example, implementation of a SN
    Map<Agent, List<Relationship>> SN =
        new HashMap<Agent, Vector<Relationship>>;

    //to hold variables and constants
    protected PythonInterpreter jythonInterpreter = null;

    protected void setup() {
        // Registration with the DF
        ...
        try {
            DFService.register(this, dfd);

            String[] behavioursNameArray =
                __behavioursNamePopulationArray__;
            for (String behaviourName : behavioursNameArray) {
                Class c = Class.forName(behaviourName);
                // get the constructor with one parameter
                java.lang.reflect.Constructor constructor =
                        c.getConstructor(new
                            Class[]{jade.core.Agent.class});

                // create an instance
                Behaviour invoker =
                        (Behaviour) constructor.newInstance(
                            new Object[]{this});

                addBehaviour(invoker);
            }
        } catch (Exception e) {
            e.printStackTrace();
            doDelete();
        }
    }

    ...
```

```
    //enumeration with a list of datasets
    String[] datasetsArray = __datasetsStringArray__;

    static {

        try {
            TreeTagger tagger = new TreeTagger(null);
            for (String dataset : datasetsArray) {
                ARFFWrapper classifier =
                    new ARFFWrapper(
                        new __classifierShortName__(), tagger,
                            dataset);
                classifiersMap.put(
                    new Integer(classifiersMap.size()),
                        classifier);
            }
        } catch (Exception e) {
            e.printStackTrace();
        }

    }

    public static void main(String[] args) {
        try {
            ...
            AgentController ac = cc.createNewAgent(
            "__agentName__",
            "__prototypeMASAppl__.__agentName__PopulationAgent",
            new Object[0]);
            // Fire up the agent
            ac.start();
        } catch (StaleProxyException ex) {
            Logger.getLogger(
                __agentName__PopulationAgent.class
                .getName()).log(Level.SEVERE, null, ex);
        }
    }
}
```

Here is the template of a population behavior instantiated through the above agent
(he specific interaction patterns for the behavior 1 in Fig. 6.14 are shown in Table 6.8
in the Java source code):

```
package __prototypeMASAppl__.behaviours;

//imports java
//imports JADE

public class __behaviourPopulationName__ extends Behaviour {

        private boolean finished_ = false;
        Agent a_ = null;
```

Table 6.8 Specific population message

Pattern	Source
__behaviourPopulationName__	Behavior name, e.g., initiator_responder_initiate_behavior_0, Fig. 6.14
__interactionMsg__	initiate_behavior, Fig. 6.14
__receiverMsg__	answer_behavior, Fig. 6.14
__receiverName__	Responder, Fig. 6.14
__skipSend__	auxiliary

```
private boolean DEBUG = false;

public __behaviourPopulationName__(Agent a) {
    super(a);
    a_=a;
    finished_ = false;
}

public void action() {
    ACLMessage msg = myAgent.blockingReceive();
    if ((msg!=null) && msg.getContent().
     equals("__interactionMsg__")) {
        if ("__skipSend__".isEmpty()) {
            ACLMessage reply = new
             ACLMessage(ACLMessage.INFORM);
            AID receiver = new AID("__receiverName__",
             AID.ISLOCALNAME);
            reply.addReceiver(receiver);
            reply.setContent("__receiverMsg__");
            a_.send(reply);
        } else {
            JOptionPane.showMessageDialog(
                null, "Done", "Interaction",
                JOptionPane.INFORMATION_MESSAGE,
                null);
        }

    }
}

...

}
```

References

André, E., Rist, T., Mulken, S. V., Klesen, M., & Baldes, S. (2000). The automated design of believable dialogues for animated presentation teams. In *Embodied conversational agents* (pp. 220–255). Cambridge: MIT Press.

Baker, J., Juneau, J., Wierzbicki, F., Soto, L., & Ng, V. (2010). The Definitive Guide to Jython: Python for the Java Platform. http://amazon.com/o/ASIN/B003VPWY4G/.

Bellifemine, F. L., Caire, G., & Greenwood, D. (2007). *Wiley series in agent technology. Developing multi-agent systems with JADE*. New York: Wiley. ISBN:978-0-470-05747-6. http://amazon.com/o/ASIN/0470057475/.

Binsted, K., Luke, S., & Building, A. V. W. (1998). Character design for soccer commentary. In M. Asada & H. Kitano (Eds.), *RoboCup-98: robot soccer world cup II* (pp. 23–35). Berlin: Springer.

Brooks, R. A. (1986). A robust layered control system for a mobile robot. *IEEE Journal of Robotics and Automation, 2*(1), 14–23. http://www.ai.mit.edu/people/brooks/papers/AIM-864.ps.Z.

Chen, X., Stone, P., Sucar, L. E., & van der Zant, T. (Eds.) (2013). *Lecture notes in computer science/Lecture notes in artificial intelligence. RoboCup 2012: robot soccer world cup XVI*. (2013th ed.). Berlin: Springer. ISBN:978-3-642-39249-8. http://amazon.com/o/ASIN/3642392490/.

Combe, D., Largeron, C., Egyed-Zsigmond, E., & Gery, M. (2010). A comparative study of social network analysis tools. In C. El Morr, P. Maret, L. Vercouter (Eds.), *Web intelligence & virtual enterprises workshop at Pro-VE 2010* (pp. 1–14). http://liris.cnrs.fr/publis/?id=4910.

Elliott, J., Eckstein, R., Loy, M., Wood, D., & Cole, B. (2002). *Java swing, second edition* (2nd ed.). New York: O'Reilly Media. ISBN:978-0-596-00408-8. http://amazon.com/o/ASIN/0596004087/.

Ellson, J., Gansner, E. R., Koutsofios, E., North, S. C., & Woodhull, G. (2004). Graphviz and dynagraph—static and dynamic graph drawing tools. In M. Jünger & P. Mutzel (Eds.), *Mathematics and visualization. Graph drawing software* (pp. 127–148). Berlin: Springer. ISBN: 978-3-642-62214-4. doi:10.1007/978-3-642-18638-7_6. http://dx.doi.org/10.1007/978-3-642-18638-7_6.

Engel, R. (2006). SPIN: a semantic parser for spoken dialog systems. In *Proceedings of the 5th Slovenian and first international language technology conference (IS-LTC 2006)*.

Gannon, M. J., & Pillai, R. R. K. (2012). *Understanding global cultures: metaphorical journeys through 31 nations, clusters of nations, continents, and diversity* (5th ed.). Thousand Oaks: Sage. ISBN:978-1-412-99593-1. http://amazon.com/o/ASIN/1412995930/.

Gatt, A., & Reiter, E. (2009). SimpleNLG: a realisation engine for practical applications. In *Proceedings of ENLG-2009*.

Hunter, J., & Crawford, W. (2001). *Java series. Java servlet programming* (2nd ed.). New York: O'Reilly Media. ISBN:978-0-596-00040-0. http://amazon.com/o/ASIN/0596000405/.

Kilgarriff, A. (1997). Putting frequencies in the dictionary. *International Journal of Lexicography, 10*(2), 135–155. doi:10.1093/ijl/10.2.135. http://ijl.oxfordjournals.org/content/10/2/135.abstract.

Kilgarriff, A. (2010). Frequency list of the British national corpus. http://www.kilgarriff.co.uk/BNClists/all.al.gz.

Klein, D., & Manning, C. D. (2003). Accurate unlexicalized parsing. In *Proceedings of the 41st annual meeting on association for computational linguistics, ACL '03* (Vol. 1, pp. 423–430). Stroudsburg: Association for Computational Linguistics. doi:10.3115/1075096.1075150. http://dx.doi.org/10.3115/1075096.1075150.

Leech, G., & Svartvik, J. (2003). *A communicative grammar of English* (3rd ed.). Upper Saddle River: Pearson Education. ISBN:978-0-582-50633-6. http://amazon.com/o/ASIN/0582506336/.

Levin, B. (1993). *English verb classes and alternations: a preliminary investigation*. Chicago: University of Chicago Press. ISBN:978-0-226-47533-2. http://amazon.com/o/ASIN/0226475336/.

Liu, H., Lieberman, H., & Selker, T. (2003). A model of textual affect sensing using real-world knowledge. In *IUI '03: proceedings of the 8th international conference on intelligent user interfaces* (pp. 125–132). New York: ACM Press. ISBN:1-58113-586-6. http://doi.acm.org/10.1145/604045.604067.

Miles, R., & Hamilton, K. (2006). *Learning UML 2.0* (1st ed.). New York: O'Reilly Media. ISBN:9780596009823. http://amazon.de/o/ASIN/0596009828/.

Moffat, A. (2012). Implementation of the sequence diagram. http://www.zanthan.com/itymbi/archives/cat_sequence.html.

Myrick, R. D., & Erney, T. (1984). *Caring and sharing: becoming a peer facilitator*. Educational Media Corporation.

Osherenko, A. (2011). *Opinion mining and lexical affect sensing: computer-aided analysis of opinions and emotions in texts*. Berlin: Südwestdeutscher Verlag für Hochschulschriften. ISBN:978-3-838-12488-9. http://amazon.de/o/ASIN/383812488X/.

Poynter, R. (2010). *The handbook of online and social media research: tools and techniques for market researchers* (1st ed.). New York: Wiley. ISBN:978-0-470-71040-1. http://amazon.com/o/ASIN/0470710403/.

Schmid, H. (1994). Probabilistic part-of-speech tagging using decision trees. In *Proceedings of the international conference on new methods in language processing*, Manchester, UK.

Sponder, M. (2011). *Social media analytics: effective tools for building, interpreting, and using metrics* (1st ed.). New York: McGraw-Hill. ISBN:978-0-071-76829-0. http://amazon.com/o/ASIN/0071768297/.

Stone, P. J., Dunphy, D. C., Smith, M. S., & Ogilvie, D. M. (1966). *The general inquirer: a computer approach to content analysis*. Cambridge: MIT Press. http://www.webuse.umd.edu:9090/.

Sun, R. (2005b). The CLARION cognitive architecture: extending cognitive modeling to social simulation. In R. Sun (Ed.), *Cognition and multi-agent interaction: from cognitive modeling to social simulation* (pp. 79–99). Cambridge: Cambridge University Press.

Tanenbaum, A. S., & van Steen, M. (2002). *Distributed systems: principles and paradigms, us ed edn*. New York: Prentice Hall. ISBN:978-0-130-88893-8. http://amazon.com/o/ASIN/0130888931/.

Valitutti, A., Strapparava, C., & Stock, O. (2004). Developing affective lexical resources. *Psychnology Journal*, 61–83.

Whissell, C. (1989). The dictionary of affect in language. In R. Plutchik & H. Kellerman (Eds.), *Emotion. Theory, research and experience: Vol. 4. The measurement of emotions* (pp. 113–131).

Witten, I., & Frank, E. (2005). *Data mining: practical machine learning tools and techniques* (2nd ed.). San Francisco: Morgan Kaufmann.

Chapter 7
Evaluation of the Prototyping Approach

This chapter describes evaluation of the proposed approach to prototyping in Chap. 6. For this purpose, it discusses SS systems implementing simulation scenarios in Chap. 3 and presents underlying interaction specifications. Moreover, it provides tables with lists of the behaviors created by SocioFramework.

7.1 Typical Culturally Homogeneous Scenarios of Social Interaction

1. Individualistic/Collectivistic scenarios (item 1 on p. 58).

1.1. Meeting someone for the first time

Figure 7.1 shows an interaction specification for analysis of the first meeting.

In Fig. 7.1, the agents *person1* and *person2* are interactants of negotiation. The meta-agents *culture1* and *culture2* represent the cultures of the interactants.

The textual representation of the interaction specification is defined as follows:

```
interaction
{
  person1.getCulture()->culture1;
  person2.getCulture()->culture2;
  culture1.$isCollectivistic() -> $ {
    person1.long_meeting();
    person1.seldom_gesture_usage();
    person1.less_body_contact();
  }
  culture2.$isIndividualistic() -> $ {
    person2.shorter_meeting();
    person2.often_gesture_usage();
```

A. Osherenko, *Social Interaction, Globalization and Computer-Aided Analysis*, Human–Computer Interaction Series, DOI 10.1007/978-1-4471-6260-5_7, © Springer-Verlag London 2014

Fig. 7.1 An interaction
specification for analyzing
first meeting

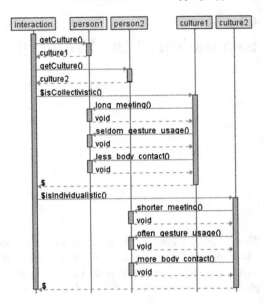

```
        person2.more_body_contact();
    }
}
```

Table 7.1 shows the names of generated behaviors in the SS system
where special characters are substituted through underscores for compatibility with name conventions for Windows files and Java classes.

1.2. Negotiating

Figure 7.2 shows an interaction specification for analysis of negotiation.

In Fig. 7.2, the meta-object *negotiation* represents the negotiation process. The agents *person1* and *person2* show the interactants of negotiation
where the variables *strategy1* and *strategy2* correspond to calculated strategies of *person1* and *person2*, respectively.

The textual representation of the interaction specification is defined as
follows:

```
interaction
{
    person1.getCulture()->culture1;
    person2.getCulture()->culture2;
    negotiation.get_negotiation_strategy(person1)
        ->strategy1;
    negotiation.get_negotiation_strategy(person2)
        ->strategy2;
}
```

Table 7.1 Behaviors for meeting for the first time

1. behavior_culture1_interaction___0;$
2. behavior_culture1_person1_less_body_contact___0;
3. behavior_culture1_person1_long_meeting___0;
4. behavior_culture1_person1_seldom_gesture_usage___0;
5. behavior_culture2_interaction___0;$
6. behavior_culture2_person2_more_body_contact___0;
7. behavior_culture2_person2_often_gesture_usage___0;
8. behavior_culture2_person2_shorter_meeting___0;
9. behavior_interaction_culture1__isCollectivistic___0;$
10. behavior_interaction_culture2__isIndividualistic___0;$
11. behavior_interaction_person1_getCulture___0;
12. behavior_interaction_person2_getCulture___0;
13. behavior_person1_culture1_void_0;
14. behavior_person1_culture1_void_1;
15. behavior_person1_culture1_void_2;
16. behavior_person1_interaction_culture1_0;
17. behavior_person2_culture2_void_0;
18. behavior_person2_culture2_void_1;
19. behavior_person2_culture2_void_2;
20. behavior_person2_interaction_culture2_0;

Legend: $ – begin/end of the scope of the conditional statement

Fig. 7.2 An interaction specification for analyzing negotiations

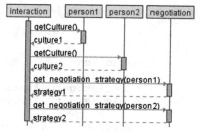

Table 7.2 lists the behaviors in the negotiation scenario where special characters in names are substituted through underscores for compatibility with name conventions for Windows files and Java classes.

1.3. Interacting with a higher-status individual

Figure 7.3 shows an interaction specification for interacting with a higher status individual.

In Fig. 7.3, the behaviors of the agents *superior* and *employee* are set according to the categories proxemics, vocalic, symbolically intrusive in the culture *culture1* and *culture2*.

The textual representation of the interaction specification is defined as follows:

Table 7.2 Behaviors for analysis of negotiation

1. behavior_interaction_negotiation_get_negotiation_strategy_person1__0;
2. behavior_interaction_negotiation_get_negotiation_strategy_person2__0;
3. behavior_interaction_person1_getCulture___0;
4. behavior_interaction_person2_getCulture___0;
5. behavior_negotiation_interaction_strategy1_0;
6. behavior_negotiation_interaction_strategy2_0;
7. behavior_person1_interaction_culture1_0;
8. behavior_person2_interaction_culture2_0;

Fig. 7.3 An interaction specification with a higher-status individual

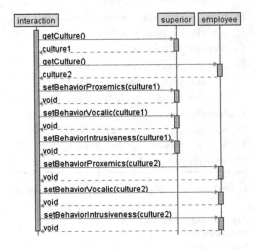

```
interaction
{
    superior.getCulture()->culture1;
    employee.getCulture()->culture2;

    //proxemics, vocalic, symbolically intrusive
    superior.setBehaviorProxemics(culture1);
    superior.setBehaviorVocalic(culture1);
    superior.setBehaviorIntrusiveness(culture1);

    employee.setBehaviorProxemics(culture2);
    employee.setBehaviorVocalic(culture2);
    employee.setBehaviorIntrusiveness(culture2);
}
```

Table 7.3 shows the behaviors of the interaction with a higher-status individual where special characters in names are substituted through underscores for compatibility with name conventions for Windows files and Java classes.

Table 7.3 Behaviors for analysis of interaction with a higher-status individual

1. behavior_employee_interaction_culture2_0;
2. behavior_employee_interaction_void_0;
3. behavior_employee_interaction_void_1;
4. behavior_employee_interaction_void_2;
5. behavior_interaction_employee_getCulture_ _ _0;
6. behavior_interaction_employee_setBehaviorIntrusiveness_culture2_ _0;
7. behavior_interaction_employee_setBehaviorProxemics_culture2_ _0;
8. behavior_interaction_employee_setBehaviorVocalic_culture2_ _0;
9. behavior_interaction_superior_getCulture_ _ _0;
10. behavior_interaction_superior_setBehaviorIntrusiveness_culture1_ _0;
11. behavior_interaction_superior_setBehaviorProxemics_culture1_ _0;
12. behavior_interaction_superior_setBehaviorVocalic_culture1_ _0;
13. behavior_superior_interaction_culture1_0;
14. behavior_superior_interaction_void_0;
15. behavior_superior_interaction_void_1;
16. behavior_superior_interaction_void_2;

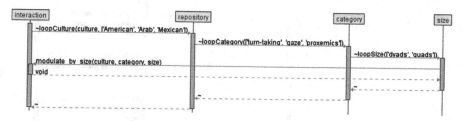

Fig. 7.4 The interaction analysis dependent on culture and the group size

2. **Influence of culture and the group size on SI** (item 2 on p. 59) (Fig. 7.4).
   Figure 7.4 shows an interaction specification for interaction analysis that distinguishes culture and group size. This specification is defined in textual form as follows:

```
interaction {
  repository.~loopCulture(culture, ['American', 'Arab',
    'Mexican']) -> ~ {
  category.~loopCategory(['turn-taking', 'gaze',
    'proxemics']) -> ~ {
    size.~loopSize(['dyads', 'quads']) -> ~ {
        interaction.modulate_by_size(culture, category,
          size);
      }
    }
  }
}
```

Table 7.4 Behaviors for the influence of the group size on social interaction

1. behavior_category_repository___0;
2. behavior_category_size__loopSize___dyads____quads____0;~
3. behavior_interaction_repository__loopCulture_culture____American____Arab____
   Mexican____0;~
4. behavior_interaction_size_void_0;~
5. behavior_repository_category__loopCategory___turn_taking____gaze____
   proxemics____0;~
6. behavior_repository_interaction___0;~
7. behavior_size_category___0;~
8. behavior_size_interaction_modulate_by_size_culture__category__size__0;

Legend: ~ – begin/end of the scope of the loop statement

Fig. 7.5 An interaction specification for expressing apology

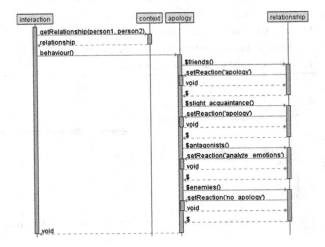

The prototype of an SS system maintains the meta-agents *interaction, repository, category, size*. Table 7.4 shows the behaviors for the scenario of the influence of group size on interaction in the SS system where special characters in names are substituted through underscores for compatibility with name conventions for Windows files and Java classes.

3. Scenarios of **Apology** (item 3 on p. 60).

In Fig. 7.5, the meta-agent *apology* represents the apology reaction; the agents *person1* and *person2* are the interactants of this SI; the meta-agent *relationship* shows the relationship between the interactants.

The textual representation of the interaction specification is defined as follows:

```
interaction
{
  context.getRelationship(person1, person2) -> relationship;
```

```
apology.behaviour() {
  relationship.$friends() -> $ {
    apology.setReaction('apology');
  }
  relationship.$slight_acquaintance() -> $ {
    apology.setReaction('apology');
  }
  relationship.$antagonists() -> $ {
    apology.setReaction('analyze_emotions');
  }
  relationship.$enemies() -> $ {
    apology.setReaction('no_apology');
  }
}
}
```

Table 7.5 shows the behaviors for analysis of apology where special characters in names are substituted through underscores for compatibility with name conventions for Windows files and Java classes.

4. Scenario of **Harmony/sympathy** (item 4 on p. 60).

Figure 7.6 shows an interaction specification for analysis of harmony/sympathy.

In Fig. 7.6, the meta-agent *dialogue* is a source of dialogue turns used to compose a pattern of SI. After a pairwise extraction of dialogue turns, the emotion models of the interactants *person1* and *person2* is adjusted, and the difference between their emotion models is calculated.

The textual representation of the interaction specification in Fig. 7.6 is defined as follows:

```
interaction
{
  interaction.getPerson('person1')->person1;
  interaction.getPerson('person2')->person2;

  dialogue.process {
    //traverse through the dialogue and read exchanges
    dialogue.~hasNext(person1, person2) -> ~ {
      //get next exchange of the dialogue interactants
      dialogue.getNext(person1, person2)->exchange;

      person1.analyzeTurn()->emotion1;
      person2.analyzeTurn()->emotion2;

      person1.storeEmotionalCourse(emotion1);
      person2.storeEmotionalCourse(emotion2);
    }
  }
  interaction.analyzeHarmonySympathy(person1, person2);
}
```

Table 7.5 Behaviors for simulating apology

1. behavior_apology_interaction_void_0;
2. behavior_apology_relationship_void_0;
3. behavior_apology_relationship_void_1;
4. behavior_apology_relationship_void_2;
5. behavior_apology_relationship_void_3;
6. behavior_apology_relationship_ _antagonists_ _ _0;$
7. behavior_apology_relationship_ _enemies_ _ _0;$
8. behavior_apology_relationship_ _friends_ _ _0;$
9. behavior_apology_relationship_ _slight_acquaintance_ _ _0;$
10. behavior_context_interaction_relationship_0;
11. behavior_interaction_apology_behavior_ _ _0;
12. behavior_interaction_context_getRelationship_person1_ _person2_ _0;
13. behavior_relationship_apology_setReaction_ _analyze_emotions_ _ _0;
14. behavior_relationship_apology_setReaction_ _apology_ _ _0;
15. behavior_relationship_apology_setReaction_ _apology_ _ _1;
16. behavior_relationship_apology_setReaction_ _no_apology_ _ _0;
17. behavior_relationship_apology_ _ _0;$
18. behavior_relationship_apology_ _ _1;$
19. behavior_relationship_apology_ _ _2;$
20. behavior_relationship_apology_ _ _3;$

Legend: $ – begin/end of the scope of the conditional statement

Fig. 7.6 An interaction specification for analyzing harmony/sympathy

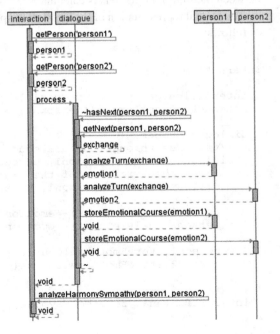

Table 7.6 Behaviors for the interaction analysis of the harmony/sympathy

1. behavior_dialogue_dialogue_exchange_0;
2. behavior_dialogue_dialogue_getNext_person1_ _person2_ _0;
3. behavior_dialogue_dialogue_ _hasNext_person1_ _person2_ _0;$
4. behavior_dialogue_dialogue_ _ _0;$
5. behavior_dialogue_interaction_void_0;~
6. behavior_dialogue_person1_analyzeTurn_exchange_ _0;
7. behavior_dialogue_person1_storeEmotionalCourse_emotion1_ _0;
8. behavior_dialogue_person2_analyzeTurn_exchange_ _0;
9. behavior_dialogue_person2_storeEmotionalCourse_emotion2_ _0;
10. behavior_interaction_dialogue_process_0;~
11. behavior_interaction_interaction_analyzeHarmonySympathy_person1_ _person2_ _0;
12. behavior_interaction_interaction_getPerson_ _person1_ _ _0;
13. behavior_interaction_interaction_getPerson_ _person2_ _ _0;
14. behavior_interaction_interaction_person1_0;
15. behavior_interaction_interaction_person2_0;
16. behavior_interaction_interaction_void_0;
17. behavior_person1_dialogue_emotion1_0;
18. behavior_person1_dialogue_void_0;
19. behavior_person2_dialogue_emotion2_0;
20. behavior_person2_dialogue_void_0;

Legend: $ – begin/end of the scope of the conditional statement; ~ – begin/end of the scope of the loop statement

Table 7.6 shows the behaviors for analysis of harmony/sympathy where special characters in names are substituted through underscores for compatibility with name conventions for Windows files and Java classes.

5. Scenarios of **Trust** (item 5 on p. 60).

Figure 7.7 shows an interaction specification for analysis of trust between two persons.

In Fig. 7.7, the meta-agent *dialogue* is a source of dialogue turns used to analyze trust. After analyzing turns, the emotion models of the interactants *person1* and *person2* is adjusted, and a behavior pattern is calculated under consideration of interactants' relationship.

The textual representation of the interaction specification in Fig. 7.7 is defined as follows:

```
interaction
{
    interaction.getRelationship()->relationship;
    interaction.getPerson('person1')->person1;
    interaction.getPerson('person2')->person2;

    dialogue.process() {
```

Fig. 7.7 An interaction
specification for analyzing
trust

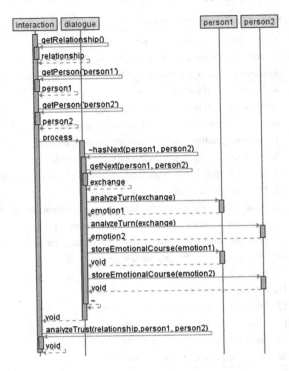

```
//traverse through the dialogue and read exchanges
dialogue.~hasNext(person1, person2) -> ~ {
    //get next exchange of the dialogue interactants
    dialogue.getNext(person1, person2)->exchange;

    person1.analyzeTurn(exchange)->emotion1;
    person2.analyzeTurn(exchange)->emotion2;

    person1.storeEmotionalCourse(emotion1);
    person2.storeEmotionalCourse(emotion2);
}
}
    interaction.analyzeTrust(relationship,person1, person2);
}
```

Table 7.7 shows the behaviors for analysis of trust where special characters
are substituted through underscores for compatibility with name conventions for
Windows files and Java classes.

6. Scenario of **analyzing SI patterns** (item 6 on p. 62).

Figure 7.8 shows an interaction specification for analysis of adaptation patterns.

In Fig. 7.8, the meta-agent *dialogue* is a source of dialogue turns used to compose a pattern of SI. After a pairwise extraction of dialogue turns, the emotion

Table 7.7 Behaviors for analysis of trust

1. behavior_dialogue_dialogue_exchange_0;
2. behavior_dialogue_dialogue_getNext_person1_ _person2_ _0;
3. behavior_dialogue_dialogue_ _hasNext_person1_ _person2_ _0;$
4. behavior_dialogue_dialogue_ _ _0;$
5. behavior_dialogue_interaction_void_0;~
6. behavior_dialogue_person1_analyzeTurn_exchange_ _0;
7. behavior_dialogue_person1_storeEmotionalCourse_emotion1_ _0;
8. behavior_dialogue_person2_analyzeTurn_exchange_ _0;
9. behavior_dialogue_person2_storeEmotionalCourse_emotion2_ _0;
10. behavior_interaction_dialogue_process_ _ _0;~
11. behavior_interaction_interaction_analyzeTrust_relationship_person1_ _person2_ _0;
12. behavior_interaction_interaction_getPerson_ _person1_ _ _0;
13. behavior_interaction_interaction_getPerson_ _person2_ _ _0;
14. behavior_interaction_interaction_getRelationship_ _ _0;
15. behavior_interaction_interaction_person1_0;
16. behavior_interaction_interaction_person2_0;
17. behavior_interaction_interaction_relationship_0;
18. behavior_interaction_interaction_void_0;
19. behavior_person1_dialogue_emotion1_0;
20. behavior_person1_dialogue_void_0;
21. behavior_person2_dialogue_emotion2_0;
22. behavior_person2_dialogue_void_0;

Legend: $ – begin/end of the scope of the conditional statement; ~ – begin/end of the scope of the loop statement

models of the interactants (*person1* and *person2*) are adjusted, and the difference between their emotion models is calculated.

The textual representation of the interaction specification in Fig. 7.8 is defined as follows:

```
interaction
{
  context.getPerson('person1')->person1;
  context.getPerson('person2')->person2;

  context.getCulture(person1)->culture1;
  context.getCulture(person1)->culture2;

  context.getPersonality(person1)->personality1;
  context.getPersonality(person1)->personality2;

  dialogue.~process {
    dialogue.getTurn(person1)->turn1;
```

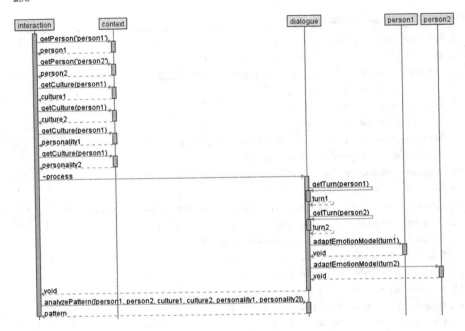

Fig. 7.8 An interaction specification for analyzing adaptation patterns

```
dialogue.getTurn(person2)->turn2;

person1.adaptEmotionModel(turn1);
person2.adaptEmotionModel(turn2);
}
dialogue.analyzePattern([person1, person2, culture1,
                         culture2, personality1,
                         personality2])->pattern;
}
```

Table 7.8 lists the generated behaviors where special characters in names are substituted through underscores for compatibility with name conventions for Windows files and Java classes.

Note that the behavior *analyzePattern* can consider the Kullback–Leibler measure in Sect. 5.7.3 to assess the changing similarity between emotion models of interactants, i.e., their HMMs for affective behavior.

7.2 Culturally Heterogeneous Scenarios of a Digital Globe

Figure 7.9 shows an interaction specification that simulates scenarios of navigation, shopping assistance, special offers in Sect. 3.2:

Table 7.8 Behaviors in analysis of interaction patterns

1. behavior_context_interaction_culture1_0;
2. behavior_context_interaction_culture2_0;
3. behavior_context_interaction_person1_0;
4. behavior_context_interaction_person2_0;
5. behavior_context_interaction_personality1_0;
6. behavior_context_interaction_personality2_0;
7. behavior_dialogue_dialogue_getTurn_person1__0;
8. behavior_dialogue_dialogue_getTurn_person2__0;
9. behavior_dialogue_dialogue_turn1_0;
10. behavior_dialogue_dialogue_turn2_0;
11. behavior_dialogue_interaction_pattern_0;
12. behavior_dialogue_interaction_void_0;
13. behavior_dialogue_person1_adaptEmotionModel_turn1__0;
14. behavior_dialogue_person2_adaptEmotionModel_turn2__0;
15. behavior_interaction_context_getCulture_person1__0;
16. behavior_interaction_context_getCulture_person1__1;
17. behavior_interaction_context_getPersonality_person1__0;
18. behavior_interaction_context_getPersonality_person1__1;
19. behavior_interaction_context_getPerson__person1___0;
20. behavior_interaction_context_getPerson__person2___0;
21. behavior_interaction_dialogue_analyzePattern__person1__person2__culture1__culture2__ personality1__personality2___0;
22. behavior_interaction_dialogue__process_0;~
23. behavior_person1_dialogue_void_0;
24. behavior_person2_dialogue_void_0;~

Legend: ~ – begin/end of the scope of the loop statement

Fig. 7.9 An interaction specification for the shopping activity

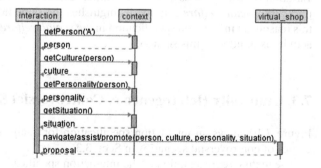

The textual interaction specification is defined as follows:

```
interaction
{
  context.getPerson('A')->person;
  context.getCulture(person)->culture;
```

Table 7.9 Behaviors in the shopping activity

1. behavior_context_interaction_culture_0;
2. behavior_context_interaction_personality_0;
3. behavior_context_interaction_person_0;
4. behavior_context_interaction_situation_0;
5. behavior_interaction_context_getCulture_person__0;
6. behavior_interaction_context_getPersonality_person__0;
7. behavior_interaction_context_getPerson__A___0;
8. behavior_interaction_context_getSituation___0;
9. behavior_interaction_virtual_shop_navigate_assist_promote_person__culture__personality__
   situation__0;
10. behavior_virtual_shop_interaction_proposal_0;

```
    context.getPersonality(person)->personality;

    context.getSituation()->situation;

    //if the person is not agitated, navigate/assist/promote
    virtual_shop.navigate/assist/promote(person, culture,
        personality, situation)->proposal;
}
```

Table 7.9 lists the generated behaviors where special characters in names are substituted through underscores for compatibility with name conventions for Windows files and Java classes.

A general specification of SI according to the *business* activity does not differ significantly from that in Fig. 7.8. It also defines an iterative process of adjusting particular personality and emotion models of an individual in a study of cultural variation of display rules or mobile market research or intercultural business. Similarly, the *social welfare* activity distinguishes the same interactional behavior. For this reason, an interaction specification in the *social welfare* activity or the *education* activity is omitted in this section.

7.3 Culturally Heterogeneous Controversial Scenarios

Figure 7.10 shows an interaction specification for analysis of probabilities of outcomes of controversial scenarios in Sect. 3.3.

The textual representation of the interaction specification is defined as follows:

```
interaction
{
    context.instantiate();

    context.getPerson('A')->person;
    context.getCulture(person)->culture;
```

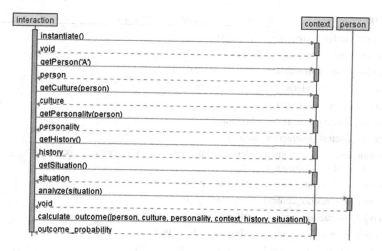

Fig. 7.10 An interaction specification of incidents

```
context.getPersonality(person)->personality;

context.getHistory()->history;
context.getSituation()->situation;

person.analyze(situation);

context.calculate_outcome([person, culture, personality,
    context, history, situation])->outcome_probability;
}
```

Table 7.10 shows the behaviors that calculate probabilistic outcomes of controversial scenarios where special characters in names are substituted through underscores for compatibility with name conventions for Windows files and Java classes.

7.4 One-Person Scenarios

This section is merely present in this book due to consistency with the narration
in Sect. 3.4. Indeed, in scenarios of SI and SS, discussion of one-person scenarios
in the context of simulation plays a secondary role since the chosen agent-specific
models are thoroughly examined in Sect. 6.6.

7.5 Summary and Outlook

This chapter reconsidered scenarios in Chap. 3 and introduced interaction specifications of SI and SS both in graphical and textual form. It also outlined necessary
simulation behaviors.

Table 7.10 Behaviors for the outcomes of controversial scenarios

1. behavior_context_interaction_culture_0;
2. behavior_context_interaction_history_0;
3. behavior_context_interaction_outcome_probability_0;
4. behavior_context_interaction_personality_0;
5. behavior_context_interaction_person_0;
6. behavior_context_interaction_situation_0;
7. behavior_context_interaction_void_0;
8. behavior_interaction_context_calculate_outcome__person__culture__personality__ context__history__situation___0;
9. behavior_interaction_context_getCulture_person1__0;
10. behavior_interaction_context_getHistory___0;
11. behavior_interaction_context_getPersonality_person1__0;
12. behavior_interaction_context_getPerson__A___0;
13. behavior_interaction_context_getSituation___0;
14. behavior_interaction_context_instantiate___0;
15. behavior_interaction_person_analyze_situation__0;
16. behavior_person_interaction_void_0;

In future, implementation of prototypes will be concluded with implementations of control elements in interaction specifications in Sect. 6.5.1 to facilitate automatic development of SS systems.

Chapter 8
Conclusion

This book studied SI and SS in the context of globalization and presented numerous theoretical, application-related, and practical contributions.

8.1 Theoretical Contributions

In Chap. 2, existing approaches to SI and SS and their shortcomings were discussed. This chapter showed both agent-specific and simulation-wide modeling dimensions that should be considered theoretically in development of SS systems. Chapter 3 presented different scenarios of SI and SS and discussed pseudocode algorithms that can build a theoretical basis for SS systems. Chapter 4 presented approaches to data acquisition for SI and SS. Since existing intercultural data is scarce, this chapter discussed heuristics to acquire data for intercultural experiments. Chapter 5 showed a framework for SS, SocioFramework, that provided means for statistical processing and prototyping. Moreover, it showed tools that can be utilized in SS, for instance, for analyzing interaction patterns. In Chap. 6, composition of software prototypes for SS systems was examined relying on a prototyping principle. It discussed an architecture of an SS system that simulates SI. A theoretical formalism based on interaction specifications was introduced.

8.2 Application-Related Contributions

Chapter 2 described existing SS systems and outlined agent-specific and system-wide modeling dimensions that should be considered in SS systems. Chapter 3 discussed scenarios that can be developed in SS systems. Chapter 4 proposed heuristics to acquire data that can be used by SS systems. Chapter 5 showed SocioFramework, a framework for statistical processing and prototyping, that provided application-related means to handle statistical datasets and to compose SS systems. Chapter 6 discussed prototypes of SS software and their programmatic implementations. It

A. Osherenko, *Social Interaction, Globalization and Computer-Aided Analysis*,
Human–Computer Interaction Series, DOI 10.1007/978-1-4471-6260-5_8,
© Springer-Verlag London 2014

examined issues that should be taken into consideration in implementing SS systems, for example, software engineering issues. Chapter 7 discussed evaluation of the SS systems and outlined their components.

8.3 Practical Contributions

This book presented the following practical contributions. Chapter 3 discussed pseudocode algorithms that can be extended to concrete SS systems. Chapter 4 proposed data acquisition for SS systems considering practical emotion-, personality-, and culture-aware issues. Moreover, it presented a case-based approach to data acquisition. Chapter 5 showed SocioFramework maintaining means for processing statistical information and composing software prototypes that can be used as a practical basis for SS systems. Chapter 6 proposed interaction specifications as algorithms of SS systems. In the proposed SS systems, issues of remote maintenance, scalability, and debugging were discussed. It showed the program code of prototypes, behaviors, and NL engines that should be taken into consideration in implementing SS. The proposed prototypes were evaluated in Chap. 7 on the basis of generated behaviors.

8.4 Answers to Research Questions

This book discussed in Sect. 1.6 various research questions:

1. *What is an advantage of SS and how can this advantage be gained in SS systems?* This book explored different scenarios of SI and addressed in Chap. 3 advantages of SS such as development of coping strategies of cultural misunderstandings.
2. *How can SS be organized computationally and what computationally feasible models can be used insofar?* In Chap. 3, this book deduced the most significant determinants of SS and showed their implementations in Chap. 6. The book illustrated an approach to compose SS systems based on interaction specifications and showed SocioFramework, a framework for statistical data processing and prototyping in Chap. 5. In Chap. 6, development of SS systems such as dialog systems, experimental testbeds, and populations was examined; a software architecture was explored, and the prototyping principle was examined. The book discussed evaluation of the introduced approach to SS in Chap. 7.
3. *What is an approach to acquire data for intercultural SS and what heuristics can be utilized for this purpose?* This book discussed issues of acquisition of intercultural data and presented corresponding heuristics and empirical data in Chap. 4.

8.5 Resolution of Drawbacks

This book discussed shortcomings of previous approaches to SI and SS outlined in Sect. 2.13:

1. *Guidelines on developing software systems.* The introduced approach defined guidelines for developing SS systems, beginning from the colloquial scenario description and ending with a programmatic prototype of an SS system.
2. *Dimensions of modeling.* The introduced approach discussed both related work and own scenarios of SI and substantiated the most significant modeling dimensions that refer to agent-specific and simulation-wide modeling dimensions.
3. *Integrative generic approach.* The introduced approach discussed domain-independent means to compose SS systems that can be used to implement SS systems simulating a SI scenario of a desired domain.
4. *Prototyping principle.* The introduced approach explored a prototyping principle that allows composition of prototypes of a certain type, for example, dialog systems.

8.6 Further Work

This book presented an outlook in regard of different issues of intercultural SI and intercultural SS concerning related approaches in Sect. 2.14, new scenarios in Sect. 3.7, data acquisition in Sect. 4.5, framework for statistical processing and prototyping in Sect. 5.8, simulation issues in Sect. 6.7, and evaluation of simulation in Sect. 7.5.

In future work, further research will focus on the following:

1. Applicability of techniques in this book to facilitate learning, for example, in neuroscience (Nagel et al. 2005).
2. Verification of sociological theories in the context of intercultural communication, for example, theories of so-called Digital Divide in Ragnedda and Muschert (2013).

This book provided a solid basis for analysis of SI and development of SS systems that can be used for experimentation in HCI. Returning to the trial-and-error at the beginning of this book, of course, nobody knows if the effort to study SI and SS repays. However, it is worth stating that it would probably succeed as it did in the cases of aviation and medicine!

References

Nagel, S. K., Carl, C., Kringe, T., Märtin, R., & König, P. (2005). Beyond sensory substitution—learning the sixth sense. *Journal of Neural Engineering*, 2(4), 13–26. http://stacks.iop.org/1741-2552/2/i=4/a=R02.

Ragnedda, M., & Muschert, G. W. (Eds.) (2013). *Routledge advances in sociology. The digital divide: the internet and social inequality in international perspective.* (1st ed.). London: Routledge. ISBN:978-0-415-52544-2. http://amazon.com/o/ASIN/0415525446/.

Index

A. Osherenko, *Social Interaction, Globalization and Computer-Aided Analysis*,
Human–Computer Interaction Series, DOI 10.1007/978-1-4471-6260-5,
© Springer-Verlag London 2014

Printed in the United States
By Bookmasters